American
Academics

American Academics
Academics
Then and Now
LOGAN WILSON

New York   Oxford University Press   1979

Copyright © 1979 by Oxford University Press, Inc.

Library of Congress Cataloging in Publication Data

Wilson, Logan, 1907–
  American academics.

  Continues the author's earlier work, The academic man.
  Includes index.
  1. College teachers. I. Title.
LB1778.W55   378.1'2   78-12118
ISBN 0-19-502482-6

Permissions to quote currently copyrighted material were kindly granted by the following:
  The American Council on Education for Tables 1.1, 1.2, 4.2, 5.1, 6.1, 6.2, 6.3, A.2 and Appendix A.
  Holt, Rinehart and Winston for Table 1.3, copyright © 1976 by Praeger Publishers, Inc.
  The University of North Carolina Press for Table 3.1, copyright © 1965.
  Teachers College Press for Table 4.1.
  Chronicle of Higher Education for Tables 7.1, 9.1, 9.2, A.1 and Appendices C and D.
  The American Association of University Professors for Table 8.1.
  The Journal of Higher Education for Tables 10.3 and A.5.
  Social Forces for Table A.4, copyright © The University of North Carolina Press.
  Change magazine for Table A.3, copyright © 1977 by the Council on Learning.

Printed in the United States of America

Acknowledgments

I am indebted to the American Council on Education for facilitating my start on this book, and to other higher education associations headquartered at One Dupont Circle in Washington for affording access to information not readily available elsewhere. For a grant to defray incidental costs in getting the manuscript completed and ready for publication, I want to express appreciation to the Ford Foundation. None of the organizations aiding my undertaking is in any way accountable for the observations I set forth, of course, and this same disclaimer applies to named individuals.

Although I am obligated to many individuals for their contributions, I want to single out some for special mention. Fred C. Cole went over an early version of my proposed commentary and made helpful suggestions. Charles V. Kidd critically reviewed several prospective chapters. Charles G. Dobbins and W. Todd Furniss painstakingly blue-penciled the entire first draft, much to my benefit in making revisions. From time to time, William F. Lasher and Irwin C. Lieb gave me some useful leads about elusive data I needed. I have also been fortunate during the final phases of my work to have the assistance of

Simona Draghici for bibliographic research, Mary Beissner for copy editing, and Suzi Patterson for typescription.

To these organizations and persons, not to mention others too numerous to list here, I am most grateful.

Contents

Introduction   1

1. Professional Recruitment   10

2. Students and Apprentices   33

3. Staff Members   56

4. Administrators   81

5. Academics and Governance   100

6. Status Appraisal   122

7. Professional Status   144

8. Economic Status   172

9. Academic Profiles and Social Status   191

10. University Prestige and Competition   210

11. Individual Prestige and Competition   234

Notes   274

Index   303

Appendices

A. Faculty Tenure and Contract Systems: 1972 and 1974 Highlights 253

B. Summary of the Forty-seven Recommendations of the Commission on Academic Tenure in Higher Education 256

C. Carnegie Commission on Higher Education Panel's Twenty-six Recommendations on Academic Governance 262

D. Average Salaries of Administrators at More Than 1,000 U.S. Colleges and Universities in 1977 266

E. Ranked Standings of Various Institutions in Selected Professional Fields in 1964, 1976, and 1977 268

F. Divisional and Institutional Standings of Graduate Faculty of Universities in Group B as Compiled from the Cartter Report 272

Tables

1.1   Professed Reasons for Being in Graduate School   15

1.2   All Current Sources of Financial Support for Advanced Study, by Sex, 1971   27

1.3.   Distribution of Financial Aid by Type and Amount, 1972   28

2.1   Rank Order of Top Twenty Fields by Doctorates Conferred, 1940 and 1969   48

3.1   Knowledge of Individuals about Specific Aspects of the Job They Accepted at Time of Acceptance   63

4.1   Comparison of Time and Skill Indices   89

4.2   Average Time Reported by 180 Presidents on 18 Activities   92

5.1   The Over-All Power Structure of American Universities   109

6.1   Frequency of Use of Various Sources of Information in the Evaluation of Teaching Effectiveness   131

6.2   Importance of Various Factors in Evaluating Faculty for Promotion, Salary, or Tenure   133

6.3   Reported Faculty Hours per Week in Teaching Activities and in Research and Scholarly Writing   137

7.1   Faculty Unionization in 1977   163

8.1   Weighted Average Salaries and Average Compensations by Category, Type of Affiliation, and Academic Rank, 1976–77   180

9.1   Attitudes of Faculty Members, by Age   195

9.2   Periodicals Ranked by Size of Faculty Readership   201

10.1   Association of American Universities   213

10.2   Comparison of the Physical Resources of the Thirty Leading Graduate Centers, 1939 and 1968   216

10.3   Institutional Standing in Letters and Sciences of Universities in Group A   222

10.4   Ranking of Divisional Strengths in Letters and Sciences of Universities in Group A, 1964   224

10.5   Institutional Standings, Letters and Sciences in Group A, 1969, by Same Divisions and Disciplines as in 1964 Report   226

A.1   Average Salaries of Administrators at More than 1,000 U.S. Colleges and Universities in 1977   266

A.2   Institutional Standings in Engineering of Universities in Group A   268

A.3   Cartter's 1976 Rankings of Schools of Education, Law, and Business   269

A.4   Cole and Lipton's 1977 Ratings of the Perceived Quality of American Medical Schools   270

A.5   Divisional and Institutional Standings of Graduate Faculty of Universities in Group B as Compiled from the Cartter Report   272

2/28/79

Introduction

This book about American academics is in some ways a belated follow-up of an inquiry a good many years ago into the sociology of a profession. When I wrote *The Academic Man* (New York, Oxford University Press, 1942), I was a fledgling academic and sociologist, curious about the folkways of my chosen occupation. In the early stages of study, I discovered that answers to many of the questions I had in mind were not between the covers of any single volume and that some topics were relatively unexplored. Knowledge about the profession as a whole seemingly could be acquired only through life experience in the college and university world, or by reference to widely scattered and unorganized sources of information.

One of my purposes in writing *The Academic Man* was to bring together the most significant observations, organize them within a pragmatic frame of reference, and present an ordered and objective view of professionals engaged in the higher learning. Although sociologists of that era had researched such assorted occupational types as railroaders, taxi drivers, and professional thieves, I was unable to locate any prototype for studying the social behavior of a higher level profession. This led me to think that prospective academics and members of the profession, not to mention others wanting to know more about the inner workings of academe, might be interested in the findings.

My conceptual mode of organization was comprised of four main parts. In Part One, I traced the course of an average academic as professional recruit, student and apprentice, staff member, and professor administrant. Part Two dealt with status appraisal, professional status, and socio-economic status. Part Three included chapters on social processes and functions and was concerned mainly with academic prestige and competition. Part Four gave my conclusions.

Since the lineage of American higher education antedates the founding of the nation, by 1942 considerable published material was available. There were numerous histories of particular colleges and universities, and I looked into enough of them to see that for the most part they were chronologies of local events that lacked interest and significance for readers having no personal associations with their institutional settings. Over the years, novelists, essayists, professors, deans, and presidents had also written extensively about various aspects of higher education, mostly from very subjective points of view. In addition to informal commentaries, numerous statistical studies had been made. The computer was not in use in those days to facilitate the compilation of massive accumulations of data about higher education, however, and broadly quantitative analyses were quite scanty.

Furthermore, higher education as a field of study was not coherently organized. Even though I have since learned that a course on higher education was offered as early as 1893, knowledge in the field, as compared with that available in the the established disciplines, was and still is somewhat inchoate, and researchers are largely persons drawn from other specialities. Dressel and Mayhew maintain that the discipline has now become professionalized.[1] Their 1974 book lists 67 doctoral degree programs in the field and estimates that upwards of 3,500 doctorates have been conferred in it. This suggests that there is now a sizable body of organized knowledge about academe, and my own experience in making a second systematic inquiry into the academic profession has shown that factual data are now abundantly available to treat more definitively some matters that in earlier years were merely topics of speculative thought.

My 1942 book did not make anybody's list of best sellers, but the reviewers agreed that the work was needed. Since then I have been intermittently urged by various persons to update it. My original reaction was that I might bring out something to be called *The Academic Man Revisited*, but other commitments led to my finally making such an undertaking a retirement years project. When the time arrived to begin, however, I soon became aware that a mere updating of what I had set forth decades earlier, with a few revisions and added commentaries, would not suffice. Too much had happened in the intervening years, and though many of the recent problems and issues appeared to be virtually the same, others were obviously new and different. Today even a referral to the generic professor as an academic *man* has become *infra dig*, and since what has come out of my writing is really a different book, I am entitling it *American Academics: Then and Now*.

When I began organizing material, I was pleased that the basic conceptualization employed originally was still viable, and that its use would enable me to make comparisons and generalizations about what had remained much the same and what had changed in academe. I was often surprised to observe how many of the personnel problems of the late 1930s and early 1940s recur and how many of the issues persist as topics of continuing debate. For some of these matters there is enough continuity of data to permit a running commentary, but for others the pertinent findings have been recorded only sporadically. Hence my *then* and *now* references necessarily are not always for identical time intervals. My main objective has been to focus on continuity and change between the early 1940s and the late 1970s.

Although little of my 1942 commentary is reproduced in this book, I have found, fortunately, that most of my former generalizations about the basic social behavior of academics are still apropos. Some of the paths I then explored are by now well trodden, to be sure, and I cannot make any claims for blazing new trails of sociological inquiry in this volume. Also, I must acknowledge that long experience from many vantage points has altered some of my earlier perspectives; my viewpoint is now the retrospective one of a disengaged educator rather than that of an inquistively engaged young academic and sociologist. All through the years, nonetheless, I have regarded the academic profession as a fascinating subject for study.

Since the problem *of* professors in their institutions and, in turn, of institutions with professors *as* problems entails more attention to dissatisfactions than to satisfactions, my approach may impress some as being too much concerned with the negative aspects of academe. I am aware, too, that reducing professors to statistics, as is necessary when their behavior is quantitatively described, may appear to dehumanize them. This is certainly not my intent; in my own opinion there is probably no other profession that values individual distinctiveness more highly, or one whose clients are as likely to cherish harmless (and sometimes deliberately cultivated) eccentricities of manner.

Evidence presented throughout this volume makes it clear, I trust, that the vast majority of academics are more satisfied than dissatisfied with their vocations, and that if, indeed, they were starting anew they would again pursue their same lines of specialization. The normal level of grousing probably is not markedly different from that in many other occupations. It should be borne in mind also that one function of the university is to be a critic of society. Thus, academics properly are more articulate critics than most persons of the world around them, not excluding themselves and their own campuses.

During the violent imbroglios of the late 1960s and early 1970s on many campuses, appreciable numbers of academics doubtless wished they were elsewhere, but with the restoration of reason in the conduct of college and university affairs, the advancement of learning is again proceeding in a less disturbed way nearly everywhere. Still, these episodes were followed by financial crises in many institutions, so that the supposedly quiet groves of academe are perhaps never as tranquil as they may appear to be from afar. In dealing with the sweep of events since 1942, I have tried to assess the evidence objectively and to maintain a detached perspective on what have often been divisively complicated situations.

Like *The Academic Man*, this book is concerned principally with those persons who will be or already are employed in universities, and more especially with those in the doctorate-granting institutions. Some of the observations pertain to all academics, but others do not. The social behavior of junior college professors, for example, may be quite different in some respects from that of university professors, and by no means do all universities replicate in detail a single model of structure and function.

Furthermore, it should be noted that doctorate-granting universities are not by definition an elitist group of institutions. It has been estimated that the several hundred such institutions enroll more than a fourth of all students in the United States and employ about a third of the total teaching faculty engaged in higher education. Since many universities are heavily engaged in mass education, their student admissions and faculty appointments may be considerably less selective than in some of the better liberal arts colleges and more specialized institutions.

Even though the most productive scholars and scientists tend to cluster in a relatively small number of universities, my guess is that effective undergraduate teachers are spread, however unevenly, across the whole spectrum of higher education. Unknown numbers of very capable and highly cultivated academics may prefer campus environs where the competition is less intense with regard to faculty research and publication. And, too, there are unknown numbers of unrenowned institutions which might get very high ratings if all colleges and universities were judged on a single scale that recorded their inputs as well as their outputs to assess their accomplishments in terms of "value added" in education.

For what readers, one may ask, is *American Academics: Then and Now* intended? My answer is that this discourse is not directed toward any special category of potentially interested individuals. Undergraduates contemplating graduate work, prospective academics, professors, administrators, and trustees should all be concerned with many of the topics covered. Experienced professors will run across diverse observations they have already made for themselves; but the exposition of matters with which the initiated are quite familiar may be very useful to potential entrants to the profession who, before making career decisions, want somebody to "tell it like it is." My general treatment, however, is not designed as a primer for the young and uninformed; my observation is that many scholars and scientists may be both indifferent to and uninformed about what goes on in academe outside their own fields of specialization.

Even as an "old pro" in higher education, I have learned some things in the process of putting these findings together, and I hope that other seasoned academics also may gain new insights here and there. Whole books have been written, of course, about certain topics that get only passing mention here, and various topics not mentioned at all are, I am aware, of great concern to some denizens of academe. My aim has been not to be encyclopedic on the one hand, nor topically exhaustive on the other. To hold the interest of general readers who are turned aside by too many footnotes and tables, I have eliminated some such entries that might have been useful to assiduous students in the field of higher education. In so doing, I know that my wide, and in places cursory, coverage risks telling some readers less than they want to know and others more than they care to learn about American academics.

However this may be, my main purpose is to inform rather than to entertain. I began with no fixed ideas about what conclusions might emerge, and with no ideology to demonstrate. It would be reassuring, for example, to be able to demonstrate that all developments in higher education during recent decades have been onward and upward, and that everything is not only bigger but also better. Unfortunately, the evidence assembled does not support such a cheerful conclusion. During the 1950s and 1960s there appeared to be a virtually unlimited demand for Ph.D.s, but in the course of just a few decades the market has run full circle back to where it was in the late 1930s and early 1940s. Even growth in size and scope, which was uninterrupted throughout most of the period under study, has come to a halt, with some decline being witnessed here and there.

Believers in the importance of institutional continuity may be pleased to observe that some things have not changed very much. The structure of graduate education is quite similar to what it was in 1942, many requirements for the highest degree have been stoutly upheld, and the merit principle of evaluating individual worth has been maintained. The egalitarian thrust for open admissions and diluted standards of achievement has in the main been resisted. Despite the encroachments of bureaucratization, the "body of equals" tradition among academics in the internal conduct of university affairs has survived.

Moreover, some of the problems frequently regarded as "new" were familiar ones in earlier years. Then as now, there were complaints about the Ph.D. stretch out in qualifying for the profession, the uncertainties and insecurities of individuals in the lower ranks, the vagaries of evaluative procedures, the "publish or perish" dictum, interferences with academic freedom, the weak bargaining power of academic employees, and the public's inadequate support of higher education.

Some of the problems of recent years, however, either were not perceived as such or else were nonexistent just a few decades ago. The differential treatment of women and various ethnic groups, for instance, was not generally regarded then as a "problem." There were no problems of academic relationship with the federal government simply because the federal involvement in higher education on most campuses was almost nil. Nobody then debated the role of students in institutional governance because in those days most students could not have cared less about such participation.

During the 1960s in particular, change for its own sake became almost a fetish in many academic circles. Time-honored policies and practices in many places were cast aside in the rush to alter admission standards, revamp the curriculum, modify modes of evaluation, reform internal governance, and in general to keep institutions abreast, if not ahead, of changes in the larger society. The public at large was sold on the importance of higher education, and most academics never "had it better."

Public disenchantment with higher education, however, developed during the late 1960s and early 1970s. Unrealistic expectations resulted in disappointments about anticipated educational outcomes. The onset of economic recession coupled with mounting inflation exacerbated existing disjunctions between ends and means. Moreover, the sweep of social change often drew colleges and universities into the middle of a conflict between forces and counterforces. The advocates of egalitarianism and of meritocracy found the nation's campuses to be very suitable places for testing the strength of their convictions. Many institutions experienced reduced autonomy and independence in confrontation with a growing collectivism of the whole social order, and even privately supported colleges and universities became increasingly politicized.

Prior to the onset of fiscal cutbacks, of course, most institutions benefited financially from the trade-offs, and higher education in general gets considerably more material support from the public than it did in 1942. Higher education is no longer an elitist enterprise, and the citizenry is now better educated than ever before. Productive science and scholarship are no longer confined to a handful of universities, and the importance of advancing learning is recognized in all parts of the country.

During the 1970s, as has been noted, job competition within academe has sharply intensified, and institutional demand for the services of new academics is likely to be reduced even further in many fields. Will a reduction in the proportion of human and material resources required in recent years for sheer expansion next bring about a reallocation, with more emphasis on improvement? This question poses both an opportunity and a challenge for American academics.

1

3/2/79

Professional Recruitment

Overview

From 1940 into the 1970s, the United States experienced marked social change and increased personal expectations. One outcome of this trend was advanced education's enlarged significance. More and more individuals came to perceive institutions of higher learning as essential to their advancement and to the welfare of society. World War II consequences and the Cold War thereafter heightened the importance of science and research. The federal government's involvement in higher education was greatly magnified, particularly after the founding of the National Science Foundation in 1950, Russia's launching of Sputnik in 1957, and later political efforts to establish the "Great Society." These and other circumstances caused private and public support for colleges and universities to rise to unprecedented levels.

Population grew rapidly and economic expansion created pressing needs for trained manpower. Occupational roles became more differentiated and specialized. Productivity and incomes rose, living standards climbed, and knowledge itself underwent what was popularly known as an "explosion."

Meanwhile, egalitarian sentiments spread and there was public demand for extended educational opportunities on all levels. These developments enhanced the importance of educational enterprise, particularly at the apex of the system in the university, or "multiversity," as Clark Kerr dubbed it.

Enrollment in the nation's colleges and universities, according to U.S. Office of Education reports, grew from 1,484,000 to 7,608,000 between 1940 and 1970. Graduate students comprised 105,000 (7.1 percent) and 946,000 (12.4 percent) of those totals. For the decade beginning in 1956, the proportion of high school graduates going on directly to college rose from 32 percent to 53 percent. Vastly increased demands for teachers and researchers led in turn to recruitment of more staff for postsecondary institutions. Similarly, business, industry, and government enlarged their cadre of advanced degree holders. The number of Ph.D.s granted per year tripled between 1960 and 1970, rising from 10,000 to 30,000.[1] Today, the population of the United States is more than twice as large as it was in 1900, but four times as many persons are employed in jobs demanding advanced education.

Prior to 1940, graduate education was almost exclusively a concern of academics. This is no longer true. But despite the growth in influence of vastly increased federal moneys for designated purposes and of other outside funding for earmarked objectives, the academic profession is still strongly in control of graduate education and basically determines the kinds of recruits to be admitted, programs to be offered, and the outcomes to be sought.

Although aspirants to academe's highest degree, the Ph.D., comprise only a fraction of those who go beyond the baccalaureate level with their formal education, this is the segment whose recruitment we are concerned with here, and more especially with those likely to become members of the academic profession. Some of the main questions include: What are their basic motivations? How does the academic profession compare in prestige and drawing power with other occupations based on a prolonged period of formal education? In what ways do sifting and sorting mechanisms affect admissions to graduate schools? What are the intellectual characteristics and social origins of recruits? How does the marketplace for talent relate to supply and demand? Have any notable changes taken place in recent years? What is the outlook for changes in the future?

Motivating Factors

To become a physician, one must first get an M.D. degree, undergo an internship and after that a residency to be a specialist, and then get certified by passing certain examinations for licensure. Lawyers must have been graduated from accredited law schools and must have passed the bar examinations. Public school teachers are required to be formally certified for their classroom duties. Many academics are heavily involved in the credentialing of these and other persons for entry into a growing variety of occupations.

It may seem anomalous, accordingly, that academics themselves have not fixed standards for entry into the profession, either by custom or law. On almost any college or university faculty there may be some individuals—artists, musicians, writers—without any degree at all. Not too many years ago, Ph.D. degree holders were a minority on the academic staffs of considerable numbers of four year institutions, and even today they are a minority among the faculties of junior or community colleges. However this may be, the doctorate has almost become a *sine qua non* for anyone who wishes to pursue a career of teaching or research in the liberal arts and science fields in senior-grade institutions of higher learning.

For most aspirants, it is a hard degree to get. The minimum period of residence is normally three years, but virtually everybody takes longer. Mere possession of the degree is no assurance of later success, to be sure, and at present as well as during the past few years, it does not even assure a job. Without the Ph.D. as a kind of "union card," however, prospective academics will find themselves handicapped.

The levels of ability and performance called for differ appreciably among institutions and even by departments within them, but getting a Ph.D. is typically an involved undertaking. A brain surgeon may spend more years preparing for the practice of his specialty, to be sure, but his later pecuniary rewards as an M.D. greatly exceed what they would have been had he opted to be a professor of biology. As will be noted later, the average lawyer has less formal education than the average professor and usually makes more money.

The academic aspirant is likely to be aware, nonetheless, of other compensations to be had. As one professor has observed, a college campus with well-tended lawns and gardens, tastefully furnished student gathering places, recreational facilities, theatrical entertainments and concerts, and a pleasing general life style affords a more appealing environment than working class and lower middle class Americans can afford from their salaries as "order takers" and "early risers."

> Students see that their professors can take off at any time of the day to run errands, and that instead of the one-and-a-half or two-day weekend, they can arrange a teaching schedule that will give them three or even four days. . . . classes can be cancelled or rescheduled. Naturally many students would like to have the very same freedoms for themselves. Academic salaries being what they are today, the economic deprivations that used to insure that only dedicated scholars would want these freedoms are no longer available to stem the flood of seekers after academic positions. It is this factor, not the draft as is so often claimed, that explains why so many undergraduates want to continue in graduate school.[2]

Most graduate students who expect to earn the Ph.D., however, profess less mundane motives than those just mentioned. Some of the students in graduate school are there because they were uncertain about what to do next after completing their baccalaureate degrees. Various reports have indicated that in many universities almost half of the graduate students were out of college for at least a year before resuming formal education. Bernard Berelson stated in 1960 that only 35 percent of 3,800 doctoral recipients had decided to go on to the Ph.D. at the time of getting their bachelor's degree.[3] Still further evidence has shown that earning a doctorate was not the primary aim of many who entered graduate school but that it later became an "emergent goal."

These tendencies have been variously interpreted as signs of procrastination, lack of drive, cautious deliberation, and intellectual versatility coupled with wide ranging interests, but a good many educators regard them as reflecting flaws in institutional sifting and sorting mechanisms.

A further point is that career decisions can be postponed by the eventual entrants into academic work, whereas commitments must be made earlier by nearly all aspirants to careers in most of the other professions. Although the institutional subsidy for training costs in some of these fields may on a per capita basis exceed those for graduate work in the arts and sciences (e.g., the per capita costs of medical education are enormous), the financial aids going directly to individuals in training are much more limited in number as compared with those available to many prospective Ph.D.s. In brief, inducements for the able but impecunious to join ranks with the able but undecided have augmented graduate school enrollments.

If what large numbers of Ph.D. aspirants have professed about their motivation is straightforward, their reasons are more complimentary to the academic profession than what might be inferred from frequent instances of vacillation. John A. Creager published an extensive inquiry in 1971, based on data about 33,199 students in 154 graduate schools, which supplies a good deal of useful information. Table 1.1 relates clues to the motivations of graduate students whose highest expected degree was the Ph.D.[4]

Table 1.1 Professed Reasons for Being in Graduate School

1.	To continue intellectual growth	96.9%
2.	To make significant contributions to knowledge in field	83.1
3.	Because of intrinsic interest in field	81.6
4.	To prepare for an academic career	81.6
5.	To increase earning power	74.9
6.	To serve mankind better	74.1
7.	Considers self an intellectual	67.9
8.	To satisfy job requirements	64.0
9.	To contribute to ability to change society	61.0
10.	To get in a prestigious occupation	57.4
11.	To get a teaching credential	41.6
12.	To find self	29.8
13.	To see whether particular field of study is congenial	20.9
14.	To engage in political activities	12.5
15.	To avoid the draft	9.7

Even though it might have been expected prior to inquiry that students would be prone to claim acceptable motives for being in graduate school, Table 1.1 does indicate, as do other findings in the Creager inquiry, that a preponderance of the Ph.D. seekers have strong intellectual motivation, a keen interest in their fields of study, and developed expectations of pursuing an academic career.

Typical graduate school procedures for searching out the ablest and best motivated students, however, have been widely criticized for being haphazard and inadequate. Admittedly, in many selective universities there is less aggressive effort to identify the most promising individuals than there is in the same institutions to recruit entering freshmen.

Until recently, most universities gave little attention to increasing the disproportionately small number of women and minority students going on to graduate school. Although some took pride in the geographic spread of their graduate school enrollments, there was much less concern with the spread of

student social origins. Because universities were influenced by
the changed ethos about extending advanced educational opportunity to all who may be desirous and qualified, lackadaisi-
cal recruitment of potential scholars and scientists is now giving way to more systematic effort.

It is important here also to take into account the relative prestige of the academic profession alongside comparable
occupations. My commentary on academics several decades
ago called attention to the generally high prestige of the profession as one of its attractions. This would be true today, and
for the intervening years. Because occupation is a basic element in social stratification and is regarded by sociologists as
"the most visible and recognizable aspect" of individual placement on society's status ladder, the prestige of a vocation directly influences its recruitment potential.

A replication in 1963 of a 1947 public opinion survey
of occupational prestige showed that U.S. Supreme Court Jus-
tices retained their preeminence, followed by physicians in
second position, with state governors and federal cabinet
members still near the top but down somewhat in popular
esteem. Scientists, particularly nuclear physicists, rose in rank,
and professors remained the same—eighth on a list of ninety
rated occupations. At both times, professors outranked lawyers, dentists, architects, civil engineers, ministers, bankers,
accountants, journalists, artists, and musicians.[5]

Other Influences on Recruitment

As Dael Wolfle has commented in *The Uses of Talent*,[6] "The
educational sector is coupled with the occupational sector by
millions of decisions made by millions of people." Nobody is
ever drafted unwillingly into the academic profession, of
course, and those individuals choosing such an option will
have their personal reasons. Even so, their motives and actions
are necessarily influenced by both educational and employing
agencies. Federal enactments, as has been demonstrated in

recent years, can widen the scope of educational opportunity. Cutbacks in governmental appropriations can also reduce the outreach of programs.

The openness of opportunity at virtually all levels of formal education in this country is unparalleled in other nations. In England and on the European continent, smaller proportions of secondary school graduates go to college, and the disproportion is even more pronounced for the postbaccalaureate level. Official Soviet statistics reveal that one of every three students gets a college-level opportunity, and that the proportion is reduced to one out of ten for Moscow State University (private estimates would lower both proportions).[7] Although no statistics are at hand for mainland China, various reports have been made to the effect that after the cultural Revolution in 1966, universities lost their elitist character, with peasants and factory workers often electing fellow workers for the privilege of advanced educational opportunity. By the late 1970s reports from China stated that the pendulum was swinging back the other way.[8]

Unlike some other nations, to be sure, the United States does not subsidize most of the individual cost of further education for those permitted to go on, but our nation does subsidize heavily the costs of operating a large number of public universities and contributes public funds to those under private sponsorship. At one time in the 1960s, community colleges were being formed at the rate of one a week. Most public senior colleges were expanded into universities, and many universities in turn became "multiversities."

The increased number of undergraduates from the mid-1950s to the early 1970s resulted in a larger pool of human talent from which graduate schools could recruit. Just how much overall improvement there was in the quality of this vastly enlarged pool is open to question. Some high school graduates who had been automatically promoted from one grade to the next entered college with reading and writing proficiency at an eighth grade level.[9] As has been reported in many newspapers and widely commented on editorially, standardized examination scores of students interested in going to college showed a progressive decline, with average College Board verbal scores dropping from 478 in 1963 to 429 in 1977, and mathematical scores down from 502 to 470. Selective admissions came under fire as being "elitist," and the tests themselves were increasingly lambasted as being unfair to the economically and culturally deprived. Some persons strongly felt that the "qualifiable" as well as the "qualified" should be freely admitted everywhere and given remedial courses, personal tutoring, and other special treatment to help bring about more equality of results.

Relaxed Sifting Practices on the Collegiate Level

Responding to both inside and outside pressure for change, many institutions during the 1960s reduced the number of required courses, activated new and more "relevant" programs of study, and substituted pass-fail evaluations for the customary letter grades. Student grading was inflated in many places to the point that "C" came actually to mean "below average."[10]

Indeed, just a few years after the appearance of John Gardner's much-discussed book, *Excellence*, in 1961, the real meaning of excellence seemed to be depreciated. The names on "deans' lists" in some institutions were more numerous than those not on them, and the rosters of "honor" graduates on commencement programs were often preposterously lengthy.[11]

By 1974, the president of Columbia University was calling for an end to low-quality expansion of educational opportunity in the United States and for less emphasis on credentialing for entry into many occupations. Many others, too, were wondering whether students were really getting "brighter and better every year" and whether the undergraduate program might be losing effectiveness as a sifting and sorting mechanism.

As a result of outcries from professional and other postbaccalaureate schools, not to mention prospective employers, the grade inflation began to taper off in 1975. Furthermore, students themselves displayed less interest in the campus distractions of the 1960s and more concern for serious study.

Although Christopher Jencks and David Riesman have asserted in *The Academic Revolution*[12] that aptitude has never played a much larger role than social class in determining who goes to college, and that once in, students with poor grades or poor aptitude scores are likely to do about equally badly whether they come from poor or rich family backgrounds, a published inquiry in 1964 showed that Harvard, Yale, and Princeton were taking fewer scions of prominent families and were thus replacing an "aristocracy of the wealthy," with an "aristocracy of the able."[13] Implementation of the Jeffersonian ideal for advanced education, accordingly, must have made gains in some places in the 1960s.

Moreover, "trendy" efforts to please students during the past decade were much less frequent in graduate schools. The least talented for the most part continued to eliminate themselves as prospects by not applying for admission. Perhaps it is true, as some say, that mediocre college graduates can always get in somewhere if they really want to continue, but there is no denying the greater rigor of admission procedures for advanced levels in the professional and graduate schools. In short, the merit principle of evaluating worth may have been weakened, but it was not abandoned.[14]

Graduate Student Quality

When I discussed graduate student quality in my 1942 book, I quoted from various persons who were dubious about the capabilities of many recruits to academe, but I went on to show that most of the evidence did not support such a view. In his 1960 book about graduate education eighteen years later,

Bernard Berelson cited data affirming that the native intelligence of the arts and sciences cadre of graduate students did indeed compare favorably with that in law and medicine. He went on to say that the quality "seems to be holding up reasonably well, despite their sharp growth in numbers. But in academic life, however good they are, they are never good enough."

Ten years later, in 1970, a Staff Report of the Commission on Human Resources[16] did substantiate two conclusions: 1) many of the very brightest baccalaureate degree holders (excepting women) do not go on to graduate school; and 2) the average aptitude test scores of those who do go exceed the average scores of degree holders not entering. Other conclusions of this inquiry were that graduates of the best colleges who do not go to graduate school exceed in quality most of the graduate school entrants from poorer colleges and that the quality of an institution's graduate program strongly influences the kinds of students attracted. In view of the creeping inflation of student grades in the 1960s, it is risky to generalize about grade averages of undergraduates who went on into graduate education in the 1940s and those who did so two decades later. Using data from a study made in 1965, Seymour E. Harris concluded that outstanding performance was not a prerequisite to graduate school attendance. As many as two-fifths of graduate students had undergraduate grades of "B−" or below, as few as 17 percent had averages of "A−" or "A".[17] Creager's 1971 study reported that 29.4 percent of those expecting to get Ph.D.s—a more select group, it should be noted—had undergraduate grade point averages of "B−" or less, with 28.6 percent averaging "A−" or better.

Nationwide averages, however, may blur notable differences from one institution to another. Over the years, for example, the City University of New York (CUNY)—with a large proportion of Jewish students whose cultural heritage, if not their socio-economic status, puts a high premium on intellectual accomplishment—displays some marked differences between the Phi Beta Kappas and others who were graduated. Eighty-nine percent of those elected to the society went on to graduate or professional school, whereas only 43 percent of the other alumni did. The honor society alumni were about three times more likely to become academics than were the other graduate school entrants.[18]

In addition to undergraduate grade point averages, another indicator of quality among applicants for graduate school admission is scores on the nationally used Graduate Record Examination (GRE) tests. Lewis Solmon's *Male and Female Graduate Students,*[19] reports a survey of doctorate-granting institutions in 1972–73. Using a cross-section of these institutions, Solmon computed mean scores by field, sex, and the Roose-Andersen ratings in 1970 of the prestige or presumed quality of the institutions to which applications were submitted. The Roose-Andersen ratings, it should be noted here, range downward from a 4.0 to 3.496 for the leading universities to 0.996 for those in the lowest *rated* category. (For further explanation of what is meant by the Roose-Andersen ratings, see Chapter 10, "University Prestige and Competition.")

Solmon's study shows conclusively that the presumably best trained bachelor's degree holders tend to go to the leading graduate schools. For the seventeen fields in which mean scores on GRE specialty tests were computed by sex, the scores virtually all ranged downward with each lower qualitative category of institution. In the field of economics, for example, the mean score of applicants for the most prestigious universities (that is, those rated 4.0 to 3.496 on the Roose-Andersen scale) was 673.15, whereas it was 505.0 for those institutions in the least prestigious rated category (rated 0.996).

Moreover, mean scores of both sexes displayed very noticeable variations from one field to another. Nearly all of the mean scores of applicants in all institutions in biology, chemistry, mathematics, philosophy, and physics were higher than 600, and none were that high in education, French, geography, German, history, music, political science, psychology, and sociology.

As has been noted earlier, women graduate students, on the average, have higher undergraduate grade point records than do men, but that is not so on the GRE specialty tests. In the seventeen fields in the four top qualitative categories of universities—those rating upwards from 1.996 to 4.0—the mean scores of men exceeded those of women. In a few fields the mean scores of women applicants did surpass those of men in the three qualitative categories of the less prestigious universities.

Solmon's monograph went on to show that whereas the most prestigious universities in his cross-section accepted slightly under half of their applicants, a majority of the other universities admitted almost three-fourths. With regard to the entry of women into graduate study, he concluded, "If discrimination in admissions exists, it is concentrated in the most elite institutions"; but he added that women tend to apply mainly to lower-quality institutions.

From all the evidence just reviewed, it seems clear that the merit principle prevails over other determinants in the admission of individuals to graduate level education, and that gaining entry signifies an achieved rather than as ascribed status. Although Berelson's 1960 comparison of IQ scores listed those of doctoral students as averaging 128, law students as 124, and medical students as 127, Ph.D. aspirants by no means include all of the "brightest and best" of those who go on in formal education after obtaining their bachelor's degrees. Other occupations compete with the academic profession for high-level talent, and in many of them the material rewards are greater for the able and ambitious. What the academic profession's "fair share" of exceptional talent should be is, of course, a matter of opinion. By reasonable standards of comparison, however, it seems to be incontrovertible that potential recruits to the academic profession are intellectually a superior group.[20]

Social Origins of Graduate Students and Potential Recruits

In 1942 I observed that the academic profession recruited more of an intellectual than a social elite, and that emphasis upon scholarly aptitude rather than general cultural attainments probably resulted in more upward social mobility for prospective academics than for young persons going into comparable occupations. I cited, for example, the following figures to indicate the occupational status of the fathers of academics (percentages): businessmen, 26.6; farmers, 24.7; manual workers, 12.1; clergymen, 10.6; teachers, 5.1; physicians, 5.1; lawyers, 4.1; professors, 3.9; chemists and engineers, 3.0; public officials, 1.9; editors and writers, 1.2; artists and musicians, 1.0.

Berelson stated in 1960 that graduate students had by then become more "heterogeneous in background and social origin. That was almost a natural accompaniment of the increase in numbers—there were too few of the 'elite' variety to support such a growth." Berelson went on to observe that Ph.D.s from the more prestigious institutions tended to cluster more at the top of the parental background ladder, partly because their families could afford to bear higher educational costs. For most graduate students, however, he said, "it is hard to overstate the importance of the graduate schools to students of high talent but low origin, and especially to those from an ethnic minority traditionally devoted to learning, like the Jews, who are over-represented in the graduate population—or its contribution in this respect to the American dream".[21]

A case in point is the study of CUNY Phi Beta Kappa alumni mentioned earlier. Only 18 percent of their fathers and 11 percent of their mothers went to college, yet 98 percent of their children did. Further illustrating upward social mobility by generation, only 10 percent of their children went to CUNY, with 49 percent going to private institutions, mostly in the Ivy League group.

In contrast with 1942, when about a fourth of those headed toward the academic profession were from farm backgrounds, Creager's 1971 report on the backgrounds of Ph.D. aspirants indicates that only 8.7 percent by then had rural origins. Of course, the work force engaged in farming had dropped drastically as a proportion of the total, as was also the case for manual laborers. But, perhaps because of more equality of advanced educational opportunity in 1971 and narrowed income gaps, the percentage of graduate students reporting fathers engaged in the lowest level of the labor force rose from 12.1 to 15.0. The percentage whose fathers were physicians declined from 5.1 to 2.7, and lawyers from 4.1 to 2.7 during the time interval. Percentages whose fathers were in public school work or were engaged in academic employment also dropped somewhat.

For the last three decades and more, it is clear that recruits to the academic profession have been in the main upwardly mobile individuals. More than half of them, in recent years, have been headed for a more prestigious and more remunerative occupation than that of their fathers. Since the gap in earnings has narrowed between those workers who did and those who did not go to college, the financial incentives of academic careers may have lessened for the upward bound. Furthermore, an open society such as our own, moving into a period of slowed economic growth, will doubtless evidence more competition between upwardly and downwardly mobile young people for beginning jobs in academe.

Other Aspects of Ph.D. Aspirants

Creager's 1971 normative description shows that about three-fourths of the prospective Ph.D.s are males, a somewhat higher proportion than their 65.7 percent among all graduate students. For both sexes of those expecting to receive the highest degree, there is this ethnic distribution by percentages: Caucasian, 91.8; Black, 1.9; Oriental, 4.5; other, 1.8. They range in age with 10.7 percent under age twenty-two to twenty-six percent over age thirty, and a fairly even scattering between these ages. Slightly more than a third have never married, but at least six out of ten report having been married at least once, with the majority not having any children.

As to religious affiliations, only 5.7 percent were brought up in no religious faith, but by the time they were prospective Ph.D.s 32.1 percent of them professed no particular religious faith. Religious groups showing a disaffiliation loss of 50 percent or more were these: Baptist, Southern Baptist, and Congregational; those showing some gain were Episcopal, Quaker, and Unitarian-Universalist. The largest single number of those brought up in a particular faith was Roman Catholic at 24.0 percent, and the next largest Jewish at 12.5 percent; at the time of the survey those still belonging to these faiths were 16.0 percent and 8.5 percent, respectively. The broad category of Protestants was numerically the most significant. Even though most of the respondents characterized themselves as being "moderately religious", it is obvious that exposure to extended formal education apparently had a secularizing influence on this large cross-section of doctorate seekers.

The respondents characterized their current political inclinations thus (by percentages): left, 10.6; liberal, 45.7; middle of the road, 21.9; moderately conservative, 18.7; strongly conservative, 3.1. In the 1968 presidential election, 21.0 percent did not vote; of those who did, 27.9 percent were for Nixon, and 44.2 percent for Humphrey.

Who Pays the Cost of Graduate Education?

Throughout the history of American higher education, the unit costs and proportional subsidies of graduate education have exceeded those of undergraduate education. Extensive data for 1942 are not available for a then-and-now comparison, but information is sufficient to show that there is nothing essentially new in the idea of subsidization. Although tuition charges on both levels haven risen sharply in recent years, a 1976 report for the Carnegie Foundation for the Advancement of Teaching concluded that the family share of higher education costs actually declined between 1929 and the current period.[22] Per capita income rose more significantly than did tuition. Government at the state and federal levels increased its share. A larger percentage of students were being educated at tax-supported institutions.

In 1942 I noted that 40 percent of the graduate students at Cornell University and 44 percent of those at Harvard were employed as student assistants. Pros and cons of the widespread use of teaching assistants were already being argued in annual metings of the Association of American Universities. Then as well as now, prospects and applicants for the more lucrative fellowships and other prestigious awards underwent highly competitive modes of selection. More frequently than on the undergraduate level, graduate students went out of state to pursue studies at leading graduate centers.

During recent decades the financial aid available to graduate students has grown enormously in amount and variety. Although sharp cuts have occurred in federal support to aid graduate students since 1971, Table 1.2 shows what the situation was in that year. As illustrated in Table 1.2, a particularly notable change from earlier years is the greatly enlarged role of the federal government in subsidizing graduate work.

The next calculation, Table 1.3 from Lewis Solmon's monograph[23] gives still further information and is useful for showing the average dollar values of direct stipends and of tuition and fee waivers.

Awards, of course, have a variety of purposes. From the point of view of particular institutions and of the academic profession as a whole, they are recruitment aids. The federal government makes such funding available to further educational opportunity for the needy and deserving, and to help channel the supply of highly trained talent in anticipation of the nation's manpower needs. Business, industry, and private

Table 1.2 All Current Sources of Financial Support for Advanced Study, by Sex, 1971

Source	TOTAL No. (N=207,208)	%	MEN No. (N=20,098)	%	WOMEN No. (N=7,110)	%
FELLOWSHIPS, SCHOLARSHIPS, TRAINEESHIPS, ETC.						
NSF	567	2	500	2	68	1
NIH, NIMH, PHS	1,626	6	1,000	5	527	9
NDEA	1,209	4	966	5	244	3
Other HEW	397	2	237	1	160	2
Other U.S. govt.	2,700	10	2,306	12	395	6
State or local govt.	1,193	4	971	5	222	3
School or university	4,572	17	3,770	19	802	11
Private foundations, organizations	1,108	4	855	4	252	4
Industry or business	657	2	563	3	93	1
Other fellowships, scholarships	551	2	411	2	140	2
EMPLOYMENT						
Faculty appointment	452	2	317	2	135	2
Teaching assistantship	4,373	16	3,756	19	618	9
Research assistantship	4,173	15	3,733	19	440	6
Other part-time during academic year	5,008	18	3,590	18	1,418	20
Other	2,732	10	2,382	12	350	5
OTHER						
Withdrawals from savings, assets	9,012	33	6,668	33	2,344	33
Spouse's earnings or funds	9,899	36	7,094	35	2,805	40
Support from parents or relatives	3,741	14	2,757	14	984	14
GI benefits	7,008	26	6,348	32	660	9
U.S. government loans	2,140	8	1,741	9	399	6
State or local government loans	919	3	769	4	150	2
Commercial loans (banks, etc.)	1,833	7	1,329	7	504	7
Other loans	1,204	4	1,069	5	135	2
Partial aid from employer (tuition reimbursement or waiver, grants, etc.)	1,423	5	940	5	483	7
Other	1,080	4	722	4	357	5

Source: Elaine H. El-Khawas and Ann S. Bisconti, *Five and Ten Years after College Entry* (Washington, D.C.: American Council on Education, 1974), p. 132.

Note: Table shows responses from 1961 freshmen.

Table 1.3 Distribution of Financial Aid by Type and Amount, 1972

	PROPORTION OF ENROLLMENT RECEIVING AWARDS		AVERAGE DOLLAR VALUE OF AWARD			
			Direct Stipend		Tuition and Fee Waiver	
	Men	Women	Men	Women	Men	Women
TOTAL NONSERVICE AWARDS	.115	.138	2389	2270	1579	1446
Awarded by institution						
Fellowships or scholarships	.081	.087	2309	2280	1353	1392
Traineeships	.028	.043	2608	2472	2114	1761
Other	.048	.042	2955	2799	1244	1179
Awarded by external (other) sources	.043	.040	2587	2442	1545	1519
TOTAL SERVICE AWARDS (other nonrepayable aid)	.306	.245	2648	2536	1311	1302
Research assistantships	.120	.079	2647	2638	1274	1337
Teaching assistantships	.219	.224	2501	2476	1260	1255
Other graduate assistantships	.072	.079	2561	2472	1120	1132
Instructorships	.069	.092	5037	3388	705	1000
Other	.101	.043	2362	2276	1206	1214
Institutional loans	.119	.136				
GI bill	.193	.027				

Source: Survey of graduate deans in which 50 schools provided usable statistics.

donors may underwrite awards for a wide range of reasons. In turn, individual students use such prospective aids in deciding where they will go to graduate school and what majors they will choose. As will be observed later, universities also may benefit financially from awards entailing the performance of service by securing a form of "cheap labor" for lower level teaching and research. Whether such "awards" are really misnomers is another question.

Berelson and others have noted that whereas families of means may accept responsibility for meeting the costs of *professional* training for their offspring, they are likely to regard meeting the costs of advanced academic training as society's business. A similar attitude apparently prevails among their sons and daughters. As one study has shown in following up a large number of students five and ten years after college entry, 45 percent of the earlier group of freshmen were unwilling to borrow any money to finance their graduate education, and only 35 percent were willing to borrow as much as $4,000; corresponding figures for the ten-year group were 35 and 41 percent.[24]

From the perspective of public policy Berelson has said, "As a matter of fact, it may cost society less to subsidize the Ph.D. training program at a relatively low rate and for a relatively short period than to provide the salaries necessary to attract the numbers to staff a mass educational system if most candidates had to pay most of their own way, as in the professions."[25]

Some Policy Aspects of Recruitment

I have already mentioned that millions of decisions affect the inputs and outputs of graduate education. Beginning in the 1950s, there was increased encouragement of holders of bachelor's degrees to continue in graduate school. The number of institutions offering graduate work multiplied, and hence the range of choice about where to go was extended.

Although standards were in the main not lowered in better universities, some of the minor institutions that moved quickly into graduate education (partly in response to inducements from the federal government) made it easier for students of marginal ability and background to go further. The emerging general attitude was not only that some college education is a "good thing" for virtually everybody, but also that still more formal education is an even better thing for many persons who obtain their baccalaureate degrees. Moved by the increasing pressure for egalitarianism, the allocators of tax moneys, not to mention others, became increasingly generous in underwriting this sentiment.

Alongside the effort to further equality of educational opportunity for all who wished to continue, however, highly selective efforts to single out the most promising for special recognition and reward became more sophisticated. A report of the Office of Scientific Personnel of the National Academy of Sciences–National Research Council summarizes how rating procedures had advanced in the selection of persons for top awards far beyond the consideration merely of grade point averages, GRE scores, and letters of recommendation.[26]

Knowledge about the reliability of instruments and procedures was enlarged and refined. Devices were developed for predicting doctorate attainment and on-the-job effectiveness among candidates. Candidate differences by field, by region, and by later employer category were more accurately delineated. In brief, as never before, improved means for implementing the merit principle of selection were made available. (Interestingly, "creativity" in scholarship and science was the single factor which proved to be most resistant to prediction.)

In the United States, as compared with many other countries where centralized planning has a more dominant role in determining the supply of recruits to meet anticipated needs for highly trained manpower, there is still a relatively free market in operation. During the 1950s and 1960s, the demand of Ph.D.s was deemed by many to exceed the supply; insofar as individual employment opportunity was concerned it was a seller's market. Not so in 1942. The saturation point of employability was being widely discussed in graduate school circles.

Before 1942 Harvard University's President Conant, for example, had stated that it might be advisable to adopt a *numerus clausus* similar to that practiced in medical schools in an effort to balance supply and demand. The Dean of the Yale Graduate School suggested in the 1930s that enrollment should be reduced by half through rigid initial selection. "Demand" was being estimated at roughly 3 percent of the number of gainfully employed Ph.D.s.

In *The Academic Man* I made these comments (pp. 30-31):

> To be sure, possible increases in demand may be brought about through population growth, changes in age composition of the population, a better appreciation for professional service, a rise in national income, the elevation of professional standards, shifts or enlargement in cultural values, and so on. Overcrowding is not merely a matter of definition or quibbling, as is proved by the vast amount of professional unemployment and maladjustment in Germany and Austria, where such conditions became factors in social upheaval. Not only does the unemployment of professionally trained persons depreciate the general social prestige of the affected occupations, but also the presence of large numbers of such individuals creates a prime source of instability in the whole social order.
>
> Because of the dangers inherent in overcrowding and in an indiscriminate selective mechanism, various forms of restriction have been proposed. Rigid examinations may discourage the less able from seeking entry into a profession, but often they only add to individual difficulties by merely prolonging and adding to the expense of training, so that general examinations coming late in the educational process are seldom highly effective as eliminative procedures. Raising fees and

lengthening time requirements penalizes those of limited means, and such measures are thus contrary to the merit system in placing a premium upon wealth or the initial class position of recruits.

Aside from examinations and other forms of limitation in the selection of graduate students, a strict *numerus clausus* such as is applied in certain of the *Ecoles* of France may aim at the production of an intellectual elite in the end, but be completely democratic in administration. Democratic ideology is on the whole antithetical to such a scheme, and in America it is only when a profession is in almost complete control of a centralized organization (e.g., the American Medical Association) that it can enforce such practices, and even then they have to be rationalized into apparent harmony with prevailing sentiments for equality of opportunity. Nonetheless, educators are going to find it increasingly imperative either to expand the market for academic work or else change the qualifications for entry into the profession.

Between 1942, when this was written, and the 1970s, the market for recruits to the academic profession has gone full circle. (I shall have more to say about this in the next chapter.) During these years, there were ups and downs in various fields—engineering enrollments, for example, being especially sensitive to the market—but in the main the Golden Age of higher education's phenomenal expansion came to an end in the 1970s.

2

Students and Apprentices

The University Syndrome

Around the year 1949 there were some 1,600 institutions of higher education in the United States, and by 1975 their number had increased to 3,055. Doctorate-granting institutions grew in number from 90 to more than 400. Not only did the proportion of Ph.D. candidates in the total student population rise steadily but also such candidates were no longer as concentrated in a few universities. By the 1960s, various observers were commenting on the decentralization, and some were beginning to ask questions about how many centers for advanced study and research the nation really needed.

Still other questions were being raised about the unacknowledged costs of resource scattering, but what has been called the "university syndrome" spread widely and in most circles was regarded positively rather than negatively. Institutional ambitions, backed by state and federal support, furthered the proliferation of graduate programs. Apprehensive about the possibility of a dire shortage of Ph.D.s, many persons believed that a sharp rise in output was needed, particularly in those areas that lacked graduate centers. New programs and centers multiplied.

Now, more than in the 1940s, the production of Ph.D.s is dispersed, and graduate students today often are in the newer schools,[1] and in public rather than private universities (the proportion of Ph.D.s awarded by private institutions dropped from 57 percent in 1940 to 36 percent in 1970). Despite the notion that the great increase in doctoral enrollments during the 1960s was largely in universities that began granting the degree after 1960, however, it should be observed that such institutions actually accounted for only 5 percent of the increase. Indeed, even in the early 1970s, almost two out of three doctoral candidates were enrolled in sixty universities.[2]

My 1942 observation was that even though students and apprentices tended to register in fairly well-known universities, they may have been recruited from obscure colleges in the hinterland. Today there is a greater probability that the undergraduate institution also is called a "university." One reason for this is that at least two-thirds of all baccalaureate degrees are now awarded by public institutions, and that spread of the "university syndrome" has left very few four-year institutions in the public sector.

Regardless of institutional origins, doctorate seekers' additional exposure to higher learning is not intended merely to be a prolongation of what they have already encountered as undergraduates. There is the added expectation that they will be prepared to contribute individually to the advancement of knowledge itself. Research becomes emphasized as an important aspect of enterprise.

Some of the persons trained in graduate schools go into nonacademic pursuits, to be sure, and they may later be employed in business, industry, government, or as independent professionals.[3] Moreover, the university is not the only social agency engaging in basic research. The graduate school is the sole agency, however, instituted for the purpose of intensively conditioning a select group for the advancement of learning *per se,* and doing so through insistent attention to research methods and processes.

In this context, a number of interesting contradictions arise. Whatever its ostensible purposes, the graduate school is in most arts and science fields a place where academics are engaged mainly in the production of other academics. The largest single number of those in training will become teachers; of those who do, comparatively few ever again do as much intensive research as was involved in writing their dissertations. The emphasis upon research in Ph.D. programs has been widely criticized, accordingly, and some other routes to the highest degree have been proposed and implemented. The Doctor of Arts Degree (D.A.) for college teachers, for example, was offered by twenty-three universities in 1975, and other degrees are available, but none as yet are in real competition with the prestige of the Ph.D.[4]

Attrition Factors

Baccalaureate holders failing to show at least average scholastic aptitude are not likely to be admitted to graduate school. Those who have not ranked above average are likely to fall by the wayside after admission. To get a more realistic and less generalized idea of what being a graduate student means, however, consider a typical recruit and observe the process and experience.

On the graduate level, the student undergoes modes of learning experienced earlier, but with stiffer requirements. More original work is expected, and examinations call for a higher order of ability and application. Rigid requirements and numerous safeguards, however, do not always have their intended effect. In my earlier study of academics, I referred to a University of Minnesota study which showed that less than 50 percent of the students in leading graduate schools ever got either the M.A. or the Ph.D., although 90 percent of the work was rated as satisfactory by their teachers. Attrition manifestly resulted from factors other than failure to make acceptable grades in courses.

In the year 1965, reported "obstacles" to completion of

the doctorate were listed in descending order of frequency as follows: financial problems, personal responsibilities, language requirements, inferior instruction, making up prerequisites, duties as assistants, uninteresting courses, thesis difficulties, limited stipends, academic restrictions, inadequate early counseling, preliminary examinations, and comprehensive examinations. Even so, financial problems were reported to be less severe than in earlier years.[5] To what extent these stated "obstacles" may veil scholastic inadequacies is a matter for speculation, but, assuming a constancy of graduate level grading standards in both earlier and later decades, it is probable that graduate student attrition during the 1960s and 1970s resulted more from other circumstances than from failure to make passing marks.

By persistent plodding, the less able students often get through the elaborate rigmarole of credits, examinations, theses, and other measures intended to sift and sort them. Not only is there no consensus about what an attrition rate ought to be in graduate education, but also there are difficulties in uniformly defining what the term means. Berelson noted in 1960, for example, that in median institutions "attrition" estimates varied from 20 percent to 40 percent.

In major universities, mere numbers of students necessitate a definite paraphernalia of accrediting, which is in effect a device for protecting and fortifying the highest degree. (As Walter Kotschnig once noted about pre-Nazi universities, "The Germans, who in their thoroughness reached a sorry perfection in this system, coined a special word for it—*Berichtigungswesen*."[6]) Accumulating the signs and symbols of scholastic approval is thus necessary for arriving at professional eligibility, and from the start the Ph.D. seeker is tied into a competitive system.

Aids and Stipends

In addition to credit courses, which do not entail student stipends, all universities have available other structured experiences designed to improve the capabilities of future academics. The most common of these are the fellowship, traineeship, and such categories as section-teaching assistant, junior instructor, science-laboratory assistant, and research assistant. Although fellowships do not couple stipends with specified duties, the other forms of "aid" are tied to the performance of assigned tasks and are thus forms of compensation.

Since the selection of fellows is often on a highly competitive, nationwide basis, with favorable publicity surrounding the naming of awardees, fellowships continue to carry more prestige than do stipends for assigned services, which leave less time for study. Other student aids, such as traineeships and research assistantships, may be directly relevant to individual attainment of the Ph.D. when pertinent to the field of specialization, but teaching assistantships (despite the pedagogical apprenticeship afforded) have been called "leftover awards" involving duties which have no relevance to getting the degree, and which actually may delay its completion, even though the experience may be helpful to some persons in getting teaching jobs.

A research assistant does assigned tasks (usually under the direction of one or more professors in charge of a project), typically involving no teaching responsibilities. A science-laboratory assistant normally supervises laboratory sections of undergraduate courses, with minimal teaching duties. One study based on 653 questionnaires returned by graduate students in "an unnamed Ivy League university" showed that 35 percent of the students were writing their dissertations, with the majority not having reached that stage. Most of the respondents (55 percent) who had held research assistantships rated that experience as "more helpful than an equivalent amount of study time, but 38 percent had an opposite reaction."[7]

The use of graduate students as teaching assistants in American universities is a practice dating back to the nineteenth century, and such designees have been variously known as readers, proctors, section-teaching assistants, junior instructors, and so on. Usually they are persons working toward advanced degrees and incidentally performing various kinds of duties connected with teaching, but they are not considered to be members of the regular faculty. After World War II, senior professors at major universities did less undergraduate teaching and more graduate students were employed to take over some of their routine responsibilities. Seymour Harris has stated that in 1965, 43 percent of all graduate students were receiving stipends for academic "scut work" of one kind or another, and that during the decade ending in 1965, the percentage increase in all fields was 283.8.[8]

It is pertinent to note surveys made at two major universities in 1965, the University of California and the University of Michigan. At California, 41 percent of all the lower division classes taken by the 1965 graduating class were taught by teaching assistants, and at Michigan the figure was 45 percent. Moreover, 31 percent of *all* undergraduate courses taken by the class of 1965 at California had been handled by teaching assistants, and in the fall of 1965 at Michigan "approximately 33 percent of the credit hours earned by undergraduates in Arts and Sciences were in courses taught by assistants."[9] This same commentary notes that at both institutions the undergraduate seeking a small class with intimate professorial contact had only one chance in three of getting such a course.

Although vociferous complaints from university undergraduates about scant opportunities for contact with senior professors are largely a phenomenon of recent years, there is nothing new about the dissatisfaction of graduate students with their roles as teaching assistants. As I pointed out in 1942, the volume of grumbling was loudest among those with subaltern statuses in the pecking order of academic employment.

Teaching assistants today appear to be dissatisfied for the following reasons: low pay,[10] responsibility without authority, role ambiguity in being regarded as students while performing as professionals, perfunctory assistance and neglectful professorial supervision, time-demand conflicts between graduate studies and assistantship duties, and wide-spread administrative and faculty indifference to their complaints about exploitation, with the "official" rationalization being that their roles are after all temporary and have to be performed by somebody. It should not be surprising, therefore, that TAs were among the leaders of some student uprisings in the turmoil of the 1960s[11] or that unionization of academic employees, which has made little headway in most major universities, did take place on the TA level at such institutions as Wisconsin, Michigan, and Oregon.

There is another side of the coin. Without teaching assistantships as financial aids, many of today's graduate students would not have had an opportunity for further education. Many universities would have found it difficult if not impossible to expand the enrollment of undergraduates very appreciably. Professorial time spent in correcting freshman and sophomore themes, drilling foreign language students, and doing other chores would have limited their chances for advancing learning *per se.* In short, the trade-offs have involved gains as well as losses, and it would be impossible to calculate precisely the balance of costs and benefits.

Moreover, many universities have been aware of the problem and have proposed and attempted solutions intended to improve not only undergraduate teaching but also the lot of teaching assistants. Cases in point may be found in the Muscatine Report for California (Berkeley); a study with recommendations made a few years ago at Cornell; a report about reforms and outcomes at the University of Utah; a project at Rochester University which involved other institutions as well;[12] and recommendations for change from various associations of institutions, such as the Association of Graduate Schools.

Ritualized Hurdles and Mileposts

Turning now from a consideration of student aids and inducements and from the various forms of apprenticeship for later

careers, we shall look next at the hurdles the prospective
Ph.D. must surmount and the mileposts which must be passed
en route to the highest degree. As an anthropologist might
readily perceive, those who are professionally initiated into
the higher learning undergo modes of treatment functionally
similar in some respects to the initiation rites primitive youth
must experience before admission to the adult circle of tribal
warriors. The academic recruit is not physically scarified or
required to fast in the wilderness waiting for a vision, but
there may be anguish prior to and during what many graduate
students regard as "ordeals."[13]

Unlike the undergraduate, who in most instances
merely has to pass the prescribed number of courses with a
"C" average to qualify for a bachelor's degree, the graduate
student normally must have a "B" average and meet still other
requirements. These latter take the form of special oral or
written examinations not directly related to any specific classroom course but to a broader field of study, tests of proficiency in one or more foreign languages, and an evaluation of
a rather extended thesis or dissertation based upon original
research.

Although the M.A. degree is not a prerequisite everywhere for progress toward the Ph.D., it does have significance
as a milepost and entails hurdles beyond meeting classroom
credit hour requirements. Moreover, it has some of the trappings of the doctorate. Traditionally, it carried a thesis completion and approval requirement, with some kind of general
examination of competence. Getting an M.A. or an M.S. en
route to the Ph.D. involves little extra effort for most seekers
of the highest degree, and many opt to take it along the way.
At this juncture, some may drop out, but others who have
been undecided may conclude that they should go on to the
doctorate.

For school teachers, the master's degree is typically terminal, but it does have a cash value for them in virtually

guaranteed salary increments. Certain kinds of master's degrees are terminal in some specialties but they also may be
generally useful for enhancing job opportunities in business
and some professions. For prospective academics the degree is
useful mainly as a symbol of exposure to some conditioning in
the graduate school, yet it has long since ceased to be worth
much as a ticket of entry into university employment. Its depreciation, in fact, has made it a rather ill-defined token of
accomplishment, illustrating in part the depreciation of symbols in inverse ratio to their scarcity.[14]

After the first or second year in graduate school the
candidate typically takes the preliminary doctoral examination,
and passing it denotes further elongation of what someone has
called "the indispensable prehensile tail for academic climb-
ing." The test's manifest function is to determine individual
worthiness for continuing up the ladder of academic apprenticeship. Although the examiners may be well aware of a particular recruit's merits or demerits, the examination can serve
to increase their insight, and regardless of this, unquestionably
it has ritual value as an "ordeal."

Such an examination can function as a status safeguard.
If it is oral and lacking in fixed standards or objective means of
gauging performance, the gatekeepers of academe can use it as
a barrier for candidates who meet course requirements but are
judged on other grounds to be unsuitable prospects.[15]

When this barricade is surmounted, the next one is
some demonstration of the neophyte's ability to read the literature of his or her specialty in two foreign languages—traditionally French and German. Such a requirement is long established, but in recent years in some fields and some institutions
other foreign languages may be chosen, or a course in statistics
substituted for one of the language requirements. The nominal
purpose of the language requirement, which usually must be
met at least a year before the candidate appears for the final
doctoral examination, is to demonstrate sufficient facility in

utilizing the languages in research. For most students, the requirement is in effect another dreaded hurdle, with possibly two or three efforts necessary after intensive "boning," private tutoring,[16] and other belated efforts to acquire at least minimal language skill.

Whatever its apparent purposes, then, the foreign language requirement undoubtedly causes some prospects to elect forms of the doctorate that omit such a stipulation, or else they may opt out entirely. In a currently glutted job market, as will be seen shortly, their dropping out may be in itself an act of service to the well-being of the academic profession.

Curricular requirements, the number of credit hours to be completed (seldom specified), and the minimum time of resident enrollment may initially seem forbidding, but the qualified candidate completes them without acute stress. A common stipulation is a minimum period of three years in graduate school on a full-time equivalence basis, with at least the final period of enrollment in the degree-granting institution. Few, however, complete the doctorate in the minimum period of required registration.

In some universities all of the courses may be in the student's chosen field, but in others at least one minor in a related field is required. Despite the lack of precise statements on quantitative requirements, broad specifications do exist as a protection of the Ph.D. as a title. Protection, which in other occupations is often secured through governmental or professional licensing, has been achieved within the academic profession largely through in-group control and agreements arrived at through institutional consensus and the sanction of accrediting agencies formed by institutions, or in some fields, by professional specialists. Since the honorary Ph.D. was abolished by agreement among universities in 1896, the Ph.D. is now exclusively an earned degree representing that its possessor has gone through a systematic form of higher education to achieve the status.[17]

The Doctoral Dissertation

The degree of Doctor of Philosophy has come to imply research competency as well as specialized knowledge and general understanding, in contrast with technical proficiency, which may be the basic criterion for other advanced degrees. The candidate is expected to acquire: 1) thorough mastery of a section of a selected field; 2) extensive familiarity with some special field as a whole; 3) acquaintance with related fields; and 4) capacity for making original contributions to the advancement of learning. In keeping with the general tendency toward greater specialization in higher education, the main emphasis is upon aspects 1) and 4), even more so than it was some decades ago.

The most important hurdle is the dissertation, or doctoral thesis. When the prospective professor is around the halfway point in his indoctrination, the dissertation looms ahead as a major undertaking. For some graduate students, finding a suitable topic is a vexing concern; for others, particularly those who as research assistants have already been involved with professors on large projects, further work on a problem already at hand may be the ready answer.

Although vastly increased funding of university research since the 1940s undoubtedly facilitates dissertation production in ways which were then virtually nonexistent, the typical graduate student is still confronted with the task of engaging in what is likely to be the most concentrated as well as sustained intellectual effort of a formal learning career. The occupational culture, however, has set up ready means for overcoming the uncertainties.

In many departments the graduate school professors have well-marked-off domains whose corners they encourage graduate students to explore for findings which may later contribute either anonymously or in acknowledged footnotes to the professor's larger "discovery." In the humanities, there are always "influences" to be traced and "sources" that are sure to be revealed by patient digging; in the social sciences there are innumerable data to be correlated in proving or disproving this, that, or another proposition; and the biological and physical sciences, too, are not lacking in their own typical projects.

The dissertation topic itself is selected by the student, subject to the advice of the professor in charge, and in some instances it must be approved by a graduate council. (Graduate students sometimes complain that the committee system places them in the role of "trying to please too many bosses.") The subject is expected to be one in which originality can be shown in proving or discovering something not known before, or by establishing one or several conflicting views already held, or by disproving an existing view widely accepted. The method of discovery, adjudication, or disproof nominally must be with reference to a topic of importance, but academic standards of importance vary from one department to another, and from one institution to another. In mathematics, for example, the candidate normally picks a problem that can be solved and has not previously been solved. Obviously, just any problem will not do, yet even in this most precise of all disciplines the criteria of adequacy with regard to difficulty and significance vary widely from one judge to another.

The unbelievably picayunish features of some doctoral dissertations that satirists have ridiculed may be less a result of choice on the part of candidates than of pressures bearing upon them. Professors may set capable students to trivial and minutely specialized tasks to fill in gaps in their own larger studies, or the candidate may pick a narrow topic of little import in order to get the job done in a limited time. Already beset by anxieties as time becomes a more precious commodity, the thesis writer is reluctant to attempt great heroic work with large risks and possibilities of infinite delay.

Some academics have proposed that the French type of doctoral dissertation, which stresses intellectual culture, be adopted alternatively as "a means of softening the hard lines of academic type," but the suggestion has had little effect in changing practices. The prevailing sentiment was and is that the prospective academic should become a real authority on at least some small domain of knowledge. When the dissertation is finished and accepted, the average candidate feels great relief—sufficient in most instances to offset any doubts about how many readers the tome might ever attract.[18]

Even though a good many universities once required that all doctoral dissertations be published at the author's expense, presumably on the assumption that they were important contributions to knowledge and ought to be made generally available, as early as 1932 at the University of Michigan only 90 of their 800 institutionally approved dissertations had ever been published. (Back in the 1930s I did a count of reader checkouts of the bound volumes of Harvard dissertations in the Widener Library there and noted that the average was 1.08 times for those of the year 1909, and 3.0 for those of the year 1929. Some of them, of course, had substantively appeared in journal articles, and others had doubtless been published in more widely read books.)

To the best of my knowledge, few if any universities now require the conventional form of publishing dissertations. Since dissertations are still considered to be public documents, however, other means have been developed for making their contents available, and at less expense, such as University Microfilms, an agency based in Ann Arbor, Michigan. In 1951, the Association of Research Libraries approved this service as a satisfactory publication medium for doctoral dissertations. The microfilm agency now publicizes the contents of about 95 percent of all the dissertations approved in the United States each year, and in an international section of *Dissertation Abstracts* also includes items from a number of European countries. Approximately 2,500 libraries subscribe to the abstract service.

Completion and acceptance of a dissertation, however, are not always the final hurdles the candidate for a Ph.D. must surmount. In earlier years, there was yet another hurdle, the doctoral examination. It usually but not invariably related only to the dissertation project. Today, some universities have abandoned this requirement.

Doctorate Profiles

A sampling in 1944 of some five hundred listings in the *Directory of American Scholars* revealed that the median age for those obtaining their doctorates was 32.7.[19] This coincides with my own observations a few years earlier *(The Academic Man)* that at this juncture the Ph.D. graduate was likely to be about thirty, as compared twenty-seven in medicine, twenty-five in the ministry, and twenty-two in engineering. I went on to note, "Occupational conditioning in the academic profession is more often interrupted by full or part-time employment and retarded by marriage, usually deterring the highest degree by five years.[20] It thus appears that far from being a callow youth, our 'fledgling' academician has already spent the most vigorous years of his life before he ever begins permanent employment" (p.52).

Then, as now, however, those who have achieved greatest prominence later in their fields of specialization have tended to get their degrees when younger than the average. Moreover, despite all efforts over several decades to reduce the doctoral "stretch-out," the median age at doctorate for 33,000 Ph.D.s granted in the academic year 1973-74 was 32.1.

After the bachelor's degree, as we have seen, the minimum time for getting a Ph.D. is three years. The total "actual time" is about four years, but in ten major fields between 1957 and 1964 the average lapsed time ranged from a low of 5.9 years in chemistry to a high of 12.7 in education.[21]

With such a stretch-out, one might guess that most Ph.D. aspirants would in the process become restive and dissatisfied individuals. A Carnegie Commission on Higher Education report in 1972 has shown that this is not the case.[22]

Seventy-seven percent of the graduate students at doctorate-granting institutions either strongly agreed, or agreed with reservations, with the statement, "I am basically satisfied with the education I am getting." Only 23 percent strongly disagreed or disagreed with reservations. Only 27 percent felt that their fields were too research oriented, and 32 percent thought that their graduate education had been a wasteful repetition of work on the undergraduate level.

Ann M. Heiss made a study in depth of doctoral student evaluations of their academic programs during the 1960s on the Berkeley campus of the University of California. Her analysis of some 2,300 questionnaire returns and 100 interviews led her to the following conclusions:

1. An average of 83 percent of the doctoral students on the Berkeley campus said they were more satisfied than dissatisfied with their over-all doctoral experiences. The greatest dissatisfaction was found among students in the social sciences and the least dissatisfaction was reported by the physical science and professional school respondents.

2. Doctoral students at Berkeley evinced a need for more personalized or individualized orientation and integration into the academic bloodstream of the university, for more interaction with their professors, and for greater interdisciplinary involvement.

3. Berkeley doctoral students reported the need for a re-examination of the rationale on which some university requirements are predicated and for a re-evaluation of the appropriateness of these requirements to specific fields of knowledge.[23]

Turning now from the feelings of graduate students about their prolonged indoctrinations, let us take a look at the main fields of study of most of those completing the doctorate, comparing the distribution by specialization in 1940 and in 1969, as set forth in Table 2.1.

In Table 2.1 it is evident that modes of classification in the data sources changed in a few instances between 1940 and

Table 2.1 Rank Order of Top Twenty Fields by Doctorates Conferred, 1940 and 1969

1940	1969
1. Chemistry	1. Education
2. Education	2. Engineering
3. English	3. Chemistry
4. Physics	4. Psychology
5. History	5. Physics
6. Economics	6. English and Journalism
7. Biochemistry	7. Biological Sciences (misc.)
8. Psychology	8. Mathematics
9. Botany	9. History
10. Mathematics	10. Fine and Applied Arts
⟶ 11. Political Science	11. Economics
12. Engineering	12. Agriculture
13. Romance Literature	13. Business and Commerce
14. Physiology	14. Biochemistry
15. Sociology	⟶15. Political Science
16. Philosophy	16. Social Sciences (misc.)
17. Bacteriology	17. Sociology
18. Agriculture	18. Biology
19. Geology	19. Religion
20. Religion	20. Bacteriology

Source: U.S. Office of Education.

1969, but that enough of them remained the same to permit some comparisons. Some of the most popular fields in 1940 were no longer among the top twenty in 1969, and some not included at the earlier time rose to the top rank during the three subsequent decades. None of the fields appearing at both times show duplicate rank orders, but most of them do not evidence drastic shifts. In brief, this tabulation illustrates once again the change and the stability which frequently are intertwined in academic enterprise.

Before getting into a discussion of how new Ph.D.s find occupational placement, it is important to note here that we are concerned chiefly with those who go into academic teaching and research. According to National Research Council figures, between 1927 and 1935 about 64 percent of doctorate holders became academic professionals, and by 1970 the proportion had risen to 71 percent.[24] In my 1942 book, I observed that chemistry was then the only arts and science field in which the chances were better than ever that new Ph.D.s would enter nonacademic employment. Now, as well as in earlier times, accordingly, the Ph.D.s who find their life careers in academe rather than elsewhere constitute the majortiy.[25]

Finding a Job

As increasing proportions of the doctorates of the 1970s are frustratingly aware, finding a suitable job these days is no simple task. Likewise, during the 1930s and 1940s, the recent Ph.D. confronted a buyer's rather than a seller's market; competition for job placement was less open then than now. In 1942, I observed that the vast majority of qualified persons were not in actual competition for the same positions, and that some were not even potential competitors. Until recent years, there was virtually no public advertising of either job openings or job applicants, and any direct approaches by candidates were typically regarded as *infra dig.* Today, on the contrary, the professional journals often run many columns of such notices, and *The Chronicle of Higher Education* (the most widely read weekly newspaper about higher education) has page after page of advertisements in every issue. There is some skepticism, to be sure, as to whether such vacancy notifications are really anything more than *pro forma* modes of compliance with federal rules and regulations, but the fact that they are there at all denotes a turnabout in apparent practices.

Then, as now, the fledgling Ph.D. was not left to fend for himself in the job quest, for the prestige of institutions and departments hinged in no small way upon what happened to their graduates. The 1940 doctorates in such relatively stabilized growth fields as philosophy, English, and the classics were experiencing problems in finding suitable jobs. The stability of faculty rosters and slow rates of turnover in nearly all places except the expanding state institutions were expressed by Harvard's President Conant for his own campus as one example: 'It is expected that there will be approximately one vacancy in the permanent staff available every four years for a department containing normally eight permanent professors; smaller departments will have vacancies less frequently, larger ones more often."[26]

During the 1950s and 1960s, employment prospects for new doctorates improved rapidly in response to the great expansion of higher education on all levels. The brightest and best of the Ph.D.s might be invited to join the staffs of the departments that had trained them, and their options to go elsewhere were much wider. Instead of beginning as instructors, they often could start as assistant professors, with reduced teaching loads and research enticements held forth as added attractions. Even the mediocrities encountered few difficulties in finding teaching posts somewhere in a nationwide bull market for academic talent.

For at least five decades, however, the marketability of recent Ph.D.s has been heavily influenced by these limiting factors: 1) their placement normally is not in an institution of higher repute than the one from which they were graduated; 2) their best employment opportunities are likely to be in places within the sphere of influence of their own university or department; and 3) if the repute of that institution or department is circumscribed, employment prospects are most likely to be within a college or university of the surrounding region.

Many years ago, the American Association of University Professors (AAUP) reported how a cross-section of 117 institutions found their replacements and additions for faculty posts: own college or graduate school, 26 percent; other graduate schools, 23 percent; friends in other institutions, 22 percent; college and university appointment bureaus, 11 percent; personal, written applications, 10 percent; commercial agencies, 5.3 percent; chance recommendations from other schools, 2.6 percent.[27] Although percentages undoubtedly are different for later time intervals, these sources of prospects for job openings are still in use. As noted, however, the market-place for academic talent is today more open (despite survival of the "old boy network") and perhaps more depersonalized as a result of equal opportunity ethos influences and the federal government's affirmative action mandates, with particular regard to race and sex. Moreover, the impact of sheer numbers of persons and jobs has also altered the picture.[28]

The annual meetings of the various scholarly, scientific, and professional societies have functioned in part as clearing houses where prospective employers and employees could come into contact. Participation in the various sections where papers are read and research work is discussed affords opportunities for the younger as well as the older academics not only to advance knowledge but also to enhance their occupational outreaches. In the 1930s and 1940s, when novitiates were anxiously casting about for $1,800 instructorships, the meetings came to be called "slave markets." Today the phrase is again in use.

The Depressed Market

Despite the continuing attractions of an academic career, many able college graduates are not indifferent to what their job prospects may be as a consequence of ups and downs in the market for highly trained talent. First-year graduate enrollments in physics during 1970-71, for example, slumped by 17 percent, while those in the health professions rose by 21 percent. In general, disciplines normally placing a large proportion of their doctorates in college and university work experienced enrollment decline and those oriented toward nonacademic fields of employment continued to grow.[29]

The bad news spread quickly, and the increasingly rough competition of new Ph.D.s for jobs was heralded in media headlines such as these: A PH.D. WAS ONCE A COLLEGE

JOB TICKET, BUT NOT ANY LONGER; DEMAND
SLOWS FOR SCIENTISTS; TEACHING JOB PROSPECTS
FOR GRADUATES WITH DOCTORATES REPORTED TO
BE WORSE.
Could this "unexpected" turn of events have been pre-
dicted? The answer is that it could have been and, indeed, was.
Bernard Berelson mentioned the possibility of imbalance be-
tween supply and demand as early as 1960. In 1965, Allan M.
Cartter pointed out serious errors in existing projections and
predicted an impending market glut in many fields, with even
worse prospects for the 1980s.[30]

Demographic data about the declining birth rate were
available, to be sure, but the proportion of young persons being
graduated from high schools did not reach its peak of 78.5
percent until 1969. Furthermore, the percentage going on to
college did not drop until 1969. The shakers and movers for
unlimited expansion of higher education apparently preferred
to ignore the likelihood of a slowdown. They also did not antici-
pate the possibility of what many economists had said could not
happen—concurrent economic recession and inflation.

In any event, by 1973 it was reported that in the field
of English, 1,402 Ph.D.s were scrambling for 139 openings,
and that just one job-seeking historian out of six was able to
find an academic post. By 1976, there were only about 15,000
new faculty "hires," but this was no temporary phenomenon—
the prospect was that by the 1980s the figure would drop to
under 5,000. (This imbalance was not confined to prospective
academics. A 1974 survey of journalism baccalaureates found
that only 62.4 percent of them were able to find jobs in news,
advertising, or public relations; the estimate was that by 1978,
about 20,000 journalism graduates would compete for only
5,680 media openings.)[31]

Higher education, of course, has other purposes than
the preparation of manpower for gainful occupations. As
Stephen K. Bailey has put it, one aim is to "make joyful persons," but one may reasonably have doubts that there are very

high levels of buoyancy among the unemployed and underemployed Ph.D.s in the recent academic job market.

Outlook

Although it is easy to blame market imbalances on the miscalculations of individuals and educational institutions, and to assume that self-correcting influences will quickly restore a balance between supply and demand, the situation is not that simple. It would be impossible, for example, to single out the decision makers who were responsible for the fact that between 1967 and 1975 the proportion of the Gross National Product going to research and development dropped from 3.0 percent to 2.29 percent.

Nearly everybody favors a leveling up of educational opportunity, of course, but there is seldom an acknowledgment that unless financial resources are unlimited (and they never are), leveling up for some may entail leveling down for others. Perhaps we should expect that in an era of pressures for equality of opportunity coupled with increasingly tighter funding for most colleges and universities, the pinch will be most severely felt in graduate education. And this is what appears to be in prospect.

In 1971, the U.S. Office of Education projected a new doctorate supply of 68,700 in 1980-81, and the next year revised its estimate downward to 52,000. We have already noted another prediction that by the 1980s the probable number of "new hires" for faculty positions would be under 5,000. The National Science Foundation has attempted to project demand for new doctorates in nonacademic research and development. Its projection states that by 1980 the figure could be as low as 7,000 or as high as 20,000. Splitting the difference between these two guesses, one gets the number of 13,500 new doctorates in science and engineering fields who may find nonacademic employment in 1980. Adding to this figure the projection of 5,000 prospective academic posts open, for a total of

18,500 opportunities, the possibility is that 33,000 of the 52,000 new Ph.D.s in 1980 may be either unemployed or underemployed. This figure does not take into account, of course, the nonacademic job prospects for new Ph.D.s in fields other than sciences and engineering, but in the humanities, for example, the likelihood of finding suitable nonacademic employment is much less than in the fields mentioned.

Despite the highly speculative nature of such forecasts, particularly for nonacademic employment, it is manifest that the future of graduate enterprise is fraught with critical uncertainties. Formed in 1969 to concern itself with such matters, the National Board on Graduate Education, after intensive study, has issued some very useful reports, including a 1975 final report which foresees the following main trends.[32]

1. A steady reduction in demand for new Ph.D.s to serve as college and university faculty members through the 1980s.

2. A reduced rate of growth of research and development expenditures relative to that of the 1960s, and hence reduced growth rates of demand for new Ph.D.s in such activities (there will undoubtedly be specific research areas, however, that grow much faster than the average).

3. A substantial supply adjustment on the part of students and universities that will reduce the number of new Ph.D.s awarded well below the numbers projected on the basis of past trends; in many fields, however, the supply of new doctorates will exceed the demand from traditional, discipline-related sources.

4. A continuing decline in the total amount of financial support available to full-time graduate students, thereby increasing the relative importance of loans and self-support.

5. Some increased enrollment demand by "nontraditional" graduate students, e.g., older students, part-time students, nonresidential students, women returning after child rearing, and nondegree students.

6. An increase in the number of women and minority students seeking graduate education.

7. Continued focus on accountability, including program evaluation, cost analyses, and other measures of program performance.

8. No large new programs to support graduate education, barring a major intellectual breakthrough in some disciplines or a substantial shift in national priorities.

The National Board recommends certain prompt adjustments, calls for further research into the whole matter, and optimistically concludes that "our national capability in this area can be strengthened and diversified, even in a period of limited growth."

My only addendum is that in a period of lessened requirements for sheer quantitative expansion of output, renewed attention can and should be given to the quest for excellence, with an emphasis on high quality as a main component for all graduate education.

3

Staff Members

Faculty Recruitment Policies and Practices

Most American universities in earlier years set their own employment policies and exercised them in what was then a buyer's market, that is, where the supply of academics exceeded the demand. During the late 1950s and 1960s, as we have already seen, the situation was reversed and virtually every Ph.D. could readily find a job somewhere. The pendulum has now swung all the way back again, with a vastly increased supply of job seekers available for a diminishing number of openings. One might mistakenly assume that filling vacancies must now be an easier institutional task than it formerly was, but in fact it has in some respects become more complicated. Universities are no longer permitted to be freewheeling in their employment policies and practices.

In earlier years, few concerted objections were voiced about policies that enlisted mainly the services of white males of certain preferred social and academic backgrounds to the exclusion in effect of women and minority groups. Employers conducted their searches largely through personal contacts, and the British practice of advertising job openings was not used and was even frowned upon in this country. Furthermore, not many persons in academic circles perceived any unfair discrimination in the avoidance of open-market practices.

Comparatively few women and blacks were to be counted in the job market for university posts. As Jessie Bernard has pointed out,[1] the peak period in the percentage of women academics was in 1879. (The percentage of black academics outside black colleges has always been minuscule.[2]) Whether as a result of dwindled demand for their services or their diminished interest in academic jobs (Bernard considered the latter situation more likely), women underwent a reduction in college and university employment between 1940 and 1960.

Despite changes in other respects, the academic and professional qualifications used by universities in making staff replacements and additions have remained relatively constant. Many of the criteria of almost half a century ago are still in use today. *The Harvard Report on Some Problems of Personnel in the Faculty of Arts and Sciences*[3] set forth the following widely used criteria: ability and training in teaching and research, intellectual caliber, capacity for leadership, general reputation, originality, personality and character, and probable future performance. I noted in 1942 that in the case of the beginning instructor, evidence of suitability was sought in the candidate's scholastic record, the judgements of those knowing him,[4] his written or published work, and the general impression made through correspondence or interview.

My further comment was that utilization of objective criteria of competence was hindered by the absence of an openly competitive market, the difficulty of judging intangible qualities on the basis of readily available information, and the intrusion of particularized attitudes favoring candidates with geographic and social proximity. A number of universities then had, and some still have, standing policies against the immediate employment of their own most recent Ph.D.s, for somewhat the same reasons underlying nepotism rules. "Inbreeding" as a mode of recruitment was regarded by some critics in that period as evidence of favoritism, but recently there has been little discussion of this matter.[5] The tendency to favor prospects having what I then termed "social proximity" has, of course, been subjected to increased attacks during the last two decades. Certain forms of discriminatory judgment once deemed acceptable and proper are now generally unacceptable and even illegal. The demographic representativeness as well as the personal capabilities of prospective faculty members must be taken into account. In an egalitarian era, it is still all right for universities to give preference to scholars as job prospects, but it is no longer legal to insist that they be gentlemen.

Amending a 1965 federal executive order banning discrimination based on race, religion, color, or national origin, a later executive order taking effect in 1968 also barred sex discrimination. It covered only those colleges and universities having government contracts, to be sure, but this meant that most of the nation's institutions of higher education were included.

The task directly ahead for the federal government and for institutions was not a easy one, and impatient activists charged both parties with foot dragging. Several years prior to 1972, for example, the Women's Equity Action League had instigated a total of about 300 class-action suits, and black political action groups were exerting pressures for speedier implementation. Meantime, many colleges and universities complained about the lack of uniformity of interpretation among regional offices, the absence of useful guidelines, the need for specific criteria to determine discrimination, the short time requirements imposed for conformity, and so on.

HEW's Office of Civil Rights and the U.S. Equal Employment Opportunity Commission began to issue guidelines and to set employment "goals" for colleges and universities. Such prestigious universities as Michigan and Harvard were thereafter threatened with cancellation of their federal contracts if they did not quickly bring their employment policies and practices into compliance. The University of California at Berkeley spent months putting together a four-inch-thick document analyzing the sexual and racial composition of its seventy-five academic departments; it projected goals and time-tables over a thirty year period for achieving—department by department—equality of opportunity in employment. Few other institutions proceeded that elaborately, but most did draw up and publish affirmative action plans and proclaim themselves to be "equal opportunity employers."

The institutions promised in general to remedy the under-representation of women and minority-group members, to eliminate salary inequities, and to adjust differentials in the bases for promotion and in the rates of promotion. Some began promptly to implement their promises.[6] Outcries of "reverse discrimination" were soon heard from white males to the effect that qualified women prospects were being favored above better qualified men competitors for job openings, and that blacks likewise were getting preferential treatment. A somewhat facetious newspaper caption of that period read: "The Ideal New Professor: She's Black."

Besides the honest effort of many institutions to bring about reform there was also protest over the uneven and heavy-handed procedures allegedly used by federal bureaucrats and courts of law. Despite official denials that Washington-set goals were intended as "quotas," even Attorney General Levi pronounced that in his opinion they were indeed quotas. There were widespread campus objections to infringements on institutional autonomy and to what was perceived as an erosion of the merit principle and the right to choose only the best qualified for particular posts.

Toward the end of 1975, Brigham Young University, for example, announced that it would not comply with the federal government's Title IX regulations against sex discrimination. Even though it voluntarily complied with most of the regulations, it denounced others as exceeding the government's legal authority to infringe on the Mormon-affiliated institution's religious freedom and the church's moral tenets. To illustrate an opposite end of the reaction continuum, however, another situation should be mentioned. In 1977, at the City College of the City University of New York, the chancellor circulated a memorandum designating Italian-Americans as an "affirmative action category," and some of his colleagues began to wonder whether Irish-Americans, Greek-Americans, ad infinitum would soon begin to want their special entitlements.[7]

An outcome of all this is that more attention is being paid everywhere to academic job opportunities for women and for "hyphenated Americans," but there is also evidence that long-established "network" modes of searching out, evaluating, and selecting new employees are still in use. Although the bona fide intent of institutions to give serious attention to responses they receive from widely advertised vacancies has been questioned,[8] one cannot dismiss lightly the fact that both jobs and applications are now being openly publicized. Most recent inquiries reveal that in many places information obtained from such sources augments rather than supplants the more informal "collegial network" in moving toward affirmative action goals.

After prolonged wrangling on all sides over affirmative action issues, the U.S. Department of Labor began hearings in the fall of 1975 in an effort to resolve the presumed differences between civil rights protagonists and institutional spokesmen, and HEW made further efforts to improve its guidelines. About the same time, the Carnegie Council on Policy Studies in Higher Education issued a report and made recommendations for better future strategies; it concluded that the greatest need was to increase the supply of highly qualified persons (mainly Ph.D.s) among the "still under-represented groups."

Of course, affirmative action issues are still very much alive. Lawsuits charging institutions with "reverse discrimination" have become more frequent, and many questions about what is fair and equitable (not to mention operable) are still unanswered. However all this may be, a research report issued in 1975[9] analyzed National Research Council files and showed that the percentage of new women doctorates in research, postdoctoral work, and teaching during the years 1967-73 "provides no evidence of discrimination against women in first job placement in R&D and postdoctoral activity, while evidence suggesting earlier discrimination in teaching appointments disappeared by 1973." The data, one should note, are for a period of general decline in academic hiring.

Still another study conducted by the American Sociological Association in two hundred graduate-level sociology departments indicated that the enrollment of women between 1970 and 1973 rose from 37.2 to 40.9 percent, of blacks from 6.0 to 7.6, and of Spanish-Americans from 1.0 to 3.0. During the five-year period from 1970 to 1974, the percentage of women in all ranks in the sociology departments rose from 9 to 18.5; of blacks, from 3.0 to 4.9; of Spanish-Americans, from virtually zero to 1.0.

As we shall note in a later chapter, however, sociologists in particular and social scientists in general are more inclined than most of their academic colleagues to push for affirmative action implementations.[10] As Betty M. Vetter, executive director of the Scientific Manpower Commission, has observed, women and blacks have been less well-represented all along in the physical sciences, mathematics, and some other fields than in the social sciences. Her finding in 1975 was that whereas "recent studies show some improvement in the participation and utilization of women and minorities in science, the position of new women Ph.D.s in a falling employment market has deteriorated over the past 5 years."[11]

Expectancies of New Appointees

Turning from a consideration of who lands where and why, one should note the continuing probability that the new faculty member will have come from another institution where the Ph.D. was obtained.[12] The further probability is that he or she will begin as an assistant professor, rather than as an instructor. In the 1940s and earlier, the beginner typically started as an instructor, but during the later boom years employee bargaining power improved and instructorships came to be occupied mainly by persons still working on their doctorates. Whether the assistant professorship will continue to be the first rung of the academic ladder for most new Ph.D.s in a depressed job market remains to be seen.

Young academics today are more likely than their counterparts of earlier decades to be informed about characteristics of their employing departments and institutions because information regarding such matters is now more widely disseminated and made use of by the professional "careerists" who are more frequently encountered at all levels. Still, surprisingly, beginners often lack important information about their new jobs, and institutions in turn often make lower rank appointments on a "sight unseen" basis. During the 1960s, to be sure, there was a pressing demand for warm-bodied Ph.D.s, and in many places travel money was in short supply.

In his 1965 monograph, David G. Brown reported the experiences of 103 newly appointed social scientists in eighteen of the largest institutions in the Southeast.[13] Forty-nine percent of them had never previously set foot on their campuses. About a third of the total number arrived unaware of salient features of their posts, and did not know what their areas of ignorance were, and about a seventh of them said they "would not have accepted their positions if they had known more about them." Of the 51 percent who had visited hiring campuses prior to job acceptance, almost all reported the visit to be "the *most* helpful means of information gathering." In view of the mutually heavy investment of both individuals and institutions in new appointments, one may wonder why campus visitation is not a part of the usual protocol for all such situations. With the prospect of fewer new appointments almost everywhere in the years ahead, perhaps campus visitation will become more common.

Table 3.1 shows what Brown found out in his interviews regarding what new appointees with fairly recent degrees knew about their jobs when they accepted appointment.

Table 3.1   Knowledge of Individuals about Specific Aspects of the Job They Accepted at Time of Acceptance

ITEMS	PERCENTAGES OF 103 INTERVIEWEES WHO KNEW ABOUT ITEM
Salary	96%
Academic rank	95
Hours of classroom teaching	93
Courses to be taught	77
Extent of library facilities	73
Office facilities	71
Fringe benefits	67
Quality of students	64
Promotion possibilities	61
Congeniality of staff	60
Availability of research monies	56
Salary advancement	49
Availability of secretarial services	48
Committee responsibilities	44

Source: Individual interviews, Brown, *The Market for College Teachers*, p. 175.

It should be remembered also that most fledgling academics find their first job in lesser institutions than those from which they were graduated. Such colleges and universities typically pay lower salaries, offer fewer staff perquisites, and load teachers with more routine assignments. Even though young academics may be aware of these differences, of course, they still may find it onerous to accept them. And too, whatever the drawbacks of their new situations, most of the recruits doubtless made their choices by rejecting other alternatives (if any) which seemed less attractive.

How do these expectations and reactions compare with those of new appointees which include in their number more experienced persons in a large university of high standing? Although the information at hand pertains to a single institution and sets forth circumstances that may now be different there as well as elsewhere, it is of interest to note the reasons set forth by new faculty members for accepting offers from the University of Minnesota, and those given by academics who declined offers. Also pertinent are the reasons given by Minnesota faculty members for accepting or declining offers to go elsewhere.[14]

The study covered a two-year period and included 150 new appointees, 51 percent of whom came from academic positions elsewhere. About a fourth came from positions in government, business, private practice, and so on; a fifth were assuming their first full-time posts. Almost two-thirds of the interviewees found things at Minnesota to be about as they had expected with regard to such matters as duties and responsibilities, professional opportunity, colleagues and associates, departmental and general administration, benefit programs, housing, commuting, and parking. Among those whose expectations were not realized, comments expressing dissatisfaction outnumbered favorable comments two to one. More than a fifth of the new staff members expressed such negative reactions as: "I have less time for research"; "more administrative duties"; "poorer students"; "heavier loads than I had anticipated." The most numerous complaints had to do with housing, commuting, and parking. Only about 10 percent reported that things were generally better than they had expected.

As will be observed later, academics are both idealistic and self-critical. Here I would remark that despite their dedication to the higher learning they are obviously not indifferent to their working environments. As the Minnesota study pointed out, the various factors drawing them to that university from elsewhere received the following rank order of importance from interviewees: 1) nature of duties and responsibilities; 2) reputation and prestige of the university; 3) salary; 4) presence of specific individuals at Minnesota; 5) research opportunity; 6) geographic location; and 7) availability of specific facilities (pp. 24-26).

Climbing the Academic Ladder

Regardless of their diverse backgrounds and attitudes, and how they came to be where they now are, all academic novitiates have in common a desire to climb the academic ladder. Moreover, there is a presumption that the average entrant to the ranks will rise. Some never get above the bottom or second rung, and they may either drop out of academe or move to another campus for a second try. Some are lured away by better prospects elsewhere, even though their prospects may be good in their current locales. Whether they leave or stay, the novices must quickly learn to distinguish between nominal and actual practices. They must acquire the set of attitudes and roles required to make a successful ascent.[15] Though there is a tendency later to eschew the role of the tyro, such would be hazardous in the earlier stages of the academic career.

In this dual role as teacher and researcher, the beginner encounters an occupational hierarchy. It is a different sort of hierarchy, however, from that of the army or a large business corporation, where there is a functional justification for an elaborate graduation of authority. Among academics there is ideally no question of superiors directing the work of others, but only a question of rank with reference to relative degrees of maturity and distinction. Yet there is a hierarchic principle in university organization. Like the army officer or the civil servant, the academic has a normal expectation of advancement according to seniority and service. Although there is much ill will provoked by status competition, from the point of view of the administration, the various gradations function as modes of stimulating and recognizing individual activity. Advancement is rarely in terms of a rigidly codified seniority;

even so, a normal expectancy within the profession minimizes the element of financial uncertainty inimical to intellectual work, and to some extent offsets moderate remuneration.

The occupational hierarchy consists typically of four ranks: instructor, assistant professor, associate professor, and full professor. In the average university, circa 1940, about 31 percent of the staff were on the first level, 23 percent on the second, 14 percent on the third, and 32 percent on the fourth.[16]

Since 1940 there has been relative stability in the proportion of academics in the top rank, a slight rise in the second rank, a much higher percentage in the third rank, and a greatly reduced percentage in the bottom rank. According to the AAUP's annual report for 1974–75, the percentage distribution by ranks, from top to bottom (not including 1.6 percent lecturers) was as follows for both sexes in the doctorate-granting universities: 33.9, 27.3, 29.7, 7.6. In these same institutions, the distribution of women faculty in terms of percentages was 12.4, 20.8, 42.3, 21.1—and lecturers, 3.4.

These changes may be attributed to such factors as accelerated staff expansion during the boom years, increased bargaining power of new academics during those years, the displacement of full-time instructors by part-time teachers and student assistants in lower-level classes,[17] and so on. (With stabilized or declining enrollments already being witnessed in many places, aging faculties will become a widespread phenomenon.) Although one might expect to find fewer individuals in each higher rank in virtually every kind of hierarchic arrangement (as in civil service, business corporations, or the military),[18] the rank distribution of academics in the average university is obviously not pyramidal.

Averages for large numbers of institutions, however, do blur quite noticeable differences between one university and another. In 1976, in the AAUP's annual report on the economic status of the profession, it was noted that at Florida Atlantic University, for example, 33 percent of the regular faculty were in the top rank, whereas at Harvard 63 percent of them were. State University of New York (SUNY) at Buffalo listed 36 percent of its faculty in the associate professorial rank, as contrasted with 11 percent at Harvard. Thirty-three percent of the Yale faculty were assistant professors, while the figure was 21 percent at the University of Michigan.

My 1942 data showed that the instructor ordinarily remained in the bottom rank from three to five years, rising to an assistant professorship at the age of 34 or 35, to an associate professorship at 38, and to the top rank shortly after the age of 40. Average ages at the different levels varied then, as they do now, from field to field, and from one institution to another. For several decades, individuals have tended to be younger in the expanding institutions, and younger in the physical sciences than in the humanities. In 1929 at the University of Chicago these were the average ages: professors, 51.4; associate professors, 44.0; assistant professors, 36.8; instructors, 32.2. At The University of Texas at Austin, where enrollment rose from about 5,000 in 1929 to more than 40,000 in 1975, the average ages of the 1,678 members of the faculty in 1975 were: professors, 52.5; associate professors, 41.7; assistant professors, 34.6; instructors, 32.9; with an average age of 41.9 for all ranks. From these and other data, it is apparent that the average age distributions of faculties by ranks in some major universities have remained relatively constant.

Seniority is not codified in most universities; in rare instances, individuals may jump ranks in promotion, and others may be delayed or permanently halted along the line. Statistics show that academics remaining in the same institution throughout their careers commonly rise more slowly (as do women) than the average academic employee. Some universities grant tenure to assistant professors, but the majority of Ph.D.-granting institutions have an "up or out" policy for the two lower ranks. Termination for mediocre performance above these normally temporary statuses is infrequent, however, so that marginal performers may be shelved in associate professorships or else sidetracked into minor administrative-assignments. A full professorship is ordinarily the top attainable rank, but distinguished professorships in the form of named chairs (outside funds are typically used to augment the usual pay limit if they do not meet full costs)[19] have been multiplying in recent years as mechanisms for attracting and retaining exceptional persons.

This movement of individuals appears institutionally as general and differential metabolism, or turnover of staff members. There is little or no downward movement (demotion) within an institution, except that academics in administrative assignments (e.g., department chairmen) may be "relieved" unexpectedly; outward movement takes place through resignations, deaths, or terminations. With the recent halt of expansion in most places, each higher stratum is again recruiting largely from below by promotion, and with the passage of time there has been a tendency toward progressive enlargement of the top stratum (the center of gravity), where outward movement of persons to posts elsewhere is least marked.

Major universities have less staff turnover than minor ones, not because they are more benevolent but because their initial selection procedures are more exacting and their retention powers greater. The University of Chicago is not one of the older American universities, but it began with top salary scales and high academic standards, which it has consistently maintained. Sixty percent of the faculty members who were there in 1918-19 were still there a decade later; 19 percent had died; 11 percent had resigned for various reasons; and less than 1 percent had resigned to go to other universities.[20] Also, it is logical to assume the existence of institutions with such weak staffs that their members receive few offers elsewhere.

During the late 1950s and the 1960s the situation changed in many universities. There was more competitive bidding among institutions for promising young academics and for those of established repute. The academic careerists had stronger ties to their disciplines and weaker loyalties to the employing institutions; "cosmopolitans" rather than "locals" were more numerous, and interinstitutional mobility became more commonplace. These changes have been delineated in some detail by Caplow and McGee in their 1958 book and by Brown, who entitled his 1967 book *The Mobile Professors*. With the slowdown of institutional expansion in the early 1970s, however, the game of "musical chairs" in academe almost came to a halt.

Turning now from these generalized aspects of individual advancement in rank, let us look at the special problems attached to the various statuses. As has been observed, the prototype of the university was a society of fellows, and academics in general are still opposed to rigid stratification by rank, or to anything resembling a caste system for their kind. With increased complexity of organization, nonetheless, the body-of-equals tradition has eroded and the modern university has moved toward a semibureaucratic pattern. Some problems of personnel are diffuse, whereas others are of primary importance at particular levels of the hierarchy. Questions of appointment, tenure, promotion, and remuneration are a concern of the whole institution, to be sure, but for organization members they have a different import in the lower statuses. Problems of research and teaching likewise permeate the whole structure, though differing in their nature for instructors and for full professors.

The Instructor or Assistant Professor

It is a matter of common observation that the largest number of critical issues of personnel problems arises in the bottom ranks. Here the tenure is brief or uncertain, the turnover highest, the remuneration lowest, the criteria for advancement vague or confused, the duties manifold, and the future full of doubt. In most institutions these statuses are regarded as a trial period, and the contractual appointment is for only one year at a time. There are always more aspirants for higher positions than there are vacancies, so that within the intensely competitive system of a large university the individual fear of exclusion may be as pronounced as the hope of inclusion where the "up or out" policy is in force. The mental anxiety may be prolonged by repeated short-term appointments, with the threat of eventual failure of renewal hanging over the novice after six or seven years of service.

A great deal of exploitation goes on. In the lowest ranks the teaching load is usually heaviest and most onerous; to the instructor or assistant professor are relegated the introductory sections (except where it is the policy to give these to the best teachers in the department), where large enrollments necessitate much paper grading, entail may student conferences, allow less freedom in course planning, and so on. Within most departments, the preferred subjects are already the prerogatives of the older faculty members, so that when the instructor or assistant professor is given advanced courses they are often those nobody else wants to teach. Because of heavy demands upon time, research activities tend to become piecemeal, and because of the individual's unestablished reputation difficulty is experienced in securing backing for projects requiring subsidy. In view of the vague and conflicting criteria by which work may be judged, there is uncertainty in the allocation of energies.

A faculty inquiry that many years ago candidly and incisively attacked personnel problems was the Harvard *Report* mentioned earlier. One item on the questionnaire to younger teachers at the institution was, "Have you been given a clear definition of what you should do, in scholarly work and teaching, in order to merit appointment or promotion?" The 164 replies were as follows: yes, 21; qualified, 20; answer not clear, 7; no, 116 (p. 46). Illustrative of the difficulties of younger men were these quotations (p. 46 ff.):

> I should say that the most crying need, so far as the instructors on annual appointment are concerned, is for some

definition of this kind.... At least there ought to be some specific understanding on what importance is attached to success in teaching.

Suggestions: Clear statement of basis for promotion. A merit system cannot work unless merit is clearly defined. And it must be watched carefully in order to keep out favoritism, nepotism, and so-called politics.... All should know exactly where they stand, and what is expected of them for a permanent job.

If I were asked to offer a one-word diagnosis of the present situation, I should simply say, "uncertainty." Uncertainty of every sort surrounds the junior instructor—uncertainty as to the policy of tenure, necessity of publication, renumeration, advisability of engaging in outside activities, etc., etc.

The reactions of the instructors also mentioned other sources of tension—the "lip service to teaching," departmental policies resting on "caprice rather than considered judgment . . . and a balanced view," the issue of judgment on intrinsic merits or cultivation of special fields, emphasis on "quantity rather than quality" in publication, and the "publish or perish" legend. Because of their precarious situations, the beginners were under a variety of pressures to "make good." Few of the junior members questioned the fact that temporary insecurity for the individual had a functional value for the institution, hence the main strain in the instructorship seems to have been the uncertain criteria for advancement.[21]

Incompatibilities still abound between the immediate demands of the instructor's or assistant professor's situation and the anticipated satisfaction of an academic career. Neither the wish for security nor the wish for recognition is adequately met. Being past thirty, the beginner is at an age when the young doctor and lawyer are starting to put down permanent roots in the community and are establishing themselves in life careers. The high geographic mobility of many young academics, on the other hand, precludes feelings of permanence and security. It is not inexplicable that they should come to regard the university hierarchy as a sort of gerontocracy setting the rules of a competitive game in which they are allowed to play only for the smaller stakes, and without knowing precisely the value of the cards.

The Associate Professor

For most individuals who remain permanently in the academic profession, the associate professorship is an intermediate status. Although some institutions limit initial contractual appointment to a specified term (e.g., five years), as they may do even for outsiders brought into the top rank, subject to review for nonrenewal or permanent status at the end of the period, permanent tenure is normally acquired at this rank. The associate professor's chief remaining source of anxiety at this stage, accordingly, is that he or she may be permanently shelved, since many institutions hesitate to reward mere timeservers with full professorships.

After spending several years at this stage, the associate professor has been in the system long enough to build up definite career expectations, and any pause that threatens to be permanent inevitably causes him to feel let down, frustrated, and even injured. Ordinarily, the individual has reached a mutual compatibility with the institution and may take permanent root in the community.

Caplow and McGee have raised and answered (correctly, I think) the question, "What happens to academics who become too old for their rank?"

> The antiquated assistant professor usually quits his job or gets thrown out. From a major university, he may either go to an institution of lesser eminence, where he is given a higher rank, more commensurate with his age, or he may leave the academic profession entirely.
>
> The associate professor who finds himself too old for his rank and peers may either go to a smaller institution or remain where he is as an associate professor until the end of his

days, probably being respected by his students and ignored by his colleagues.

The older full professor, if he is unhappy in his department or if his department is unhappy with him, may be in serious trouble. His mobility is highly limited. From the standpoint of the hiring institution, there are many anxieties attendant upon hiring him. Because of his rank, he will be expensive. Because he must be hired on tenure, he will be permanent. Because he is in his declining years, he may fail to produce the quantity and quality of scholarship that is expected from a man of his rank and salary. Yet, on the other hand, if his eminence is so great as to make the risk of such failure worthwhile, he may be so identified with the department from which he comes that his transfer will reflect no glory on the new university. Once he reaches a certain point of seniority, then, his *potential* mobility declines sharply. The data seem to place this point at about twenty years of service, or about fifty years of age. [Pp. 44–45]

The Professor

Despite the incongruences which may develop between academics who have achieved the top rank and their departmental, not to mention institutional, colleagues, personal adjustment to the organization is usually so complete and status so secure that few problems stem from mere occupancy of the rank. It is an achieved rather than an ascribed status, and once the individual is there, the competitive pressure shifts from rising in rank to the urgency of living up to expectations. Hence it is by no means a fixed position entirely removed from the competitive game. The control forces behind such a status can be strong and can create internalized drives through such negative sanctions as a sense of shame, fear of moral condemnation, or through such a positive sanction as pride. Gossip and other control mechanisms remind the professor that strains develop in an organization when symbols of achievement are felt to be unjustly held.

It is true that responsibilities have been increased along with rights and privileges, yet the professor's position as an employee is sufficiently secure to remove the constant pressure of the stresses and strains of lower levels. Barring serious misconduct, the individual will not be removed from office, so that almost the only pressure experienced is the desire to avoid a salary freeze and to sustain or enchance an established reputation. The position is assuredly no sinecure, for special demands upon time are likely to be greater than on lower levels. Administrative tasks, committee work, public service, and numerous other duties in addition to teaching and research draw upon individual energies.

Professors who have gained academic recognition beyond the confines of their own campuses are more likely than their junior colleagues to hold offices in learned societies of professional associations, to be on advisory boards, to serve on panels in Washington, to do outside consulting, and—if they are of sufficient repute—to become statesmen in and for their fields. One reason for this is that the experience and discernment required for such assignments usually increase with age. Another, of course, is that capacity and drive in research accomplishment tend in most persons to diminish by middle age; this slowdown typically occurs in the earlier years among mathematicians and physicists and later for historians and philosophers.

During the later 1950s and throughout the 1960s, in a good many universities there were more relatively early promotions to the top rank, and as a consequence some institutions now find themselves heavily loaded with professors. Since virtually all of them are tenured, there is not much these institutions can do about those professors who meet their classes regularly but have ceased to be productive scholars and scientists. The pressures from below to do *something,* however, will undoubtedly increase, and the lot of the least deserving in the highest rank is likely to be made less comfortable than it once may have been.

Regardless of the discomforts that may be experienced by some hitherto secure professors in the uncertain times ahead, their lot is not likely to be as perilous as in a fictitious South American university described by the University of Chicago economist, George J. Stigler, in an amusing essay entitled "An Academic Episode." There, according to the author, the dictatorial rector decreed that each June any member of the faculty could challenge the person immediately above him in rank to undergo a competitive examination. "If the challenger won, he exchanged position and salary with his former superior."[22]

Institutional Aspects of Tenure and Status

Although it would be an error to assume that employee and employer interests in tenure and status necessarily must be in conflict, it is patent that personal and organizational objectives are not always identical. The university that desires to be something more than a pleasant place to work must exert pressures to maximize staff performance. Secure tenure in all ranks undoubtedly would be regarded as a boon by the least productive staff members, but it would be a liability to the institution employing them and also to the status of the profession as a whole. Accordingly, to some extent the university must systematically yet subtly invoke the prospect of the professor's loss of position for purposes of stimulus and control. It may utilize both positive and negative sanctions, pride in participation, and fear of loss. Informal controls may be in certain instances inadequate, so that a central authority is necessary. (Of late, teachers unions have been promising to eliminate much of this by insisting upon early tenure and a detailed spelling out of the "objective" criteria in contracts.)

As many critics have observed, a defect in the academic system of tenure is that a shelter is provided for faculty deadwood in the upper ranks. Another frequently noted defect is that in some places tenure is not really secure. Since institu-

tional improvement requires noiseless riddance schemes for
the incompetent functionaries, resultant disjunctions are often
the points at which issues of academic freedom arise. From the
employer's perspective, noncooperation may be defined as a
form of incompetence, and by definition the compliant staff
member of limited capability may be given preference over
the more troublesome but abler academic. Unorthodox and
outspoken professors often invite attention to themselves, of
course, and in an earlier era the most widely publicized instances of breaches of academic tenure and freedom often
resulted from outside pressures, yet more recently other pressures just as damaging may well arise within an institution.

Even if the academic profession were able to enforce a
uniform system of tenure, such as that advocated by the
American Association of University Professors, this enforce-
ment might eventually defeat some of its purposes by causing
the initial selection of "safe" recruits and thus stifling individu-
alism. Hence, forcing tenure demands too far is necessarily
detrimental to the profession itself. The complexity of the
whole issue appears when unions and professional associations
find themselves inadvertently defending exhibitionists and in-
competents who are ever ready to fall back upon real or alleged violations of the ethics of tenure. In short, tenure is a
necessary but not a sufficient condition for academic freedom
in its broadest sense.

Another institutional problem involving both tenure
and promotion (largely the latter) is that the present system
ultimately produces a disproportionate number of employees
in the highest status. If the rule of seniority were complete, all
individuals who remained in the system long enough would be
full professors. Although such a situation is more hypothetical
than real, universities often find themselves with too many full
professors, and the consequent closure of opportunities for
younger staff, budgetary difficulties, and other perplexities.
The presence of a large number of persons in the highest
ranks can imply advancement on length of service rather than

merit, and, if so, the professorship is cheapened. Since the institution can no longer recognize exceptional individuals, its bargaining power is weakened and it is able neither to hold its own best academics nor to attract outstanding persons from other places.

In its efforts to control both general and differential staff metabolism or turnover, the administrative organization guards against routinized promotions and stagnation by a graduated "system" of qualifications. Present methods are certainly far from systematic, but there are periods of review and protocols to determine status changes. Even though many academics feel that the prevalent scheme of rank and tenure is too complicated in application and too protracted, thus resulting in a cumulative expectation on the part of the individual and a cumulative commitment for the institution, I think it should be observed that a salient characteristic of leading universities is the greater care they exercise in such matters.

Still, most university hiring procedures do not involve the detailed scrutiny of prospects utilized by some professional football teams (where performance data are often computerized), and usual modes of evaluating employees for tenure and promotion are not as elaborate as those of the military. Unlike the Air Force second lieutenant, who can calculate that he has a 90 percent chance of being a major in eleven years, and a 50 percent chance of being a colonel in twenty-one years, the young academic finds himself in a career fraught with many more uncertainties.

Delinquent academics commonly point to their extenuating circumstances, and even average faculty members like to think of themselves as special cases, so that the specific persons may be more interested in seeing absolute standards applied to others than to themselves, when such an application is not in their own interests.

Lower staff members normally consider themselves in line for the rank just above their own, and there is a constant pressure by departments upon central administration for the promotion of their younger members. This pressure is frequently brought to bear in situations where the candidate in question receives an outside offer. In such situations, whether or not the candidate seriously considers the outside offer, individual bargaining power is often enhanced. Indeed, outside offers may be solicited with no other purpose that using them as levers to elevate the recipient's local status. It is a game which both sides have been known to play, however, for there are departments and institutions where advancement may be slower for those faculty members who never get any bids from other places.

To maintain and improve its own institutional standing, a university obviously has to pursue a careful course to encourage and retain its ablest faculty members and simultaneously to avoid bestowing recognition and reward on the undeserving. The pursuit of excellence requires attention to the principles of equity as well as merit to uphold the levels of faculty morale necessary to the university's functions as a productive enterprise.

Recent Exigencies

In view of the depressed job market of the 1970s, various individuals and groups, many of them nonacademic, have urged that tenure be abolished, rank quotas be established, and so on. Various researches into the whole matter have been undertaken. The American Council on Education (ACE) conducted a survey in 1972 which showed that 42 percent of all the reporting institutions that year gave tenure to *all* eligible faculty members; the next year the percentage dropped to 37. Somewhat later the ACE found that a third of the nation's institutions had made some changes in their tenure policies and procedures, and that two in every five had problems under review. Some of the outcomes were longer probationary periods, shorter initial-term contracts, and tightened appeal procedures, but Todd Furniss, the council's survey director, reported no major shifts.[23]

In 1971, the Association of American Colleges and the AAUP initiated the formation of a Commission on Academic Tenure in Higher Education to make an independent inquiry and recommendations. Underwritten by a Ford Foundation grant, the commission, under the direction of William R. Keast as chairman (with John Macy as cochairman), published its report in 1973. In general, it recommended the retention of tenure as the "most tested and reliable instrument for incorporating academic freedom" and expressed the view that a tenured membership in excess of one-half to two-thirds of any full-time faculty roster was inadvisable. In the opinion of many, the report did help counter movements to abolish tenure and gave useful institutional guidelines for a more rigorous approach to staff evaluation.[24]

The fiscal crunch that began around 1970 caused about fifty small colleges to close by 1974, and even some public universities with enrollment drops and/or decreased funding had to take drastic actions. According to reports appearing from time to time in the *Chronicle of Higher Education,* some well-established institutions were affected. The University of Wisconsin, for example, gave notice a year in advance to 88 tenured faculty members and to 200 nontenured faculty and staff members that effective July 1, 1974, they would be terminated. At the University of Maryland, 31 of 60 untenured faculty members did not have their contracts renewed, and officials there foresaw a future in which nine out of ten junior academics would have to go out rather than up. By mid-1976, the nine senior institutions of CUNY were having to inform tenured academics of impending terminations.

Adversely affected academics are understandably reluctant to accept their changed circumstances, and the recalcitrants among them are seldom quietly submissive. Where they are unionized, the counter demand may be tenure for virtually everybody. Or, aided and abetted by the AAUP, the American Federation of Teachers, or the National Education Association as their bargaining agent, they may take their cases to court, charging unfair discrimination or abridgment of their constitutional rights as citizens.

The kinds of problems arising from the recent exigencies just reviewed stem in part from the unpreparedness of some institutions to make cutbacks or even to level off after an extended period of academic growth and seemingly limitless staff expansion. Since the 1980s will witness a continuation of "no growth" prospects for American higher education, universities should be able to cope more effectively with a clearly foreseeable future. In most places, the best that can be hoped for is steady state staffing, with some institutions needing to do contingency planning for a further decline in student enrollments.[25]

All of this means that there will be fewer openings for new academics, more care exercised in their appointment and advancement, a slower climb up the academic ladder, and progressively older faculties. Modifications in tenure and retirement policies and practices will doubtless be made in some universities. Such circumstances may have the effect of weeding out the least capable all along the line, but diminished advancement opportunities may also discourage some of the ablest individuals from entering academic careers. What the net outcome will be is, of course, a matter of speculation.

4

Administrators ³⁄₆⁄⁷⁹

American academics, as has been noted, progressively occupy various statuses as professional recruits, students and apprentices, and staff members. Although many professors eschew full-time administrative roles, considerable numbers of them do become involved in such assignments, and virtually all of them engage from time to time in some administrative tasks. Every university has its discrete cadre of administrative employees or "bureaucrats," to be sure, but faculty professionals retain extensive powers of administration in most places, and thus play dual roles, both successively and simultaneously.

In my 1942 book about academics, I commented on the fact that there was an average of one administrative officer for every six persons engaged in teaching. David C. Knapp has pointed out that small colleges as well as complex universities progressively invested more in administration, both absolutely and proportionately, between 1929 and 1958, with administrative expenditures increasing more rapidly than those for instruction.[1] Only spending for organized and department research showed a greater rise, and by 1976–77, according to a U.S. Office of Education analysis, there were in private institutions 35.7 administrators for every 100 faculty members, and in public institutions 19 per 100. By way of contrast, as Halsey and Trow have mentioned, British universities have small administrative staffs which are more likely to be composed of part-time academics, with committee chairmen often performing key administrative roles.[2]

According to the prototype, a university faculty is a body of equals, and there is still a nostalgic preference for the club-like plan of institutional operations. The conventional rhetoric of academic governance refers to the department chairman, dean, provost, or even the president as being merely *primus inter pares,* and nonacademic administrators are regarded at best as being ancillaries and at worst as being supernumeraries. Even though some nonacademics are highly trained professionals who make important decisions, they typically are without academic department status and lack voting rights in matters of university governance.[3]

University administration and governance display some rather curious anomalies and contradictions. Egalitarianism and elitism exist side by side. Power moves up as well as down. Insisting upon independence of action for themselves as teachers and researchers, academics are reluctant to accord much leeway to many of their administrative confreres. Requiring high professional qualifications for entry into their own ranks, they are wary of professionalizing qualifications for academic administration and often relegate very complex assignments to complete amateurs. Their willingness to delegate routine and onerous administrative chores to staff specialists is frequently accompanied by an unwillingness to trade off any faculty authority.

The same academics who complain about the lack of strong leadership in their institutions may stoutly defend governance schemes which make such leadership difficult if not impossible. (In this regard, I call to mind one major university where the faculty rather prided itself on maintaining "weak deanships," as if the corollary were "strong professorships.") Understandably, of course, no faculty wants to be "managed," but widespread academic distrust of specialized competence in administration does seem to be an anomalous attitude on the part of those who could be its main beneficiaries.

Turning now from these ambivalences, anomalies, and contradictions, let us take a look at the social organization of the university and examine what someone has called the "sprawl" of authority and responsibility.

Departments and Chairmen

The importance of the subject-matter department to average academics is illustrated by the fact that their initial appointments, their employment continuity, and their academic advancement—and, in part, their salaries—are largely determined within their particular departments. Ever since 1900, there has been an increase in the importance of departments. The rise of specialization and professionalism in academe, together with the growth in size and complexity of institutions, have bolstered departments as the basic units of university organization. A university is something more than a mere agglomeration of departments, to be sure, but its academic repute stems mainly from the prestige of its various departments. The department, moreover, is the organization unit most resistant to bureaucratic intrusions, the place where average academics perform most of their basic functions as teachers and researchers, and the milieu in which they interact most intimately with colleagues and students.

Despite the familiar view of the department as the place in a multiversity where one is most likely to find a true community of scholars, the late Robert M. Huchins regarded it as a basic impediment to liberal education. He felt that it spawns overspecialization, discourages faculty interest in broader university affairs, often stands in the way of needy reforms, and is mindful mainly of its own expansion and prestige. Others have criticized departments for being political and social blocs, for eroding unity of purpose and organization, and for being the chief instigators of an attenuated curriculum which spreads resources ever more thinly.[4]

Even so, no major university has as yet come up with an equally satisfactory unitary basis for academic operations. The higher learning itself is compartmented principally along disciplinary lines, as are most departments. Moreover, academics obviously like to have their own power bailiwicks and commonly use them to help counter the larger hierarchy and more impersonal bureaucracy of the complex university.

However egalitarian a department may be, it too requires some centralization of authority and responsibility in the form of a head (now a largely outmoded designation), chairman, or "chairperson." In those departments where none of the ablest members want such a responsibility, or in those where nobody really desires strong leadership, it may well be that the recent neuter-gender designation is the most appropriate title for the officeholder.

Contrary to what some academics contend, however, chairing a department is not an inconsequential responsibility. A number of longitudinal inquiries have shown that the quality of academic departments is correlated with the capabilities of their chairmen. The functions to be performed by such individuals have been described by Paul Dressel and others as follows:

> Tradition and faculty demands require the chairman to be a scholar, but the demands placed upon the chairman include many functions: Chairmen initiate action of budget formulation; selection, promotion, and retention of academic staff; faculty salaries; sabbatical leaves; interdepartmental relationships; research grants; educational development and innovation; university committee membership; discipline representation; professional growth; advice to dean on departmental matters; administration to faculty relationship; new faculty orientation; departmental meetings; adequate nonacademic help; student personnel records; faculty load; graduate student application approval; grading standards and practices;

and curriculum changes. Also, they have knowledge of the administrative routine of the college; institutional legislative organization; government grants procedures; policies relating to graduate students; and scholarly productivity of department faculty.[5]

These varied duties, particularly in large departments, are necessarily time consuming, but, even so, most chairmen carry substantial teaching loads, get no extra pay, and serve for limited terms. Often the turnover is more frequent than the length of tenure would suggest, and some chairmen feel great relief in getting back to full-time professorial posts.[6] Others have more zest for the challenges, nonetheless, and some of them may go on to become deans, provosts, or presidents.

Marvin Peterson[7] has indicated that in institutions of lower prestige, chairmen appear to be more responsive to influences from central administration, whereas those in higher-prestige universities seem to be more sensitive to departmental and disciplinary attitudes. Although no causal relations between particular kinds of departmental organization and academic excellence have been clearly demonstrated, the better and the larger departments are in general less oligarchic (as are their parent institutions). As we shall note in a later chapter, strong departments tend to be more numerous in strong institutions where the resources to support quality are greater, and it is uncommon to find even a single distinguished department in a generally mediocre, much less a weak, university.

As to mode of selection and tenure of chairmen, the AAUP recommends election by department members for limited terms of office (subject to re-election). Officers of central administration, on the other hand, usually prefer appointive procedures, and particularly so in emerging universities where the resources may be available to upgrade as well as expend the faculty. A shortcoming of too much departmental autonomy is that weak departments tend to perpetuate themselves, to become inbred in their ideas as well as personnel, and to obstruct the recruitment of academics who are manifestly superior to those already on deck. Thus, institutional ambitions often leave no alternative to outside prodding—not to mention restraining—of departments which are out of step.

Institutes and Directors

In addition to academic departments, other widespread modes of organization in academe include institutes, centers, bureaus, special offices, and named research laboratories. They were rather uncommon in 1942 but are frequently found today in all major universities. In a smaller institution there may be only a limited number of them, but Paul Dressel reports that one university has more than 200.[8] Why this proliferation? One reason is that some academic pursuits simply do not fit logically into any conventional subject-matter department—as, for example, an institute of Latin American studies, or a special program of energy studies. Another is that one or more academics with strong innovative zeal may opt for an end run rather than a line buck to reach their goal. Still another is that the university's central administration may want to institute quickly a new program without going through the normally protracted deliberations used by departments, divisions, and schools to launch such enterprises.

The heads or directors of these various entities, incidentally, may or may not have status in teaching departments, and the other professionals employed in them often lack tenure and other perquisites of the regular faculty. Funding may be entirely from sources outside the regular university budget, and it is seldom on a permanent basis. Institute directors, accordingly, are frequently impelled to display promotional capabilities, both to launch and keep such enterprises going. Regardless of their uses and abuses, institutes and similar entities unquestionably increase the flexibility of university organization, and indeed some add luster to an institution's reputation.

Schools or Colleges and Deans

The nomenclature of academe is not always clear-cut. Some universities call themselves colleges or institutions, and others calling themselves universities are really more like colleges in basic purpose and organization. In this country, however, a university is usually defined as being comprised of a college and one or more graduate or professional schools.

Each of these latter typically has its own faculty and is presided over by a dean. Its faculty members may participate in wider university affairs through dual appointments, by service on special committees, or through their elected representatives to senates or other broadly designated bodies. In a large and complex university, nonetheless, the average academic's participation is limited largely to his or her own department and school or college. The individual's formal line of communication is directly to the department chairman, who, in turn, reports to the dean of the college or school.

Although large and complex universities, as well as statewide university systems (as in California and Texas), may have high-level designees—e.g., executive or academic vice-presidents, provosts, or other deputies—to whom deans report directly rather than to the president or chancellor, deans are normally the most important liaison officers between the academic staff and the institution's chief executive officer. Unlike a presidency, which is by definition the most prominent institutional post, regardless of who occupies it, a deanship may vary widely in power and importance. A medical school deanship, for instance, is almost invariably a complicated and difficult job, and this may account for the high turnover rate among medical deans. The deanship of a college of pharmacy or a school of social work typically involves a more limited scope of operations and perhaps fewer exasperating problems. An architecture or fine arts dean may find that he has to give most of his time to reconciling extremely divergent and often conflicting faculty perspectives about what should be taught; and a graduate school dean,[9] whose faculty members draw their pay in other schools, may devote more time than he would like to dealing with other deans.

In the multiversity, the dean may be aided by associate and assistant deans and by assistants to deans, whereas in smaller or lesser institutions he may have his energies consumed by paper shuffling. With some persons, the office becomes a mere clearing house; with others, it becomes a source of university policy—and readily so when departments are too immersed in their own interests to care, and presidents are too busy raising money on the outside or "putting out fires" to have much time for basic questions about the means and ends of higher education per se.

One analyst of the roles of academic deans has concluded that they are "as likely to represent ad hoc action as sustained leadership," and that "a great many deans regard themselves not as leaders but as catalysts of faculty opinion and decision making." He cites an information survey about what 163 well-regarded academic deans deemed to be their main concerns and the order of skills required, as indicated in Table 4.1.[10]

In deanship circles one still hears the old quip that "a dean is one who does not know enough to be a top professor, but who knows too much to be a president." Much less frequently quoted in such circles is the equally familiar definition of an assistant dean as a mouse studying to be a rat—there are after all some limits to the indulgences deans can be expected to display in the furtherance of faculty relations and morale.[11]

Presidents

With the growth of multicampus university systems and the spread of statewide coordinating boards to the point that they now have jurisdiction over public higher education in virtually all states, it is more difficult than it once was to determine who the kingpins are in the social organization of some universi-

Table 4.1   Comparison of Time and Skill Indices

RESPONSIBILITY	TIME	SKILL	COMBINED
(1)	(2)	(3)	(4)
Faculty relations and morale	33	69	102
Recruitment of faculty	30	26	56
Curriculum work	24	28	52
Budget work, promotions, evaluation of personnel	22	27	49
Committee work	33	11	44
Routine administrative duties: correspondence, scheduling, catalog, reports, questionnaires	35	9	44
Student counseling	27	6	33
Work with other administrators, advising the president, relations with other colleges in the university	4	14	18
Work with department heads	4	12	16
Policy making, planning, goal setting, institutional studies, study of other institutions	6	10	16
Public relations, alumni relations, speaking engagements, professional association meetings, college functions	4	3	7
Admissions problems, registration problems, foreign students	5	0	5
Seeing parents, students	1	3	4
Enforcing regulations, discipline	0	2	2

Source: John Wesley Gould, *The Academic Deanship*, New York, Teachers College, Columbia University, 1964, p. 27. The figures in columns (2), (3), and (4) are index numbers indicating the demands upon deans of their various involvements.

ties,[12] particularly those in the public sector. Even in the private sector, there may be both a chancellor and a president on the same campus. Chief executive officers, however, are commonly designated as presidents, and this is the generic term we shall use here.

In a sense, when academics become presidents they cease to be academics. Except in rare instances, they no longer teach or do much research. Although professionals, such as lawyers, engineers, physicians, and others, may continue to pursue their occupations when they are employed by universities for nonacademic administrative posts, there is no profession of *academic* administration. This anomaly is witnessed in the fact that no specified training and certification are required, and in the lack of any widely accepted definition of the amount and kind of experience needed to quality. To be sure, there are now a good many departments of higher education that offer Ph.D.s and are in part designed to prepare administrators, but presidents come from a diversity of disciplinary backgrounds, and few of them have ever had any courses in higher education.

Contrary to the notion that presidents frequently are deficient in academic qualifications, most of them are persons who have climbed the academic ladder rung by rung. More often than in earlier years, the preponderance of them have earned doctorates, have risen to full professorial rank, and have taught for ten to fifteen years. Most of them are not new to academic administration, for they average more than ten years of prior experience in previous administrative posts. The majority of them are recruited from other institutions and have had more varied institutional connections than most of their academic colleagues.[13]

These common circumstances make it evident that there is at least an implicit mode of preparation and selection. In short, the president may be a transmogrified academic in the eyes of professors, but the probability is that not many academics are as widely experienced as their chief executive in the ways of academe. It is true, of course, that few presidents come into office after having achieved international renown as scholars or scientists, but if this kind of distinction were made a qualification it could be a dubious trade-off between the two sectors of academe.[14]

Professor Herbert A. Simon has pointed out that colleges and universities are not exempt from the operation of a pecuniary calculus which necessitates justifying institutional claims on society's resources. He has contended that the president is primarily an executive,[15] even though he may not have had as many as three semester hours of training for administrative work, just as professors have had little formal training for their main function of teaching. The president's main functions, as Dr. Simon has lined them out, are these: 1) to raise money; 2) to balance the budget; 3) to participate with others in setting institutional goals; 4) to work with the faculty in creating an environment that encourages learning, for faculty and students; 5) to recruit and maintain a high quality faculty. The president's role is obviously not one for the individual whose aim is to be comfortable and well liked, but it can be a source of deep satisfaction when institutional opportunities are realized.

To find out what presidents do with their working time, the New York Regents Advisory Committee on Educational Leadership had a study made in the 1960s, and 180 of the 194 college and university presidents in the Empire State made reports which yielded the data in Table 4.2.[16]

Academic administration, of course, has its abuses as well as its uses. Because of hazy or inappropriate job criteria, faulty modes of selection, and inadequate mechanisms of preparation, the wrong kinds of individuals sometimes get drawn or propelled into administrative jobs. There are often widespread misconceptions of both what needs to be done and what can be done. Even with good people in key posts, the effective operation of a university may flounder because of structural gaps, inadequacies, and weaknesses in its social organization. Authority may be too tightly held at the top of the hierarchy, or too loosely diffused throughout the structure.[17]

Although a 1974 study has shown that presidents are now spending more time on their campuses (about 65 percent) than during the prior decade, the varied demands made on them seem to have increased rather than diminished. The campus turmoils of the 1960s had no sooner quieted down than campus uproars over the financial cutbacks of the 1970s again made scapegoats of many presidents who, despite the ubiqui-

Table 4.2   Average Time Reported by 180 Presidents on 18 Activities

ADMINISTRATIVE	Percent
Administrative planning with trustees	4.1
Administrative planning alone	9.6
Administrative planning with subordinates	13.5
Reviewing and analyzing reports	5.5
Authorizing and approving expenditures	2.9
Total	35.6
EXTERNAL	
Meeting with outsiders on college affairs	4.0
Meeting with outsiders not college related	3.4
Correspondence	6.7
Preparation and delivery of speeches	5.0
Fund-raising activities	8.5
Official entertainment	3.8
Total	31.4
COLLEGIAL	
Working with faculty on curriculum	5.1
Meeting with students	5.6
Teaching	2.2
Counseling faculty on personal problems	3.1
Informal interaction with faculty	6.7
Total	22.7
INDIVIDUAL	
Writing, study, and scholarly work	4.8
Private thought and reflection	5.3
Total	10.1
Grand Total	99.8

tous desire of administrators to keep the faculty happy (as Jencks and Riesman noted in *The Academic Revolution*), were once more blamed for circumstances not of their own making.

Somebody once remarked that a new president needs five years to learn the ropes, five more to decide what ought to be done, and another five to do it. This observation obviously was made a long time ago. In 1972, I looked into the median tenure of the forty-eight presidents of the major institutions belonging to the Association of American Universities and found that between 1968 and 1972 the average term of office had dropped from six to three years. Twenty-six presidents had been in their jobs for less than three years, and only eleven of them had served for ten years or more.

Beginning in the 1960s, some well-known presidents of prestigious institutions were opting to bail out rather than be shot down, and still more were quietly resigning for publicly stated reasons that usually gave no hint of their real frustrations and harassments. By the summer of 1969, it was reported that 200 institutions had vacancies in the top post. Discontent about governance and other circumstances in academe had reached the point in the summer of 1976 that the almost-unheard-of phenomenon of faculty votes of "no confidence" in the top administrator was being reported in a few places.

In 1962, Harold W. Dodds, then a retired president of Princeton, discoursed about the presidential problem of the "honorable exit,"[18] and since then the problem has become even more critical. One difficulty, of course, is that many presidents are well aware that they are out of touch with their former academic fields of specialization and would often not be welcomed back into academic ranks. Only the fortunate few can go into foundation posts, ambassadorships, and other high-level assignments outside academe. Thus, unknown numbers of top administrators in universities undoubtedly have few options to hanging on as long as they can, and may feel trapped in their office.

Academic Managers

No faculty wants to be managed, and justifiably so. Unlike many other employees of large organizations, academics are professionals, and close supervision and control have a stultifying effect on professionalized functions. Insofar as teaching and research are concerned, this is indeed the main rationalization for academic freedom. To survive as viable organizations, however, universities require a good deal of management, under whatever guise.

William H. Danforth, chancellor of Washington University, has pointed out that waning public confidence in higher education and continuously rising costs in a time of inflation are resulting everywhere in more "calls for accountability" and for improved control of operations.[19] He has made reference to the Western Interstate Commission for Higher Education's sponsorship of a National Center for Higher Education Management Systems involving over 800 institutions from 50 states as participating members. Some of the main thrusts are these: "1) Cost-finding principles are being explored. 2) Information exchange procedures are being developed for comparative analysis among institutions. 3) A series of output measures are being developed by which an institution's total output in terms of education *and* other activities can be measured both qualitatively and quantitatively. 4) A faculty activity analysis is being developed" (p. 135).

While acknowledging such dangers as oversimplifying in order to quantify the inherently unquantifiable; moving the locus of decision making even farther away from those who perform the basic functions of teaching, research, and public service; using arbitrary and erroneous standards of performance for all campus units; and risking that "bits of information taken out of context can be used to mislead the public," Dr. Danforth concludes that better management information systems will, if properly conceived and utilized, benefit the academic community. Moreover, he urges faculty leaders to keep abreast of the whole movement.[20]

John D. Millett has described governance as a procedure for policy planning and action—a method for accommodating power and directing its use to common ends. He defines management as the implementation of a university's policy decisions of governance. The two are, of course, related, but are separable. According to his definition, leadership provides the linkage between governance and management, and it is usually identified as "the administration."[21]

Management functions are to be found at three levels: department, school or college, and the entire university. A department's main functions are teaching and research, of course, but these require management with regard to the number of students to be instructed, faculty work loads, allocation of financial resources, and so on. Constraints on individual and departmental autonomy also must be applied. Colleges or schools often supply management guidelines to their departments. In time, more formalized procedures of university management tend to evolve with regard to such matters as the budget, space inventory and utilization, student records, personnel practices, instructional evaluation, and course offerings.

Academic management is also to be noted in such support services as the library, the office for student admissions, the registrar's office, audio-visual services, and in the whole area known as student services. "The fact that so many discussions of governance tend to overlook or ignore problems of management, and especially the problems of business management," Dr. Millett observes, "has helped to gain for higher education its reputation of inefficient management. Few discussions of governance ever set forth efficient management as an objective. Little is ever said about the careful husbandry of all assets of a college or university." (p. 231)

It is encouraging to note, however, that colleges and universities, not to mention other organizations concerned with higher education, are now paying much more attention to the improvement of managerial practices. For example, through their professional associations business officers have published manuals of desirable practices, and they frequently exchange information and hold short-term institutes for the continuing education of their members. The American Council on Education, in cooperation with a large number of colleges and universities, has for more than a decade offered internship programs for prospective recruits to academic administration. The ACE also regularly conducts institutes for presidents, deans, business officers, student personnel officers, and others. The Carnegie Commission on Higher Education in a 1973 report even called attention to a frequently overlooked management agenda item, that of "emergency of unprogrammed decision making," and set forth recommendations for coping effectively with campus disruption. In light of these and related developments, there is now less excuse than there once was for administrators to work mainly by improvisation.

Leaders and Goals

Another Carnegie Commission on Higher Education study has concluded that most universities over which top administrators are assumed to have some jurisdiction should be realistically described as "organized anarchies," with ill-defined goals, confused procedures and technologies, and too many ambiguities of decision making and implementation.[22]

Although the Carnegie study focuses on the internal disarray over which presidents are expected to preside, their administrative ambiguities do not stem entirely from intramural sources. A good many of the decisions and actions affecting academic endeavors are now made by outsiders who rarely set foot on the campus. I would not agree with Lyman Glenny's categorization of these outsiders as "leaders" in the conventional sense of that term, but he correctly emphasizes both their influence and their anonymity.[23] To most academics they are faceless and perhaps unknown, but their number has become legion. Resource allocations for local expenditures, for example, are increasingly determined in the state or the nation's capital. Educational programs are heavily affected by accrediting agency standards over which university entities often have little control. Statewide coordinating and governing boards and governors' and legislative budget office edicts are influenced by staff professionals who may shape as well as assemble data. Federal legislation for higher education may be so vague that its application is molded by Washington bureaucrats. With litigation being increasingly resorted to by some members of the academic community to settle disputes, courts of law rather than faculty committees, administrators, or trustees are being handed the authority to set ground rules.

I do not subscribe to Glenny's conclusion that "the ostensible leaders of institutions of higher education, that is their presidents and governing boards, are the leaders of institutions mainly in title and visibility," but I do agree that local leadership roles have become eroded and further confused by an indeterminate number of outsiders.[24]

Most universities, as I have said elsewhere, must somehow be better institutions than their denigrators would have us believe. They are models of economy, for example, as compared with hospitals; of efficiency compared with courts of law; and of effectiveness, alongside most political agencies. Unlike many other productive enterprises, private as well as public, universities do not charge all the traffic will bear for their services. Their campuses, like businesses and industries, have been at times shut down, but rarely because the faculty and staff were striking for shorter hours and higher pay. Although urban universities are accused of inattention to the problems of their immediate physical environment, I have heard of none charged with polluting it. In brief, there must be a good many things right about the way universities are operated.

One gauge of their social usefulness is their durability. Despite nervous talk about their fragility, they tend to outlast most other kinds of organizations. Universities, however, are not indestructible, and nearly everybody can call to mind places where operations have been seriously interrupted, missions perverted, and viability threatened.

One major cause of the widespread disjunctions of recent years has been the ascendancy of mistaken ideas about university goals. Ignoring the functional distinctiveness of the

university as an institution intended to focus on gaining, sharing, and using knowledge, some militant reformers have contended that it should be a microcosm of the larger political
community, with its directions decided on a one-person, one-
vote basis, and the course offerings determined by some academic equivalent of the Nielsen rating system in commercial
television.

Still other reformers of recent years have tried to trans-
form the university into a kind of welfare agency. They would
saddle it with responsibilities ill-suited to its established purposes, shift to it burdens more logically belonging to other
social agencies, and substitute, as Sidney Hook has said, "good
works off campus . . . for good works on campus." Disregard-
ing the fact that education cannot be bought and sold like
many other services and commodities, and that it certainly
cannot be given away to all who may want and need it, these
reformers would pull the university apart in the futile endeav-
or of having it try to mean all things to all people.

A third category of dissidents has believed that the
campus ought to be a retreat or enclave providing many special rights and freedoms with few special duties and responsibilities. Conveniently forgetting that the public supports colleges and universities as socially useful institutions, advocates
of the secular sanctuary idea would convert them into places
where everybody's existence would be justified by his simply
"doing his own thing."

Of all the forces impinging on the university in recent
years, however, the most destructive in terms of its time-
honored purposes have been those exerted by the cohorts of
conflict who would make it into an arena or battleground for
fighting out the main issues of the day. Although it has long
been recognized that the university should be a testing ground
for diverse ideas, and a place of keen intellectual competition,
this has not satisfied those activists who have been bent on
imposing their will on others through organized disruption
and obstruction.

Fortunately, the popularity of these mistaken ideas has diminished. It would be delusory to maintain that all institutions have emerged unscathed, or that appreciable numbers of them have actually been improved as social organizations subsequent to their embroilments. The toll levied on duly constituted administrative leadership in many places was indeed heavy, and in some places the concessions made under duress may prove in the long run to have been disastrous.

Even so, the vast majority of the nation's universities have been upheld as bastions of rationality and civility, and as intellectual institutions. It is again being agreed on many sides that an institution of higher learning prospers most as a nonpartisan enterprise, and justifies public support most effectively when it is widely upheld as a socially indispensable undertaking.

5

Academics and Governance

By now it should be clear that the basic hierarchy of academe is traditionally one of competence rather than power. Members of the academic community, including students, seldom act under intramural orders from anybody, and coercion is a rarely used sanction in the orderly conduct of university affairs. There has to be authority, or course, but in most institutions it is carefully legitimated. Professorial authority over students, for example, stems largely from the fact that academics are more experienced and knowledgeable and can transmit to them what they presumably want and need to know. Moreover, professors are duly authorized to evaluate student efforts, and thus have influence and a measure of power over their destinies. Faculty members elected to councils, senates, and other bodies also have legitimated powers to regulate the behavior of their colleagues, as do elective or appointive administrative officers.

Depending upon the kinds of decisions and the institutions being talked about, powers may be tightly held or loosely spread. Although the university more closely resembles democracy than any other form of government, we have already observed that students, nonacademic staff members, and untenured academics are frequently excluded from voting privileges in matters of general university governance.

As Kingman Brewster has pointed out,[1] it is also generally acknowledged that certain kinds of decisions are best made in camera—e.g., status evaluations of individual faculty members, certain pending real estate transactions, some dealings with outside adversary interests, and winnowing a list or prospects for a top administrative post.

Thirty or forty years ago, a common faculty complaint had to do with authoritarianism. In many places, the faculty meeting was ridiculed as a farce. The AAUP was continuously critical of the lack of consultation between the regents and the president on the one hand, and the president and the faculty on the other. Appointive, promotional, and dismissal procedures were frequently found to be arbitrary. In large numbers of institutions, faculty committees were not named by their colleagues but by the administration. Autocracy, gerontocracy, and authoritarianism were more prevalent in the lesser and more insecure institutions, however, than in those of major stature.

During intervening years, even though the autonomy of universities had been noticeably eroded by outside agencies, internal decision making had become more dispersed. Regents or trustees (who, according to a 1968 study, spent just over five hours a month outside board meetings on institutional concerns, and who, according to another study in 1973, showed "some improvement" in this regard) came to delegate much of their legally constituted authority to govern. Administrative departments acquired more independence. In some universities, particularly in the private sector, schools and colleges were treated as tubs standing on their own bottoms, even in such concerns as securing additional funding. Faculty and students showed less hesitation about demanding a voice in many matters of university governance.

Distinctive Aspects of the 1960s

Alienation and general disquiet over the nation's involvement in Vietnam combined to foment of spirt of rebelliousness in

American youth during the 1960s and a good many campuses were caught in the uproar. For long years, students in virtually all institutions had their own separate schemes of governance (if any), which dealt largely with minor issues of little institutional import. In many places during the 1960s, however, students began to demand and get a voice in large educational concerns. Stanford University, for example, added students as voting members of academic council committees and authorized three students as nonvoting participants at trustee meetings. The State of Kentucky made student government presidents from state institutions nonvoting members of institutional governing boards. (Although nonvoting status gave them no real power, it did provide a more direct opportunity to exercise influence.) At the State University of New York (SUNY) in Binghampton, a revised governance plan entailed a membership ratio of five faculty members to three students to two administrators. Columbia University circulated a reply form to nearly 23,000 of its students and faculty (8,400 made returns) to get advice about reforms of governance.

The dissidents were not always well informed about existing mechanisms of governance in their own institutions, and indeed, were at times misinformed about who actually decided what, yet they were insistent upon change. In retrospect, it is interesting to note what changes they proposed and why. How did faculties and administrators assess the feasibility and desirability of proposed reforms? What were the outcomes?

One undisguised intent of the militants was to denigrate centralized authority by denying its legitimacy. Although many administrators were already familiar with the wry definition of their vocation as "the roughest profession," most had never before experienced such open onslaughts. In a campus gathering at a well-known eastern institution during the 1960s, for example, a rather hysterical student said to the president in an open meeting, "This university is faculty and students and we need you for only one thing—to get money. You and the deans should have no say in education. You administrators get in the way. . . . " Paul Goodman tagged administrative machinery a "mere excrescence." J. Kenneth Galbraith, presumably advocating syndicalism, proclaimed that "only the faculty can govern . . . the mature university."

There was no acknowledgment that governing boards and presidents had long since abandoned in fact, if not in law, any pretensions to absolute power. However anachronistic they may have become as symbols of bygone oligarchy, however, it was convenient to conjure them up as authoritarian devils responsible for most of the shortcomings of academic governance. Even though a good many trustees in various places may have still clung to the "dated and impossible charge of 'governing' their institutions" and handing decisions down from the top in all important matters, Morton A. Rauh expressed the view that such perspectives were in the main either ill-advised, or, more probably, at odds with what actually was happening in their institutions. Rauh went on to suggest that trustees should concentrate on five basic responsibilities: 1) select the president; 2) evaluate the management (especially the president); 3) hold the assets; 4) act as a court of last resort; 5) maintain a balance between competing constituencies; and 6) relate the institution to the larger society.[2]

Somewhat similarly, in a report issued a few years later, in review of what he considered to be the "more and more demanding" task of such boards, John W. Nason had this to say:

> In the face of multiple and sometimes conflicting purposes, of divided faculty loyalties, of competing student expectations, there is no other group than the trustees, both deeply concerned and yet above the fray, to insist on the clarification of mission. Once directions have been agreed upon, it is the responsibility of governing boards to examine progress and to assess institutional performance. This is one way of discharging their responsibility to protect the independence and the integrity of their institution. Pressures from the outside are increasing. Only strong boards which command pub-

lic respect for the kind of job they are doing can effectively champion institutional autonomy. Educational programs are a mix of requirements of intellectual disciplines on the one hand, the needs of society on the other. A nation in social motion will not leave educational patterns at rest, and the interpretation of social needs to academic experts will be an increasing function of trustees. To the extent that higher education is moving into an era of governance by conflict rather than by consensus, rights become important and challenges to authority more prevalent. It would become intolerable to take all local issues to the public courts; in the last analysis governing boards must serve as courts of last appeal. And finally trustees must evaluate their own performance. To do what comes naturally or what has been habitual is no longer good enough.[3]

Despite the recent lull on most campuses, many academics and others can vividly recall the institutional disruptions of the 1960s. They will remember the Students for a Democratic Society's advocacy of a complete student takeover of universities, with view to making them vantage points for launching "the social revolution." Activist student newspaper editors had a field day issuing new demands for reform. Many professors thought that it would all simply "go away," and in some instances it did, but students were not the only urgers of change. Growing dissatisfaction of faculty and others with the shortcomings of academic governance led to the issuance in 1966 of the *Joint Statement of Government of Colleges and Universities* by the American Association of University Professors, the American Council on Education, and the Association of Governing Boards of Universities and Colleges. The "call to mutual understanding" set forth the general rights and responsibilities of the faculty as follows:

> The faculty has primary responsibility for such fundamental areas as curriculum, subject matter and methods of instruction, research, faculty status, and those aspects of stu-

dent life which relate to the educational process. On these matters the power of review or final decision lodged in the governing board or delegated by it to the president should be exercised adversely only in exceptional circumstances, and for reasons communicated to the faculty.

With regard to students, it stated:

> Ways should be found to permit significant student participation within the limits of attainable effectiveness. The obstacles to such participation are large and should not be minimized: inexperience, untested capacity, a transitory status which means that present action does not carry with it subsequent responsibility, and the inescapable fact that the other components of the institution are in a position of judgment over the students.

Although university presidents and trustees have issued few collective statements about their desired reforms of governance, a Canadian university head complained in 1969 about how the rise of faculty power in North America had sapped the powers of presidents. He regretted the "lack of speedy and effective powers of decision-making, of academic foresight, and of rising to sudden crises." While being "cheered by the death of the old campus despotisms," he concluded wearily that after having worked in several universities—some almost wholly professor-governed, others wholly lay-governed, and others with mixed boards—he had found the facts of academic life to be much the same in all.[4]

Professorial Roles in Governance

Student interest in academic governance seems to have subsided since the 1960s, but to the best of my knowledge none of the concessions made during that period have been rescinded. The fact of the matter is, of course, that the professors themselves exercise the largest influence on academic policies and practices. Students come and go annually, department chairmanships may rotate, presidents seldom last out a decade, and most trustees (especially those in public institutions) serve for limited terms, but tenured members of the faculty usually remain as long as they choose to do so. They have the main jurisdiction over what will be taught and how. They pass critical judgments on students and their colleagues. In most universities they continue to comprise a majority on many of the policy-making committees and other academic bodies that really decide what the university should do. (Student revolutionaries in the 1960s and early 1970s sometimes mistook the real seats of power in academe and blockaded the wrong offices!)

The lines of authority and processes of government, however, may be uncertain and confused. A few years ago at the University of California in Berkeley, for example, a researcher who considered the school to be "well-advanced" in governance stated that for many years the faculty senate made basic policy which the administration then carried out. Even so, in some spheres the administration was accustomed to formulating policy and holding faculty groups responsible for implementation. In still other spheres, the custom was for the administration to make as well as implement policy.

In many institutions, decision making and implementation historically have not evidenced a simple or unitary process, with clear and unmistakable lines of authority and responsibility. During the 1960s, some faculties seemed not to understand that they could not reasonably engage in sporadic intervention while also refusing to play a major role in day-to-day administration. On many sides then and now there seems to be reluctance in acknowledging that direct participation in an area of concern calls for a commitment of time, energy, and intelligence to the solution of problems.

In earlier days, when the average university community was smaller and less complex, "town meeting" governance, with the president presiding over sessions of the entire faculty, was fairly common. Everybody was eligible to participate and vote. By contrast, at Columbia University, the Faculty's Executive Committee pointed out in its March 20, 1969, report that in the contemporary university such a faculty body can work only if most of its members pay no attention to it, for often there is not even an assembly room large enough to seat them all. Furthermore, experience there showed that attendance at meetings was normally only about 15 percent of the eligible membership, with a rise to 25 percent at a time of crisis.

The American Council on Education in the mid-1960s conducted a study of governance procedures in more than 1,000 colleges and universities. The unpublished results showed that 104 of them had faculty senates; 196 had faculty organizations other than a senate; 149 had faculty representation through a council or committee; 441 had faculties meeting under administration leadership; 14 had faculty representation through an AAUP chapter; and only 77 were without designation of faculty organization or leadership. Still another ACE inquiry, made in 1969, indicated among other things that there was some system of student government. Only 16 percent reported that neither faculty nor students had any appreciable influence in policy making.[5]

Perceived and Preferred Roles

Most of the extensive literature on academic governance, unfortunately, represents authors' opinions rather than any systematic inquiry into what the various participants perceive and prefer. To correct this deficiency, an inquiry was made in 1968 that brought together the attitudes of a cross-section of presidents, vice-presidents, academic deans, department chairmen, directors, trustees, and faculty members in 68 universities.[6] They responded to a questionnaire that included a list of 47 goals, rating each goal on a five-point scale according to how much emphasis they felt each goal received at their institution and how much it ought to receive.

The rank order of the top ten *perceived* goals was as

follows: 1) protect academic freedom; 2) increase or maintain prestige; 3) maintain top quality in important programs; 4) ensure confidence of contributors; 5) keep up-to-date; 6) train students for scholarship/research; 7) carry on pure research; 8) maintain top quality in all programs; 9) ensure favor of validating bodies; and 10) ensure efficient goal attainment.

The rank order of the top ten *preferred* goals, on the other hand, was thus: 1) protect academic freedom; 2) train students for scholarship/research; 3) cultivate students' intellect; 4) maintain top quality in all programs; 5) disseminate new ideas; 6) keep up-to-date; 7) maintain top quality in important programs; 8) develop students' objectivity; 9) ensure efficient goal attainment; and 10) protect students' right of inquiry.

Among the 47 perceived and preferred goals, it is pertinent to report the following lower rankings in each category: involve faculty in university government (25 and 19); run university democratically (29 and 22); protect students' right of action (41 and 40); and involve students in university government (45 and 46).

With regard to the perceived goals of the university, the respondents were also asked to give their opinions about how much influence each of 16 agencies, groups, or persons had in determining major goals of the institution as a whole. To give the overall picture in the 68 universities sampled, the survey tabulated the following mean scores, along with the standard deviation for each as given in Table 5.1.

Gross and Grambsch concluded that, in general, the administration and the faculty share much the same values and work toward essentially the same goals, with no evidence of any deep-rooted conflicts. Moreover, no appreciable dissonance was found between perceived and preferred objectives.[7] Institutional size and location were negligible factors in goal perceptions and preferences, but elitist institutions tended to emphasize scholarly qualities, whereas other universities tended to be more service-oriented.

Table 5.1   The Over-All Power Structure of American Universities

POWER-HOLDER (rank-order)	MEAN SCORE	STANDARD DEVIATION
President	4.65	.62
Regents	4.37	.82
Vice-Presidents	4.12	.82
Deans of Professional Schools	3.62	.84
Dean of Graduate School	3.59	.89
Dean of Liberal Arts	3.56	.89
Faculty	3.31	.97
Chairman	3.19	.93
Legislators	2.94	1.37
Federal Government	2.79	1.06
State Government	2.72	1.21
Large Private Donors	2.69	1.06
Alumni	2.61	.90
Students	2.37	.82
Citizens of State	2.08	1.02
Parents	1.91	.87

Archie Dykes's *Faculty Participation in Academic Decision Making*[8] sets forth the findings of another empirical study of academic governance. The author interviewed a random sample of the liberal arts faculty in a large public university in the Midwest to get at their conceptions of a "proper" role for them to play in decision making, to find how they perceived the status quo in campus governance, to ascertain reasons for participation in governance, and to gather their complaints.

Five main tentative conclusions were drawn from the findings:

1. Faculty members have ambivalent attitudes about participation in decision making. While believing that they should have an important role, many of them are unwilling to give the time required by the role.

2. Few faculty persons recognize that institutional growth causes shifts in the nature of decision making. The necessity in larger universities for representation rather than

direct democracy seems to be poorly understood. Moreover, there is little historic evidence to support the common faculty view that professors have steadily lost power to the administration.

3. In view of the impossibility of neatly separating all decisions into "educational" and "noneducational" categories, a faculty should not be too choosy about its areas of concern. Decisions about student affairs, for instance, which most academics want to pass on to the administration, may radically affect an institution's educational purposes.

4. A source of much faculty-administration tension is the academic tendency to disregard the mutual relations existing between faculty and administrative power, and to see each party as being engaged in a kind of zero-sum game with the other.

5. There is a serious discrepancy between faculty role perceptions and actual roles. Many respondents displayed an indifference to faculty government but at the same time were critical of the administration for failing to communicate.

Finally, Dykes concluded that the faculty holds a simplistic view of the distribution of institutional power, stating that "the faculty members interviewed attributed to the administration vastly more power than it actually possesses" (p. 42). He expressed the further view that the pressures on the administration, both internally and externally, are only dimly recognized by many academics, and that widespread misconceptions are impediments to more effective decision making.

At the time of campus disturbances, McGeorge Bundy wrote an article ("Faculty Power")[9] pointing out that effective university governance calls for much hard work in which professors should share. His view was that they can work through committees and accept administrative assignments or respect others who do so for the right reasons. To effect feasible and desirable changes, they, more than any other group, are required to lend their best efforts to the processes of government. Neither they nor any other university group can have absolute power, because the concept has no place in a properly functioning university. Where faculty governance has in effect been a gerontocracy, the younger members need to be involved to offset their alienation and to incorporate their efforts in the common cause. For day-to-day university business to be carried on, however, decisions have to be made which the faculty as a corporate body simply cannot handle. "It needs an agent, and that agent is the administration."

Many universities, as Martin Trow has observed, carry on under two forms of governance—the complex administrative apparatus and the departmental structures. Administratively formulated rules and regulations tend to coordinate the whole enterprise and give it coherence, while departments foster diversity and may produce fragmentation. The one centralizes decision making, and the other decentralizes it. This arrangement has its advantages, to be sure, but the resulting roles are often ambiguous, and jurisdictions may become confused. A further complication in many institutions is that student government is an entirely separate arrangement.

Collegial Senates

Although college and university senates have long been familiar as governance mechanisms in academe, it was not until the campus disruptions beginning in 1968 that such a venerable institution as Columbia University set about devising its "new" plan of governance.[10] The main outcome was the formation of a university-wide senate, which held its first meeting about a year later. It was a unicameral body, consisting of 101 members, including the following: 9 administrative officers; 57 faculty members (42 tenured and 15 nontenured); 22 students; 5 members from affiliate institutions (Barnard, Teachers College, and Union Theological Seminary); 2 professional library staff members; 2 research staff members; 2 from higher levels of the classified personnel staff; and 2 from the alumni.

After considering alternatives in governance, Columbia

rejected both the "town meeting" type of body, with everybody eligible to vote, and the bicameral type, with separate
student government. The size of the senate, it was believed,
would allow for free debate without elaborate rules of procedure and without a highly organized and controlled system of
leadership. Subject to the reserved power of the trustees and
certain other limitations, the University Senate was established
as a policy-making body to consider all matters of university-
wide concern, all matters affecting more than one faculty or
school, and all matters pertaining to the implementation and
execution of agreements with other educational institutions
that were then or might thereafter become affiliated with the
University.

The body was charged with these main responsibilities:
development and review of plans and policies to strengthen
the university's educational system; work on a long-range
master plan of physical development; advancement of academic freedom and protection of faculty interests; promotion
and enhancement of student life and welfare; and initiation
and review of policies to govern the university's relations with
outside agencies for research, instruction, and related purposes. Unless its acts required trustee concurrence, they were
to become final on passage, except that in certain instances the
president was to advise the senate no later than its next regular
meeting that trustee concurrence would be necessary. When
trustees did not concur, their reasons were to be explained to
the University Senate.

Faculty and student reactions to the structure and functioning of the senate were diverse, as one might expect. In
response to a query I made in the summer of 1977 as to how
successfully it was operating by then, I received this comment
from a faculty member who was also a key officer of academic
administration:

> Opinions on the effectiveness of the Senate vary enor-
> mously. On the one hand the Senate does provide a forum

for the airing of important matters. On the other, a good deal of what the Senate has actually done seems trivial to many of its constituents. That a certain disillusionment concerning the Senate has set in is evidenced by the fact that early Senate elections were hardfought contests between a substantial number of nominees but in the last few years there have never been more faculty nominees than vacancies (at least in the Arts and Sciences). Last year, despite an enormous amount of arm-twisting, the Graduate School was unable to produce a sufficient number of nominees to fill the vacancies.

The Administration of the University seems committed to using the Senate, and in some areas, e.g., faculty affairs, the Senate has contributed substantially. In others, e.g., budget (as might be imagined), success has been elusive.

Noting that senates seemed to be "springing up every-where," the Center for Research and Development in Higher Education at the University of California at Berkeley launched a study in 1971 under the direction of Harold Hodgkinson.[11] A survey was made of 1,863 institutions; of those responding, 688 currently had broadly based senates, 40 had had them in the past but had discontinued them, 303 were currently consider-ing establishing them, 52 had plans for the future, and 545 had never considered the idea. One difficulty in generalizing from the Hodgkinson data is that the total number of institutions surveyed included 32.8 percent junior colleges and 23.0 per-cent four-year institutions, with only 17.4 percent of the sample of 688 institutions being Ph.D.-granting universities. (Since our concern is mainly with universities, it should be observed here that familiarity with the idea of a senate is probably much less commonplace in junior colleges and in many four-year institu-tions than in the more complex institutions.)

Hodgkinson found that such governing bodies are vari-ously called councils, assemblies, and senates, with senate be-ing the most frequent designation in advanced level institu-tions. Many institutions, incidentally, had senates long before the beginning of student protests.

The most frequently given reason for the formation of senates was "the desire to democratize decision-making and broaden the input base for policy questions" (p. 19). In 48 percent of the doctorate-granting institutions, students were included in such bodies. Ratification procedures for actions taken by such bodies varied from one institution to another, with little uniformity by types. In some instances, the formation of a senate resulted in the elimination of other governmental groups on campus (e.g., separate student government, an administrative council) and in others it did not. On some campuses, the president was the presiding officer, and on others not; the president might or might not be a member, with or without the power to veto.

Although the senates and similar forms of representational government undoubtedly democratize the decision-making process, they afford no intrinsic assurance of either efficient or effective conduct of academic affairs. Except in time of crisis, the ablest and busiest professors may find their deliberations to be taken up too much with time-consuming and unproductive debate (as apparently was the case at Columbia University, for example). Important decisions may be made without regard to the fact that institutional resources are limited, and that mandates for action are rarely, if ever, as budget balancers know, "cost-free." Moreover, total immersion of the faculty in the multitudinous tasks of trying to govern complex institutions may make serious inroads on time normally given to teaching and research.

In light of his experience at Berkeley and elsewhere, Roger Heyns has advocated more power and effective responsibility for administrators at all levels, with new practices for holding them accountable. Instead of diffusing responsibility loosely, he has suggested better identification of major decision-making points, and a concentration of responsibility, accountability, and authority in specific persons. More freedom would be accorded administrators, with specification of what it is they are expected to do and an auditing of their performance.[12]

Changed Loci of Academic Governance

It has been widely observed that the loci of decision making have become more dispersed on many campuses in recent years, but an almost concurrent shift of controls away from campuses to other locales has been in the main an unpublicized movement. Virtually none of the rhetoric about individual academic freedom, for example, has been directed toward institutional freedom as its corollary, even though the autonomy of virtually all colleges and universities has steadily eroded. Many academics, I would guess, are hardly aware that nearly every state now has a statewide board, council, or commission giving policy direction to public higher education. The mandates of HEW and other federal agencies specifying student admissions policies, faculty and staff employment practices, and teaching and research objectives are accepted without organized protest on the part of the academic rank and file. (To be sure, administrators do on occasion complain.) Strong as well as weak institutions yield formerly cherished autonomies, moreover, as they voluntarily enter into consortia and other arrangements designed to further collective improvement.

Although autonomy is still considered important and a diversity of institutional goals and their freedom from central contol continue to be proclaimed as virtues of the American system of higher education, the fact of the matter is that local control of colleges and universities has been appreciably diminished. Shortcomings of self-governance are in part responsible, but the whole movement stems fundamentally from changes in contemporary society. Egalitarianism has made advanced education a right of the many rather than a privilege of the few, and no institution of higher education is in a position today to maintain both viability and complete independence.

Responding to public demand, the whole enterprise of higher education has become larger, more costly, and increasingly politicized. Institutional independence has been displaced by interdependence. In an era of growing collectivism, it is not surprising that the movement of authority in higher education's governance has been from the local to the state or national level, and from the private to the public arena. Many initiatives have in the process changed hands.

Statewide boards or commissions typically engage in analysis of institutional budgets for construction, operational cost studies, the development of uniform systems of accountability, and similar matters. Some engage in master planning for the state system of public education. Such planning entails attention to the role and scope of existing institutions, the formulation of criteria for establishing new branches and new institutions, and efforts toward the more efficient use of staff and facilities. Some of the boards must approve and authorize construction plans for new buildings. Most review institutional budget requests and make recommendations to the governor and legislature. Some have devised programmatic formula approaches which institutions must follow in making their requests for funds. In at least one state, the agency has authority to veto individual course offerings.

Such agencies have negative as well as positive reasons for existing. In some states, a wasteful duplication of programs among public institutions, disregard for a sensible institutional division of labor, dysfunctional rivalries, and seemingly limitless ambitions to expand vertically and horizontally all pointed to the need for a central coordinating body. Positively viewed, there was also a desire to allocate public funds more equitably and effectively, and to insulate the legislature from the pressures of lobbying groups whose prime interests were not necessarily the best interests of the state as a whole.

Even though the existence of statewide coordinating or governing bodies for higher education is no guarantee of economy, efficiency, or equity in the use of resources, the operations of such agencies are likely to become more rather than less important in the years ahead. The mushrooming of academic programs and the increase in number of publicly supported institutions in recent times have greatly increased the competition for public funds, and hence it is to be expected that central agencies will continue to search out and refine common denominators for evaluating budget requests. In such a situation, unit costs, formula approaches, and similar devices will be widely utilized. There is the danger, to be sure, that application of such concepts will tend to disregard institutional differences in quality and purpose. Excessive bureaucratic control from a state capital can reduce a system to a Procrustean bed if mediocrity is permitted to become a common denominator.

Moreover, in an increasing number of states public financial aid assists the private sector of higher education, and such aid usually comes with strings attached. To preserve the advantages to society of a pluralistic system of higher education, a problem ahead will be to keep state support (and control) from resulting in what would amount to a monolithic system.

Since institutions compete among themselves and with other organizations and groups for public and private support, they have to be partisans for their own causes. To minimize jockeying among state-supported institutions, some detached and nonpartisan entity between claimants and the legislature can be useful to them and to the public in evaluating how resources ought to be allocated. Because voluntary institutional associations cannot reasonably be expected to perform amputational operations on their own members, to fix institutional roles and scopes, or to undertake other tasks requiring an insulated perspective, some other coordinating agency can be more objective. For the necessary autonomy of colleges and universities to be maintained, however, civil service status for faculty and staff, centralized prescriptions of curriculums, and detailed directions about how all funds must be spent should be shunned as agency involvement.

I have called attention in another publication to the need to resolve some basic issues and to answer more knowledgeably such questions as the following:

1. What kinds of decisions are best made by local authority and what kinds by central authority? The institution itself, for example, is in a better position than any outside group to decide which faculty members are entitled to promotion and which students to graduation, but by the same token it is in a much worse position than a detached agency to advise the governor and legislature about *where* a new state-supported law school or medical school should be established.

2. Which aspects of institutional autonomy should be most carefully safeguarded? A distinguished educational leader, Sir Eric Ashby, formulated a check list several years ago, and in reviewing it I have noted that some of this nation's most prestigious universities would not be in the clear on every count. No institution receiving federal funds is free to employ, retain, advance, or let go faculty members in strict accord with its internal criteria. Colleges and universities no longer have the same jurisdiction over their students which they once held. Despite the inroads on institutional independence, and in part because of them, there is a pressing urgency nearly everywhere for some firm positions about priorities to be upheld.

3. In systems where there are both institutional and statewide boards, how can their respective roles be made more compatible and mutually supportive? My only comment here is that in some states the enabling legislation ought to be redrafted.

4. Since many of these statewide agencies tend to relegate even the ablest institutional leaders to roles as advisers and observers in public policy formation, what other arrangement would make better use of their expertise without introducing partisanship into the decision-making process? Some states, of course, do make good use of the advice of such leaders, and their experience in this regard deserves more attention elsewhere.

5. In view of growing demands for more institutional accountability, who should be responsible for what and to whom? Answers to this question will and should vary from one setting to another, but whatever the lines of communication, they must be widely perceived and clearly understood by all who will be called upon to use them.

6. Although evaluating productivity is admittedly more difficult in educational than in commercial enterprise, need the former be limited largely to such measures as class hours taught weekly, books and articles published, student credits completed, degrees awarded, and so on? Some methods for assessing the impact of different kinds of institutional environments on student learning are already available, but, unfortunately, not used extensively.

7. To avoid the leveling effects of centralized coordination or control, how can the importance of quality in higher education be more surely delineated and encouraged? The main problem in this regard is to develop and utilize reliable indicators of quality.

8. If the resources of higher education are to be coordinated as effectively as possible in serving the public interest, the private sector needs to be included in the purview of statewide agencies, but how can this be done without undermining the educational dualism considered to be important in a pluralistic culture and democratic society? A first step would be to hold out real inducements to private institutions to participate in coordination.[13]

Turning from the outside influences exercised politically within states on the governance of institutions of higher education, it is also important to observe the vastly increased role in recent years of the federal government in the support, direction, and control of the nation's colleges and universities. In 1942, the federal government's role was so minor and indirect that my earlier book about academics hardly made mention of it.[14] Now the situation has drastically changed. By the late 1970s, the Congress was appropriating around 10 billion dollars a year for higher education, with institutions involved in almost four hundred federal programs, and operating in conformity with the rules, regulations, guidelines, and audit requirements emanating from several dozen congressional committees and approximately fifty executive agencies. Few of these federally funded programs were intended directly to help colleges and universities as such, to be sure, but they all entailed involvements with central government.

These involvements in the main have been mutually beneficial and have yielded incalculable dividends for the whole society, but the growth of governmental interest has also been accompanied by a growth of governmental control which has reduced institutional autonomy and further politicized the process of educational decision making. In the mid-1970s, university presidents were beginning to sound like conservative businessmen in complaining about the interference coming from Washington bureaucrats in the conduct of academic affairs. The presidents of Harvard, Yale, Ohio State, and numerous other institutions began to speak out against what one of them termed an "outrageous" federal intrusion "upon academic self-governance."[15] About that time the ACE conducted an inquiry which showed that at six representative institutions compliance with a dozen federal programs was costing them from 9 million to 10 million dollars a year, amounting anywhere from 1 up to 4 percent of their operating budgets. While approving the intent of most federally mandated social programs, institutional heads were critical of the poorly thought out schemes that added uncontrollable costs to their budgets. These schemes included equal employment opportunity regulations, affirmative action, elimination of age discrimination, wage and hour standards, unemployment compensation, Social Security measures, retirement benefits, wage and salary controls, occupational safety and health mandates, special provisions for the handicapped, and environmental protection. A further complaint was that as many as four different federal agencies might be holding institutions accountable for administering a single enactment.

Perhaps the most flagrant instance of federal intrusion on institutional self-governance was the attempt to dictate to medical schools receiving federal aid a requirement that they would admit hundreds of Americans who enrolled in foreign medical schools after being rejected for admission here. When the medical deans rebelled, Congress did modify the legislation it had passed earlier with little debate in order to permit more flexibility.[16]

Regretting the fact that institutions and the federal government were too frequently becoming adversaries during the late 1970s, with overregulation on the one hand and overreaction on the other, Ohio State's President Harold L. Enarson has called for a restoration of partnership, with both parties again working amicably and effectively together to solve national problems.[17]

It is unrealistic, of course, to expect drastic deregulation, and perhaps the most that can be anticipated is a more sensible procedure for accountability in the expenditure of what are, after all, public funds. Collective and organized actions on the part of institutions through their Washington-based associations undoubtedly can help effect more consultation to improve the whole regulatory process without unduly impending institutional autonomy.

However all this may be, the trend in all industrialized nations has been and is likely to continue to be one of increased governmental involvement in both the finance and control of educational institutions. Just how far this trend can go without reducing institutional autonomy to the point that the efficiency and effectiveness of colleges and universities in serving the larger society is also undermined is an unresolved issue.

6

3/9/79

Status Appraisal

Since academic statuses are mainly achieved rather than ascribed, occupancy of them implies satisfactory performance of certain functions. A status, translated into action, becomes a role. In performing their various university roles individual academics may fulfill normal demands, fall short of meeting them, or go beyond usual requirements. Most academics share commonly held expectations of occupational recognition and reward, but desired statuses are not achieved merely by longevity of service, and by no means does every beginning academic get to the top statuses. As a consequence of prolonged indoctrination, few academics falter or fail because they are technically incompetent, but they are in competition with other individuals for advancement, and performance levels among the competitors are necessarily unequal.

Appraising individual differences of performance in intellectual activity is not a simple task, however, and evaluations for purposes of status assignment are complex. In universities, how are determinations reached regarding which members of the untenured faculty will be kept on and which ones terminated? How are promotions made? What are the criteria? Who makes the assessments? What are the rewards and penalties?

These are the main questions to be considered with regard to status appraisal.

The Merit Principle

Regardless of their political systems, all advanced, technology-oriented societies tend to be achievement-based in their divisions of labor for productive enterprise. Even though some practices run counter to principle, the merit principle of evaluating the worth of human services still finds wide acceptance. It is not surprising, accordingly, that the merit principle of status appraisal is the most familiar one in American university circles. In recent years, to be sure, collisions between meritocratic and egalitarian forces have become more frequent, and the nation's campuses have often been the locales of hotly disputed issues.[1] Despite attempts of egalitarians to politicize colleges and universities, however, certain hard realities are apparently inescapable. One such reality is the inherently meritocratic character of organized intellectual endeavor. The functional underpinning for such a structuring of the higher learning derives logically from the fact that nobody becomes educated by inheritance, gift, or decree—nor does anybody educate others or advance knowledge in these ways.

Since the sifting, sorting, and cultivation of human talents are major missions of the univeristy, it is to be expected that problems should arise in differentiating between the less and the more capable, including faculty as well as students. William J. Goode has noted that whereas many groups have devices for protecting the inept and for protecting themselves against the damaging effects of ineptitude, sports and basic scientific research represent the closest approximations to structured situations in which individual rewards stem mainly from performance.[2] Unlike unionized laborers whose preferment is based on seniority more than merit, or public school teachers, who in general resist any differential evaluation of job performance, academics are members of a system formally committed to the merit principle.

Nonetheless, there are complicating factors. Like other professionals, such as physicians and lawyers, academics like to claim exclusive competence to evaluate members' capabilities, are reluctant to rate one another publicly through invidious comparisons, and are at times prone to use academic freedom as a shield against full public accountability. In spite of what Goode calls "achievement rhetoric," academics are often hostile to rigorous efforts to measure their productivity and may oppose anything smacking of managerial attempts to increase institutional "efficiency" as an interference with time-honored professional prerogatives.

The indoctrination of academics is such that the completely inept are seldom found in professorial ranks, but every institution has its misfits, and the productivity of some academics is disappointing. The complaint about "faculty deadwood" can be found nearly everywhere and, with progressively aging faculties in prospect during the years immediately ahead, is more likely to be prevalent in the future. Moreover, the average academic of advanced years undergoes some decline in productivity, but, like virtually all wage and salary earners in an inflationary era, continues to expect an annual increase in pay.

Evidence of institutional compromise of the merit principle also may be seen. In 1974, for example, Frederick Burkhardt, then president of the American Council of Learned Societies and former chairman of New York City's Board of Education, noted that at CUNY 25 out of 26 persons were getting tenure, and that its routine bestowal suggested mediocrity as a standard. (At that time CUNY, incidentally, had one of the highest salary scales in the nation.) Concurrently, a spokesman for the Professional Staff Congress (the CUNY faculty union) was protesting the Board requirement that departments had to justify exceeding a 50 percent tenure limitation on their staffs.[3] As already noted, the fiscal crunch of the

1970s was a harsh reminder to many institutions throughout the country that laxity of judgment had overloaded them with tenured personnel.

As I remarked in my 1942 book, the proper evaluation of faculty services was then a crucial concern, and the end of the expansionist boom in higher education makes it even more critical now. Technical competence continues to be the most important single criterion of appraisal, but age, maturity, length of service, and peculiarities of each individual situation, now no less than then, can hardly be ignored. No basis for promotion has yet evolved that provides ready-made answers to all employer and employee perplexities. Fundamental disharmonies result from the "up or out" system, carefully codified rules of seniority, or rigid adherence to any inflexible scheme of evaluation (not to mention arbitrariness, the most disliked of all procedures) which ignores the fact that university people, like all other human beings, do not want to be treated as mere instrumentalities.

Type Situations

We are here concerned less with general cautions and admonitions, however, than with procedures to be observed in existing universities. What are the more important problems of type situations encountered in evaluating what the academician does and is expected to do? Whom does an institution dismiss, retard, or promote, and how does it determine who its best academics are? The real state of affairs is less well integrated than it superficially appears to be, and attaching recognition symbols to achievement, though institutionally valued, is often not well articulated. Any administrator will grant the verisimilitude of the following hypothetical instance:

> . . . The university president in his swivel chair is still confronted by the enigma of qualitative evaluation. A promotion is to be made, and there are four available candidates.

One has written two books, but the pundits in his field call them "unsound" and "theoretical." Is he a genius or a fool? The other has written only three somewhat incomprehensible articles on esoteric subjects, but the wise men and great consider them promising of better things to come. The third has written nothing, but the great professor whom he is assisting swears that he possesses the most searching mind he has ever come in contact with. Number four has written one book which is declared fair, one article which suggests the same promise as number two. One and three are acclaimed by students as brilliant teachers; two, one hears, is a dull lecturer; four has had little teaching experience. What is the administrator going to do? Evidently, all four are men of some ability; appointing any one of them will not wreck the university. Yet, he is supposed to pick the one who will be the most brilliant and distinguished at fifty. I am glad I do not have to make that selection.[4]

In his further analysis of the problem of selection, Professor Friedrich pointed out that Kant, who published nothing of consequence until he was fifty-seven, would have been eliminated in the modern American university long before beginning *The Critique of Pure Reason.* An opposite type of career is represented by Hume, who did his most important work at the age of twenty-seven. Administrative selection faces a difficult problem of predicting when the best work will be done, not to mention deciding whether an individual's productivity has already peaked.

As Harriet Zuckerman and Robert K. Merton have noted, "Nobel laureates in physics, for example, were on the average 36 at the time of doing their prize-winning work; laureates in chemistry, 38 and those in medicine and physiology, 41 ... [yet] we sometimes need to be reminded that median ages at time of discovery tell us that half of the discoveries were made after the median age as well as before."[5] Zuckerman and Merton go on to show that whereas some scientists are still heavily engaged in research in their later years, many of their careers show a diminution of time allocated to research and an increase in administrative engagements, or in such roles as advisers, "gatekeepers," referees, sages, and statesmen. Observing that the average age of members in the prestigious National Academy of Science is 62, "with about a quarter of them being 70 or older," one might conclude from evidence at hand, despite claims that science is a young man's field, that a gerontocracy does exist.

Faculty appointments and promotions, accordingly, always involve imponderable factors, even when the merit principle of evaluation is rigorously applied, and more commonly than not other considerations also enter into the evaluation of services to complicate matters still further. Lionel S. Lewis has published a book which attempts to refute the notion that "in the last analysis university professors are judged primarily by the quality of their work."[6] Although his focus is on departure from rather than adherence to the merit principle in the appraisal of faculty services, his extensive findings do illustrate that in many institutions impartiality of judgment is confounded by the intrusion of factors having little if anything to do with professional merit per se.

Many universities have complained in recent years about federal and other outside intrusions as impediments to the operation of the merit principle of assessing individual worth, and justifiably so if excellence is to survive as a goal for institutional achievement. Ironically, however, longstanding personnel policies and practices in many places already display departures from the principle. The rank and file of academics are often resistant to more objective bases for assessing their productivity in teaching and research, administrators are frequently remiss in utilizing improved procedures already available, and length of service together with "institutional loyalty" are all too commonly substituted for more meritorious criteria in the retention and promotion of staff members who may contribute little to the advancement of higher learning.

In our society, which supports upwards of 3,000 institutions of higher education, a case certainly can be made for having many campuses where excellence is not an institutional aspiration and where criteria for judging individual worth are based on more considerations than merit. The faculties in these places ought to be competent and dedicated teachers, but they need not be creative thinkers in scholarship and science. Like public school teachers, they should be effective schoolmasters and schoolmarms, but on a somewhat more advanced level of knowledge.

In universities, however, and particularly in the several hundred of them which grant Ph.D. degrees, it can be argued that academic staff members presumably have responsibilities for advancing as well as disseminating higher learning. Whether the nation ever needed so many supposedly research-oriented centers is doubtful, and especially so in view of the fact that in some fields about 90 percent of the significant research continues to emanate from only a couple of dozen or so universities. It is obvious by now, moreover, that the "university syndrome" is producing a glut of Ph.D.s, and that programmatic cutbacks are inevitable. With intensified competition among universities in the years just ahead, will Gresham's law prevail or will the merit principle of evaluating university academics be strengthened?

Appraisal Criteria and Procedures

Despite inherent difficulties in evaluating faculty services and the admitted impossibility of unerring discrimination in attaching symbols of achievement to the deserving and withholding them from the undeserving, academics have long been accustomed to varying schemes of rewards and penalties. The rewards may be salary increases, job security, advancement in rank, titular or honorific recognitions, special grants or prizes, and so on. Conversely, penalties may range from the denial of various improvements in status to outright dismissal. It is no wonder, accordingly, that the AAUP has over the years concerned itself more intently with the whole matter of faculty appraisal than with any other single topic except possibly academic freedom.

Institutional data regarding various forms of faculty advancement are systematically recorded and often widely publicized. There is an understandable silence about the withholding of rewards, of course, unless the individual "victims" choose to make a noise about their felt grievances. In recent years, there has been a growing litigiousness about such matters, and this may in part account for the trend in many places toward across-the-board pay increases and toward increased skittishness about making the hard decisions required to build and sustain institutional excellence.

In 1929 the AAUP made a study of dismissals in thirty-one institutions which yielded the following rank order: 1) poor teaching coupled with some other shortcomings; 2) personal incompatibility or failure to get along with colleagues; 3) failure to achieve excellence in any direction; 4) lack of scholarly output, together with some other weaknesses; 5) lack of scholarly output as the sole factor; 6) poor teaching as the sole factor; 7) "race"; and 8) religion.[7] Other factors occasionally mentioned were "erratic judgment and tactlessness," "sex," and "feud in the department." These itemizations are of historic interest because some of the stated reasons are now illegal and others would no longer be considered sufficient or justifiable causes for termination of faculty services. It is worthy of note, however, that, contrary to widespread impressions, faculty members have on occasion been fired for professional inadequacy or incompetence.

A few years later a study was made at the University of Minnesota to ascertain the factors affecting promotions there between 1913 and 1931. Tabulated results were these: teaching, 43.4 percent; productive scholarship, 27.6 percent; student counseling, 11.6 percent; administrative work, 11 percent; and public service, 6.4 percent. At Indiana University a similar study was published for that institution in 1940, and the findings give almost the same order: teaching, 35.4 percent; productive scholarship, 22.9 percent; administrative work, 9.9 percent; student counseling, 7.1 percent; and public service, 5.1 percent. No similar statistics were then available for such prestigious private institutions as Harvard, Columbia, and Chicago, and hence comparisons could not be made with such high ranking public universities as Minnesota and Indiana. However, a sampling of subjective opinions I made then indicated that productive scholarship or research loomed larger as an evaluative criterion among the major independent institutions.

Shifting the time perspective three decades or more ahead, one can observe much more systematic and widespread attention to the evaluation of faculty services. There has been increased recognition of the need to provide a more objective basis for administrative decisions about such matters as faculty advancement, for assessing more accurately teaching effectiveness in order to improve it, and to provide better criteria for gauging teaching and learning. One investigator, John W. Gustad, compared the results of a survey he made in 1961 and repeated in much the same form in 1966.[8]

For that time interval he reported a decline in the use of informal student opinions, systematic student ratings, classroom visitation, and longtime follow-up of students as a means of teacher evaluation. For both of the reported years, the department chairman ranked highest as a source of judgment, and colleagues' opinions also ranked high, as did the evaluations of deans. Increased significance was being attached to committee evaluations, grade distribution, and enrollment in elective courses.

Gustad noted that few institutional researches had been conducted to determine the validity of the measures being employed or of criterion performance to ascertain whether observable events could be judged relevant to any conceptual criterion utilized. Some of his suggestions were these: there are too many kinds of good teaching for any numerical rating of competence. With regard to systematic evaluation, laziness among faculties is more endemic than fear. Two extremist attitudes are to be avoided: first, the monistic ideal of the Great Teacher; second, the flabby latitudinarianism which regards education as being so complex that every kind of teacher is valuable in one way or another.

In 1966, when Gustad made his survey, Alexander W. Astin and Calvin B. T. Lee also made an extended inquiry into practices regarding the evaluation of college and university teachers.[9] They sent a questionnaire to a large number of institutions and got well over a thousand usable returns. Most of the responding institutions maintained that teaching effectiveness was considered to be a major factor in determining a faculty member's usefulness. The sources of supply for pertinent information and comparative frequency of use are reported by Astin and Lee in Table 6.1.

Table 6.1 Frequency of Use of Various Sources of Information in the Evaluation of Teaching Effectiveness

SOURCE OF INFORMATION	Used In All or Most Departments (%)	Not Used (%)
Chairman evaluation	85.1	3.4
Dean evaluation	82.3	5.8
Colleagues' opinions	48.9	8.7
Scholarly research and publications	43.8	21.6
Informal student opinions	41.2	9.6
Grade distributions	28.0	37.4
Course syllabi and examinations	26.4	28.0
Committee evaluation	25.1	52.4
Student examination performance	19.6	35.8
Self-evaluation or report	16.3	57.2
Classroom visits	14.0	39.5
Systematic student ratings	12.4	47.6
Enrollment in elective courses	11.0	49.9
Longterm follow-up of students	10.2	47.1
Alumni opinions	9.9	46.8

Source: Completed questionnaires from 1,110 academic deans.

Noting that classroom visits were reported to be infrequent and even taboo in almost 40 percent of the responding institutions, Astin and Lee concluded that deans, department chairmen, and professional colleagues with evaluative responsibilities must necessarily base their assessments on opinions rendered by other persons. Moreover, since almost half of the institutions did not use systematic student ratings, the unanswered question is who these "other persons" might be.

To the best of my knowledge, nobody has done a comprehensive survey of the kinds of records universities maintain and use systematically in assessing faculty productivity, but one study of a group of state universities has shown that the majority maintain records.[10] In addition to listings of published research, inclusions often cite such items as translations, reports, fiction, poetry, essays and printed speeches, radio and t.v. programs, concerts, art designs and exhibitions, musical compositions, and patents. These recordings are frequently published on an annual basis, mostly for intramural distribution.

Aside from kinds of information gathered for purposes of faculty evaluation, and who uses it, there is the more significant question regarding the relative importance attached to the various factors in deciding which members of the academic staff go up, out, or have no change in employee status. Astin and Lee's findings are set forth in Table 6.2 (p. 304). From the data shown in Table 6.2, it is clear that the responding deans in all types of institutions considered classroom teaching effectiveness to be the most important single criterion. From the other computations noted, it is also clear that chairmen and deans are the main sources of information about teaching effectiveness, and the main evaluators of it. Astin and Lee go on to state: "However, in light of the data about how teaching effectiveness is actually evaluated, the apparent overall importance assigned to classroom teaching is not as reassuring as it at first appears to be." They suspect that "teaching ability is more likely to be evaluated on the basis of scholarly research and publication rather than on information more directly rele-

Table 6.2 Importance of Various Factors in Evaluating Faculty for Promotion, Salary, or Tenure

PERCENTAGE OF DEANS CHECKING ITEM AS A "MAJOR FACTOR"

SOURCE OF INFORMATION	All Colleges (N=1,110)	Junior Colleges (N=128)	Teachers Colleges (N=133)	Liberal Arts Colleges (N=484)	University Colleges				
					Arts and (N=110)	Education (N=48)	Engineering (N=109)	Business (N=65)	Agriculture (N=33)
Classroom teaching	95.9	98.2	94.0	97.6	93.6	91.7	93.7	95.3	93.8
Personal attributes	56.8	69.2	53.8	61.3	33.7	46.8	53.9	50.0	70.0
Length of service in rank	47.4	63.3	47.4	59.9	21.3	33.3	24.3	18.8	46.9
Research	46.6	1.0	27.1	31.7	92.7	79.2	82.0	84.4	87.5
Supervision of graduate study*	40.8	—	16.0	17.8	55.2	52.2	59.6	38.7	61.3
Publication	39.9	1.0	22.0	24.5	83.3	70.8	70.9	82.8	80.7
Student advising	39.5	42.5	37.7	46.8	20.2	38.3	29.6	22.2	62.5
Campus committee work	29.2	41.5	35.6	32.6	15.7	21.3	13.9	21.9	34.4
Activity in professional societies	25.3	18.3	28.2	23.9	19.8	33.3	28.4	35.9	31.3
Public service	20.5	15.7	22.0	16.1	23.2	48.9	14.8	29.7	43.8
Competing job offers	13.2	3.1	10.9	9.8	31.1	10.4	16.8	15.6	31.3
Supervision of honors program*	12.4	4.3	2.5	14.3	21.7	3.2	11.5	10.3	12.5
Outside consulting	5.3	4.0	12.3	2.4	2.8	17.4	5.7	6.2	9.4

*Percentages are actually based on considerably smaller Ns because of the relatively high number of deans who checked "not applicable."

vant to effective performance in the classroom." They also observe that in the university colleges the weight attached to research performance is almost on the same level as that for teaching.[11]

Insofar as universities are concerned, the situation has not changed much in the last three or four decades. Institutions are now in the main considerably larger, but even then a third of all academics were employed in institutions with 500 or more faculty members, and half of them were in institutions having 200 or more. The chief evaluators of their services could not have known very well personally most of those being evaluated. Then as now, evaluations must have relied mainly on indirect sources of information.

Although individual achievement in teaching cannot be surmised by study of anything equivalent to the published research bibliographies used (however crudely at times) to appraise research productivity, a fairly substantial body of objective knowledge has displaced some of the old mystiques about teaching effectiveness. Impressionistic evaluations are still in widespread use, of course, but there is no longer any justification for proclaiming, as did the dean of a large state university back in 1937, that it is futile to attempt appraisal of teaching competence when it is "something about which so little can be determined."

Service Load and Productivity

The academic's personal estimate of how many hours he works during the average week may be prone to error, of course, but the time budgets of large numbers of professors reveal a great deal about the allocation of their energies. In its 1933 survey of the faculty[12] the University of Chicago found that for the average academic there, 41.6 percent of the service load was for teaching, 24.6 percent for research without special compensation, 12.7 for departmental services, 5.4 for administration, 4.5 for extramural activities without compensation, and the remaining lesser percentages for miscellaneous activities. Time budgets varied from one subject-matter division to another. The total working day appeared to average around 8.5 hours.

Generalizations about the academic working day tend to ignore what are undoubtedly greater variations than will be encountered among many other kinds of employees; moreover, like every other community, the university community harbors some drones alongside the workers. For the capable but lazy professor in an institution where little attention is paid to research productivity and other nonclassroom functions, the academic profession may be a sinecure. For the diligent and ambitious, however, employment in the higher learning can be one of the most strenuous of all intellectualized occupations. What many persons outside academe fail to realize is that the hours academics spend in their classrooms, laboratories, or offices give an incomplete idea of their total working-time budgets.

In 1942, I observed a marked contrast between such an institution as the University of Chicago, where upwards of 70 percent of the faculty were engaged in research and publication, and many other institutions, where only 32 percent of the academics had made any contribution to the literature of their fields in a five-year period. My comment then was that the hierarchic pyramid of typical colleges and universities would have shown few academics at the top if their rank and status had depended on their published contributions to scholarship and science. Although the "publish or perish" phrase was bandied about in those days, too, it obviously had no more, and probably less, application as a local criterion in most colleges and universities than it does now. Furthermore, persons outside academe who blame the so-called neglect of teaching upon an exaggerated institutional attention to research output should be aware that even though most universities have policies prescribing teaching loads (though these are rarely uniform for all of the teaching staff), they normally leave it to the individual academic to set his or her own time budget for research.

Bayer's 1972–73 survey shows that about three-fourths of all the academics employed in universities have teaching as their principal activity, with 95.6 percent of them currently engaged in teaching.[13] Almost a third of them report spending no time in administration, and of the largest proportion of those teachers so engaged in a limited way, 43.5 percent gave no more than eight hours a week to such duties. As to their time budgets for teaching and research, Table 6.3 is revealing (pp. 23–24).

About 20 percent of the university teachers report having one class, and 32 percent have two classes. During the current teaching term, the majority (almost 70 percent) have no more than two *different* courses, and about half have no introductory courses for undergraduates. Of those having introductory courses, 68.9 percent have no more than 25 students in them; 91.4 percent of those with advanced undergraduates have 25 or fewer students enrolled in such courses; 86.8 percent of those with graduate-level courses in their teaching assignments deal with 25 or fewer students on that level. Bayer's data give no figures for total numbers of students dealt with by individual faculty members, but his findings make it obvious that not many university teachers have cause for complaint about excessive teaching loads.

Even so, 37 percent of them (32.6 of the men and 60.0 of the women) either did not respond to the item or else had no published writings to report for the previous two years; percentages for the other categories were: 27.3, one to two publications; 18.3, three to four; and 17.2, five or more. Thirty-nine percent reported no involvement in research, scholarly writing, or creative work which received some support during the prior twelve months. Such evidence suggests, accordingly, that academics whose research involvements interfere with their teaching commitments must be only a small minority.

Table 6.3   Reported Faculty Hours per Week in Teaching Activities and in Research and Scholarly Writing

NUMBER OF HOURS PER WEEK	PERCENTAGES REPORTING HOURS INDICATED
Scheduled Teaching	
None, or no answer	7.2
One to four	17.8
Five to eight	32.6
Nine to twelve	25.2
Thirteen to sixteen	8.8
Seventeen or more	8.4
Preparation for Teaching	
None, or no answer	8.4
One to four	14.6
Five to eight	23.2
Nine to twelve	22.0
Thirteen to sixteen	13.6
Seventeen or more	18.2
Student Advising and Counseling	
None, or no answer	11.8
One to four	42.9
Five to eight	28.1
Nine to twelve	11.8
Thirteen to sixteen	3.4
Seventeen or more	2.0
Research and Scholarly Writing	
None, or no answer	23.2
One to four	19.7
Five to eight	14.0
Nine to twelve	13.0
Thirteen to sixteen	9.2
Seventeen or more	21.0

Incidentally, Bayer's separation of percentages for men and women shows that lower proportions of women engage in administration; higher percentages of women than of men spend nine or more hours in scheduled teaching, in preparation, and in advising and counseling. However, women give markedly less time than men to research and scholarly writing.

Not only do most university professors have lighter teaching loads now than in earlier decades, when nine to as many as fifteen hours were not uncommon for academics in a considerable number of senior-level institutions, but also more of them are now secure in their jobs, as evidenced by the fact that more than half of them are in the two top ranks. Also, secretarial, clerical, and research assistance is more likely to be provided. There is now less sharing of offices with other professors; more latitude in scheduling to permit uninterrupted time for research, consulting, advising, and so on; and more funding institutionally for professional travel and from various granting agencies for research and special projects (even though federal funding began to decline after 1971).

Scholarly Productivity and Its Attributes

Consistent with the low level of research productivity on the part of many members of university faculties, Bayer found that only about a third of them would want lighter teaching loads in order to devote more time to research, and that only one academic in five maintains that institutional demands for doing research interfere with teaching effectiveness. Moreover, almost seven out of ten faculty members believe that teaching effectiveness, not publications, should be the primary basis for faculty promotions. In light of these circumstances, it is evident why productivity in scholarship and science is in some respects an elitist enterprise, both institutionally and individually, as will be detailed in the last chapters of this book.

Since the most esteemed recognition and rewards go to creative scholars and scientists rather than to academics who are proclaimed to be devoted and effective classroom teachers, however, it may be surprising that more academics everywhere do not busy themselves with research and writing for publication. As Lazarsfeld and Thielens observed in their 1958 book,[14] there are these payoffs: 1) the likelihood that professors will be named to prestigious off-campus positions increases with their volume of publication; 2) the freedom of geographic and interinstitutional mobility is greater among the more "productive" academics; 3) the higher the quality rating of an institution, the higher the proportion of productive social scientists (and, as will be seen later, of other productive scientists and scholars) on its faculty.

It is of interest to note here Halsey and Trow's findings about British academics during the 1960s (Chapters 12 and 13). Roughly a third of the Britishers said they were primarily interested in teaching, but of the remaining two-thirds, only 10 percent described themselves as being interested in research to the point of being almost willing to exclude any teaching. Only 4 percent agreed that research is the first duty of university faculties. The number of published articles in a large sample of them was (by percentages): none, 7; one to four, 22; five to ten, 23; and ten to twenty, 27. Most had published no books, but half of them said they were "preparing a book for publication." Oxford and Cambridge included more productive researchers on their faculties than did the Redbrick institutions; over three-fifths of the academics at Oxford, Cambridge, and London had published ten or more articles, as compared with about one in ten of those at the former colleges of advanced technology (CATs), and slightly more than a third of those elsewhere. These observations point to some similarities between Great Britain and this country.

With regard to the whole matter of productivity and individual appraisal and advancement, however, there are some marked contrasts. Except for some complicated differentials at Oxford and Cambridge, compensation scales are state regulated and relatively uniform throughout the British university system. Moreover, in the British universities not more than about 10 percent of the academics were professors (occupants of "chairs"), whereas in the United States in 1968 about 27.2 percent of university academics occupied the highest-level post.

Qualitative Evaluation

It is by now evident that academics are appraised both inside and outside the institutions where they are employed. Although widely renowned scholars and scientists tend to have high faculty standing wherever they may be, the local repute of an academic as a teacher or valued member of the community may hardly extend beyond the confines of the campus. One reason for this is that the classroom teacher is heard only by those he addresses directly, most of whom are postadolescents; his influence on them tends to become so dispersed in time and space that objective assessment is difficult. True, if he is a professor of mathematics in the graduate school he may get credit from his peers elsewhere for helping to train an unusually large number of mathematicians who later become distinguished in a particular field; or the renown of a professor of torts who has never published very much may become fairly well known in the legal profession. In general, however, professorial accomplishment in pedagogy lacks universal currency. (More will be said about the relative prestige of teaching and research achievements in later chapters.)

This is not to say that the importance of teaching is deliberately played down as a matter of policy in most universities. Faculty work load, as we have observed, is still calculated largely in terms of hours of formal instruction. Student-credit hours constitute the basic unit for arriving at teaching costs and for allocating the major part of financial resources. Since faculty members who teach fewer students, at least in the arts and sciences, usually are paid higher salaries than their lower-level colleagues who teach more students, the reward scheme for teaching duties alone is obviously somewhat complicated.

Some campuses are making use of the notable advances by educational researchers in recent years in our knowledge about the criteria of effective teaching, the loci of evaluation, and the modes of utilizing reliable procedures. In other places—and among some academics everywhere—there is an

understandable resistance to attempts to quantify faculty pedagogical proficiency. Because most faculty persons do more
teaching than research and prefer this division of their own
professional labor, it is unfortunate that better means of recognizing and rewarding superior teaching are not more widely
utilized.

Even if the best-known means of identifying effective
teaching were used universally, however, the standards of judgment would still differ from one campus to another, and it is
doubtful that any consensus could be reached about common
units of measurement. The assessment of performance in scholarship and science is a somewhat different matter, for in these
lines of endeavor appraisal standards are very much the same,
not only throughout the nation but also throughout the world.
In its upper reaches, the competition for excellence knows no
geographic bounds (as is illustrated in Nobel science awards).

Although the "publish or perish" dictum is obviously a
myth in many institutions, it is certainly valid for all academics
who wish wider recognition. The aspiring academic may draw
his paycheck locally, but the most valued kudos of recognition
and reward are often conferred elsewhere as a consequence of
the judgments made by members of the larger community of
scholars or scientists who are "referees" and "gatekeepers" of
merit symbols. The most widely publicized estimates of scholarly and scientific worth—special fellowships, distinguished
lectureships, major awards, listings in citation indexes, honorary degrees, editorial appointments, board and panel memberships, memberships in the National Academy of Sciences, and
so on—are all symbols of visibility and esteem. The recipients
of such awards are not always prolific publishers (though they
tend to have high ratings in citation indexes) or the "brightest"
in their fields, but by and large they are clearly superior in
intelligence, motivation, and stamina (as Merton, Zuckerman,
and others have noted).

Thus, the more productive the individual academic, the
less his or her total status as a professional will depend on

local appraisals. Although recipients of the highest-level awards are more numerous on the faculties of the leading universities, they are sufficiently rare to be exceptions in any department, and in lesser universities and departments they are likely to be regarded as real adornments, widely publicized to the "greater glory" of the institution. Moreover, the spread of the university syndrome in recent years has caused emergent and developing institutions to get caught up in a nation-wide competition for "big name" scholars and scientists— sometimes when they are known to be well past their prime and are recruited in the largely mistaken notion that their past accomplishments at one institution will somehow add luster to the next one.

Institutional appraisal of professional endeavor cannot be entirely clear-cut and impersonal, and reputation is not reducible to precise categories. The unfortunate aspect of the whole situation is that objective orientation for the individual is rendered difficult by tangential and often conflicting demands; teaching, research, and other work are judged by a number of standards, one set often being at variance with another. And the hierarchy of prestige in academic fields, as in all others, is never identical with merit. Judgments of merit, in turn, as well as the capacity to assess it, differ according to the level and segment of the hierarchy rendering the verdict. The competitive system and whatever scale of values academics may choose or have forced upon them determine their ideology of success. Pressures vary from department to department and institution to institution, so that functionaries work toward the kind of attainable results that bring approval from those whose verdict is worth most.

Everywhere there are to be found a few rare individuals so absorbed in performance for its own sake as to be relatively indifferent to the symbols that may be attached to achievement. Even the most perfunctory performers experience occasional moments of real zest, for much institutionalized activity proceeds in the form of voluntary projects to be carried forward rather than as assigned tasks to be finished. Yet a competitive system necessitates expedience in the allocation of time and energy and causes the functionary to concentrate on teaching if this brings the greatest rewards, or on research if the local stress lies in this direction. In lesser colleges and universities most staff members are relatively nonproductive of published work, and hence an individual's publishing record cannot be made a generalized criterion for the evaluation of staff services in respect to employee status. On the other hand, the staff members of a major university are placed in a situation where the innovative function is precedent to the disseminative function, and, because of the universality of science and productive scholarship, they are judged according to competitive standards that come from outside as well as inside the institution.

In these central institutions the wish for recognition is tacitly backed by administrative imperatives, so that the intensity of competition and the large number of competitors multiply enormously the real and alleged contributions to the advancement of learning. That a strong emphasis on scholarly productivity results in tremendous positive values from leading universities is generally known. That it interferes with the performance of other functions, and in marginal cases produces flamboyancy, exhibitionism, quantitativeness without regard for quality, and results indirectly inimical to knowledge itself is not so generally acknowledged. When the evaluative system prevailing in leading universities is indiscriminately used in lesser colleges and universities it can only multiply such consequences. Indeed, it is no exaggeration to say that a critical problem confronted in the social organization of any university is the proper evaluation of faculty services and the giving of due recognition through the impartial assignment of status. Not to mention its utility in removing unnecessary sources of anomie and frustration in many organization personalities, a more adequate and rational basis for the differential appraisal of faculty services would unquestionably afford a less wasteful division of labor.

7

Professional Status

Although the faculty members of a university are likely to display greater ideational diversity than members of the surrounding community, all academics do have some common characteristics. They share, for example, familiar status designations in the professorial hierarchies of their particular institutions and are readily identifiable as specialists in the various disciplines they pursue. Most importantly for our purposes here, they are all professionals.

What is the meaning of professional status? In what ways is the academic profession like and unlike similar vocations in society's division of labor? Codes of ethics are regarded as being essential denominators of professional behavior. How are they formulated and applied in academe? Every profession has some kind of overarching organization. Beyond the confines of their own campuses, in what kinds of organizations are academics most involved? How do these organizations reinforce and advance the collective status of their members? Under what circumstances do professorial and professional roles entail conflict? What major changes, if any, have taken place during recent decades? What are the functional relations of these various matters to academic freedom and professional solidarity?

The Meaning of Professional Status

The professions, it should be noted, differ significantly from other occupations. Their distinctive aspects are in the main as follows:

1. They entail prolonged and specialized training based upon a systematic intellectual tradition and body of knowledge, rarely acquired through mere apprenticeship.

2. There are commonly rigorous standards of licensure (but not, as was observed earlier, for all types of professorial positions). Fulfillment of these requirements may confer upon the functionary a degree (e.g., M.D.) or title (e.g., C.P.A.) signifying specialized compentence.

3. Professional work often involves the application of techniques so complex that competency cannot be tested on a simple continuum scale. The tasks to be performed do not lend themselves to close supervision.

4. Unlike unionized wage earners in industry or entrepreneurs in business enterprise, professionals are not expected to engage in a calculated limitation of output and an exploitative attitude toward productivity.

5. Ethical codes limit the self-interest of the practitioner, and insulate certain professional considerations from such extraneous matters as private opinions, economic interests, and class position.

6. Membership in a profession entails obligation to the profession and its clientele.

Some other generalizations are pertinent. The professions are more autonomous than most other occupations in setting and upholding their own standards. Control by outside groups is resisted, and legal restrictions tend to be less conspicuous than other types of controls. Any given profession tends to be monopolistic; only physicians can practice medicine, and only members of the bar can practice law. Members of professional groups are strongly identified with their professions, typically prefer them to other occupations, and normally pursue their entire careers within them.

From these desiderata, it is obvious that the professions involve not only more responsibilities but also more privileges than do most other occupations. Some professions are both highly prestigious and quite lucrative for many of their practitioners. It is no wonder than in an era of rising expectations many occupations should want to emulate them. Insurance agents, realtors, auditors, public relations specialists, financial analysts, morticians, and numerous others strive to enhance their status by acquiring at least an "air of professionalism" through the formation of national societies and associations, the establishment of training programs, and the installation of certification requirements.

Not many years ago, universities had no schools of nursing, social work, or library science; today many do. Indeed, there are in some institutions what are called schools of mortuary science. Since universities are the seedbeds of the traditional professions, the rise of these new fields is suggestive of increased university involvement in such new movements.

Egalitarian thrusts have also been felt in the long-established professional fields. Because of the inherently exclusionary nature of high entrance standards, prolonged and often arduous curricular requirements, and strict standards of licensure, some of the professions and the schools maintained for them are being increasingly subjected to political and other pressures to "broaden" their modes of access. Examinations for licensure are likewise under attack for their "unfairness" when disproportionately large numbers from disadvantaged groups fail to pass them.

Manifestly, then, the university is caught in some crosscurrents. On the one hand, the labor force is becoming increasingly professionalized, with marginal groups attempting to become full-fledged professions, and still others seeking at least some of the trappings; this trend implies more restricted entry requirements. On the other hand, some of the established professions are experiencing outside pressures to relax such restrictions. Whether the rise of some occupations will be attended by a decline of prestige for others, with the net result a kind of zero-sum game, is still uncertain.

Academics as Professionals

Historically, the professional ethos for academics has deep roots both here and abroad. In their treatise *The British Academics,* Halsey and Trow make this comment:

> There was support for, even idealisation of, the professional man among dons, but the word "professional" had ethical and status as well as occupational connotations. The professional man, it was argued by those who distrusted and feared the ethical implications of the acquisitive aspects of industrialism, thought more of duty than of profit. The gratitude of his client rather than the market defined his reward, and technically he was not paid but granted an honorarium. He earned his reputation by discretion, tact and expert knowledge rather than by advertising and financial success. He was a learned man, and his education was broad and comprehensive. Unlike the businessman, who operated within an impersonal market situation, the professional man was involved with his clients at a personal, intimate level. Ideally he did not have to compete with others of the same profession, at least not to the same extent as the businessman. The professional society, with its principles of restricted entry, embodied in the professional examination and the *numerus clausus,* insulated him from the severer pressures of supply and demand. There was, therefore, a certain self-restraint in his manner, a gentlemanly quality which distinguished him from the brash and aggressive industrialists of the Midlands and the North. [pp. 48–49]

Although the contemporary American academic may not invariably possess a "gentlemanly quality" to the extent cherished by the British dons of bygone times, most university faculties in this country still have extensive privileges. By and large, theirs is the main say in the selection, retention or termination, and promotion of colleagues; few employees in other organizations have such powers. Faculties determine essentially what will be taught, how students will be evaluated, and the kinds of roles they will perform individually in their largely unsupervised teaching and research. Academics rather than nonacademics make most of the decisions about appropriate work loads.[1] Their professional productivity as scholars and scientists is judged largely by fellow specialists, and many of the judgments are rendered in distant places. Thus, the extramural repute of academics is in many respects more important than their intramural standing as a factor in professional prestige. The prestige of demographers, for example, is determined by the appraisals of other demographers, and not by their students, their colleagues in other disciplines, and certainly not the the local administration, the board of trustees, or the general public.

None of this is to say, of course, that academics as professionals are free from other controls. Employing universities are likely to be fairly large and complex organizations with unavoidably bureaucratic aspects. Most of them have faculty handbooks setting forth certain policies and practices which employees can disregard only at their own peril. Unlike physicians in clinics or attorneys in law firms, academics are subject to a good deal of administrative jurisdiction stemming from both inside and outside sources. Some of the decisions affecting their behavior and determining their rewards are made by persons not in their professional spheres. In brief, the endeavors of academics as university employees and as professionals are not invariably in the same context, and outcomes are frequently weighed on different scales.

Whether occupational controls in academe will move closer to or farther away from the jurisdiction of professional specialists, and whether "locals" who find approval mostly within their institutions will gain ascendancy over "cosmopolitans" who primarily desire widespread peer approval remains to be seen. Meanwhile, as we shall note shortly, some of the cleavages in academe are becoming more pronounced as increasing numbers of academics opt for trade union rather than professional association models. A strength of the professional ethos in academe, however, is suggested by the fact that thus far few major university faculties have chosen to trade off their traditional heritage for presumed monetary gain.

Professional Ethics

The vocational ideology of the academic world supports the tradition of collegiality, with corporate decisions in collaborative enterprise, and the evaluation of individuals largely in terms of their technical competence and accomplishment. University autonomy, in turn, presupposes self-imposed as well as professionally enforced duties and obligations. Though not isolated, academics are insulated against outside interference—the assumption being that they will do their work disinterestedly or objectively, not to mention conscientiously. As has been known since the time of Francis Bacon, however, objectivity in scholarly enterprise is not simply a matter of writing in the third person singular. Higher education is ideally organized to minimize bias, careerism, and other factors injurious to the dedication and disinterestedness necessary for best professional performance, but the academic ethic results from a combination of certain positive factors and a negation of others. Thus, the scholar-scientist is not a person with no values, but one with disciplined values.[2]

In 1942, I stated and would now repeat that ethical codes are to some extent unenforceable in a legal sense, and that their sanctions are usually nonlegal. Laws in the main apply to territorial groups, whereas professional codes apply to functional groupings. Sanctions exist positively in the desire for approval and negatively in the sense of shame; taboos, publicity, education, and the effects of clarifying and interpreting individual cases all serve as sanctions of a sort.

Although moral aspects of professional behavior are regulated more by ethics than by law, professors, doctors, and lawyers are in no sense beyond economics and the ultimate value system of the community. Standards of licensure and ethical codes are not merely arbitrary in-group formulations: they must have a general social acceptance. Group opportunism, esoteric cultism, or monkish idealism in small, independent associations may be tolerated by society, but it is hardly conceivable that these tendencies would be allowed to develop unrestrained in any major profession.

The professor's independence is limited by his institutional connection, and especially so if he cannot distinguish between freedom and license, yet there are in most universities few positive hindrances upon his intellectual initiative. There is no universal acceptance in the academic profession of any explicit statement analogous to the Hippocratic oath, and for some members there is merely a vague understanding of norms and conduct. Be they explicit or implicit, however, institutional codes help to define situations for individual members; they set up rules that insist upon something more than "a merely economic logic of production." The fact that many verbalized codes are nothing more than ideologies in no way negates the importance of having them. For a group to maintain itself, special conditions of success must be formulated, error penalized, and deliberate deviation punished.

Despite the absence of any explicit code of ethics that all American academics are expected to live by, there have been some widely distributed statements issued by important educational associations. In 1953, the Association of American Universities (AAU) adopted a statement called "The Rights and Responsibilities of Universities and Their Faculties"; the Association reprinted the statement and again circulated it in 1962. The section pertaining to faculty obligations and responsibilities pointed out that in terms of the law, the university scholar has no more and no less freedom than other citizens.

Like judges, however, university professors have tenure to protect them "against undue economic or political pressures and [to ensure] the continuity of the scholarly process." The statement goes on to note, "There is a line at which 'freedom' or 'privilege' begins to be qualified by legal 'duty' and 'obligation.' The determination of the line is the function of the legislature and the courts." As an institution, the university is a guarantor of standards, but it does not necessarily endorse its members' views. Since the reputation of the university depends upon the capability and integrity of its members, all of them have an obligation to maintain this reputation.

The AAU statement then gets into these specificities:

> As in all acts of association, the professor accepts conventions which become morally binding. Above all, he owes his colleagues in the university complete candor and perfect integrity, precluding any kind of clandestine or conspiratorial activities. He owes equal candor to the public. If he is called upon to answer for his convictions it is his duty as a citizen to speak out. It is even more definitely his duty as a professor. Refusal to do so, on whatever legal grounds, cannot fail to reflect upon a profession that claims for itself the fullest freedom to speak and the maximum protection of that freedom available in our society. In this respect, invocation of the Fifth Amendment places upon a professor a heavy burden of proof of his fitness to hold a teaching position and lays upon his university an obligation to reexamine his qualification for membership in its society.
>
> In all universities faculties exercise wide authority in internal affairs. The greater their autonomy, the greater their share of responsibility to the public. They must maintain the highest standards and exercise the utmost wisdom in appointments and promotions. They must accept their share of responsibility for the discipline of those who fall short in the discharge of their academic trust.
>
> The universities owe their existence to legislative acts and

public charters. A state university exists by constitutional and legislative acts, an endowed university enjoys its independence by franchise from the state and by custom. The state university is supported by public funds. The privately sustained university is benefited by tax exemptions. Such benefits are conferred upon universities not as favors but in furtherance of the public interest. They carry with them public obligation of direct concern to the faculties of the universities as well as to the governing boards.

Legislative bodies from time to time may scrutinize these benefits and privileges. It is clearly the duty of universities and their members to cooperate in official inquiries directed to those ends. When the powers of legislative inquiry are abused, the remedy does not lie in noncooperation or defiance; it is to be sought through the normal channels of informed public opinion.

The AAU stand stresses that unless a faculty member violates a law, his discipline or discharge is a university responsibility and not one to be assumed by political authority. Moreover, the association deprecates special loyalty tests for faculties and other forms of discrimination to which other citizens are not subjected, and asserts that political insistence upon the conformity of academics to current beliefs and practices would do infinite harm to the principle of freedom as a central American doctrine.

Since its founding in 1915, the American Association of University Professors has issued a number of statements recommending standards of policy and practice for the academic community. The majority of these policy papers and special reports have to do with two topics: academic freedom, tenure, and due process; and institutional governance. More than fifty years after its founding, the Association adopted and distributed a "Statement on Professional Ethics," which read as follows:

I. The professor, guided by a deep conviction of the worth and dignity of the advancement of knowledge, recognizes the special responsibilities placed upon him. His primary responsibility to his subject is to seek and to state the truth as he sees it. To this end he devotes his energies to developing and improving his scholarly competence. He accepts the obligation to exercise critical self-discipline and judgment in using, extending, and transmitting knowledge. He practices intellectual honesty. Although he may follow subsidiary interests, these interests must never seriously hamper or compromise his freedom of inquiry.

II. As a teacher, the professor encourages the free pursuit of learning in his students. He holds before them the best scholarly standards of his discipline. He demonstrates respect for the student as an individual, and adheres to his proper role as intellectual guide and counselor. He makes every reasonable effort to foster honest academic conduct and to assure that his evaluation of students reflects their true merit. He respects the confidential nature of the relationship between professor and student. He avoids any exploitation of students for his private advantage and acknowledges significant assistance from them. He protects their academic freedom.

III. As a colleague, the professor has obligations that derive from common membership in the community of scholars. He respects and defends the free inquiry of his associates. In the exchange of criticism and ideas he shows due respect for the opinions of others. He acknowledges his academic debts and strives to be objective in his professional judgment of colleagues. He accepts his share of faculty responsibilities for the governance of his institution.

IV. As a member of his institution, the professor seeks above all to be an effective teacher and scholar. Although he observes the stated regulations of the institution, provided they do not contravene academic freedom, he maintains his right to criticize and seek revision. He determines the amount and character of the work he does outside his institution with due regard to his paramount responsibilities within it. When considering the interruption or termination of his service, he recognizes the effect of his decision upon the program of the institution and gives notice of his intentions.

V. As a member of his community, the professor has the rights and obligations of any citizen. He measures the urgency of these obligations in the light of his responsibilities to his subject, to his students, to his profession, and to his institution. When he speaks or acts as a private person he avoids creating the impression that he speaks or acts for his college or university. As a citizen engaged in a profession that depends upon freedom for its health and integrity, the professor has a particular obligation to promote conditions of free inquiry and to further public understanding of academic freedom.[3]

In addition to this very generalized pronouncement, the AAUP has from time to time formulated statements with strong overtones of ethics for the guidance of individuals and institutions with regard to such matters as extramural utterances, professors and political activity, academic freedom and tenure in the quest for national security, representation of economic and professional interests, participation in strikes, recruitment and resignation of faculty members, late resignation of individual academics, conflicts of interest, and leaves of absence.

The range of topical coverage in the AAU and the AAUP statements, incidentally, is suggestive of the more common trouble spots giving rise to ethical issues in academe. Even so, several years ago the *Chronicle of Higher Education* carried an article by a University of California teacher under the title: "Needed: A Code of Ethics for Teachers."[4] The author was critical of an academic reluctance to examine the central ethical defects of the profession. In particular, he felt that questions of morality are imbedded in such familiar occurrences as these: slovenly preparation for undergraduate classroom teaching; frequent professorial absences from classes and offices; carelessness in student advising and evaluation; dubious practices in shared research recognitions; discrimination against women; and sexual misconduct with students.[5] Asserting that a "major dimension of education involves the teacher as a role model," the commentator concluded that a formal ethical code dealing explicitly with what is expected of a professor and what procedures should be used to deal with misconduct ought to be widely adopted and made contractually binding to enable the academic profession to exert more fully the ethical as well as intellectual leadership society expects.[6]

John D. Millett has written that ethical issues are essentially moral issues, and that in academic circles it has become unfashionable to discuss moral questions. He finds that there is nowhere a definitive statement of the standards to be observed and enforced in the academic profession, and he notes that the statements at hand frequently set forth "an excess of virtue" when what is needed is a reassertion of a mean between the vice of excess and the vice of defect.[7]

Despite some criticisms inside academe about gaps between professed piety and actual practice, however, a Gallup poll survey conducted in 1976 showed that the public has a higher esteem for the ethical standards of medical doctors, engineers, and academics (in that order) than for any of the other occupational categories under review. In light of disclosures in recent years, respondents gave lower than average ratings to business executives, members of Congress, labor union leaders, and advertising executives.

Professional Associations and Learned Societies

Paradoxically, the whole of American education is underorganized in some respects and overorganized in others. Unlike many other nations, the United States has no ministry of education exercising overall control and no nationally formalized "system" on any level. On the primary and secondary levels, for example, it has been estimated that there are at least 48,000 basic administrative units, and that each of our 3,000 or so colleges and universities has at least some degree of institutional autonomy. However this may be, American higher education does have a complex scheme of centralized organization as manifested in the large number and almost bewildering variety of groupings.

There are those consisting of individual members drawn from a wide range of scholarly, scientific, and professional fields, such as the American Astronomical Society, the American Chemical Society, the American Economic Association, and the Modern Language Association of America. Their members congregate periodically by localities, states, regions, and on a nationwide basis. More encompassing alignments of allied disciplines are to be noted in the National Research Council, the American Council of Learned Societies, the Social Science Research Council, and the American Association for the Advancement of Science. The first three of these, along with the American Council on Education, have formed a kind of "holding company" known as the Conference Board of Associated Research Councils. In addition, there are the more inclusive associations of educators, such as the American Association of University Professors, the American Federation of Teachers, and the National Education Association of the United States, which all engage in collective bargaining and have purposes comparable to those of union workers in business and industry.

Administrative and staff employees—presidents, deans, directors, athletic coaches, purchasing agents, and others—also have their voluntary associations. To complete the picture, there is a national association of governing boards. It is not surprising, therefore, that some academics spend a lot of time away from the campus in workshops, seminars, conferences, meetings, and other extramural activities.[8] Such participation is mostly unpaid and intermittent, but it does strengthen voluntary, collective enterprise and helps promote coherence and unity in the structuring of higher learning.

These groupings, for the most part, are associations of

individuals, but there are other organizations where participation is largely representational of the various segments or divisions of a college or university, e.g., the Association of American Medical Colleges and the National University Extension Association. Even more inclusive are the groupings of entire institutions—e.g., the American Association of State Universities and Land-Grant Colleges, the Association of American Universities, and the Association of American Colleges. Most inclusive in its membership is the American Council on Education, which encompasses all types of institutions of higher education, together with nearly two hundred educational and professional associations.

Although academics have no overarching organization comparable to the American Medical Association or the American Bar Association to which even a majority of them belong, the average professor in a university is a member of the national organization of professionals in his or her particular field. The associations themselves range in size from a few hundred members to many thousands. For most of the well-established fields there is just one major association (e.g., the American Historical Association), but there also may be specialized associations for subfields (e.g., the American Indian Historical Society).

All of the large associations have headquarters with a paid secretariat, hold annual meetings, and elect their officers annually. Their financial support derives mainly from membership dues. Many of them publish one or more journals, issue newsletters, and circulate special committee reports. By and large, their publications contain the writings of specialists in the discipline and are addressed to them.

Aside from the importance of these professional associations and learned societies for the advancement of knowledge in their respective fields, they are also useful to individual academics for advancing themselves. By reading papers, serving on important committees or commissions, getting elected to offices, having articles published in their journals, having their books reviewed and brought to the attention of specialists elsewhere, and by various other modes of participation, individual academics gain recognition as professionals.

The key figures in such organizations have traditionally been leading scholars or scientists in their disciplines and have been regarded as "the establishment." For many years, younger academics often felt that their elders tended to form a kind of gerontocracy, with too much emphasis on conventional values and perspectives, but it was not until the late 1960s that open confrontations began to occur in annual meetings. *Science* magazine, one of the most widely read periodicals among academics, in its issue of May 19, 1972, carried an article entitled "Professional Societies: Identity Crisis Threatens on Bread and Butter Issues." It said:

> Perhaps there was a time when scientific and engineering societies dealt solely with traditional professional and technical issues. But even if this ever was true, it no longer is. Protest against the Vietnam war, charges of discrimination against minority groups, and even a bit of tomato throwing at annual meetings have been known to ruffle the solemnity of their deliberations.
>
> Possibly the most far-reaching challenge to U.S. professional societies in recent years, however, has been the demand that they act in some decisive fashion to alleviate rising unemployment and underemployment among the membership.

Interviewing spokesmen for various professional and scientific groups, *Science* encountered disunity of response, even from such organizations as the American Chemical Society and the American Physical Society, both of which have traditionally been led by academics. There was reluctance, for example, to be drawn into employee welfare considerations as contrasted with technical questions, and to becoming involved in lobbying.

American Learned Societies in Transition by Harland G. Bloland and Sue M. Bloland[9] makes similar observations. It notes the impact of dissent and recession on such organizations, with radical students' and faculty members' attempts to take over annual meetings during the 1960s, and efforts beginning in 1970 to shift from ideological concerns to the "job crisis." The authors state:

> Given the possibility that under present employment conditions only those faculty members at the top of the academic hierarchy will sustain a primary identification with national disciplinary organizations, while the majority of academics have increasing incentive to identify more actively in the local units of collective bargaining agencies, it seems reasonable to predict that the size and character of learned-society members will undergo major change in the next decade. [p. 111].

With these considerations in view, let us next examine the roles being played by such organizations as The American Association of University Professors, the American Federation of Teachers, and the National Education Association of the United States. In a sense, all are unions, for they all engage in collective bargaining. What are their purposes and accomplishments?

Status Protection Associations

Since its formation in 1915, the American Association of University Professors has been the most important single organization concerned with the general welfare of the academic profession. It began with 867 charter members, and steadily increased its roster to 97,102 by 1972, and thereafter underwent some decline in membership. Its general functions have been to establish and articulate criteria and sanctions governing the mutual relations of members, to influence the relations between academics and institutions, and to develop a more favorable public attitude toward the academic profession. An early and continuing concern of the association has been the

upholding of academic freedom. It has given consistent attention to such matters as faculty job rights and tenure, due process in the appraisal of faculty services, improvement of compensation, and enhancement of academic roles in institutional
governance.[10]

Contrary to the impression given in some recent writings about "unprecedented" faculty militancy and the rise of
sentiments favoring collective bargaining, similar issues were
being debated at the time the AAUP was founded. James M.
Cattell, a prominent psychologist at that time, was urging a
militant type of organization. In his famous book *The Higher
Learning*,[11] Thorstein Veblen deplored the lack of a strong
bargaining position for the academic profession and scoffed at
the prevailing notion that the professor should meekly accept
"an expensive increment of dignity attaching to a higher rank
than his salary would indicate."

Twenty years later, there was still no consensus about
what kind of organization was best suited to academic ends.
Professor Arthur O. Lovejoy, a well-known philosopher and a
leader in AAUP affairs, authored an article entitled "Professional Association or Trade Union?"[12] He showed that in
some respects the AAUP was analogous to a trade union because of legal similarities between the economic status of
teachers and industrial workers. Unlike many independent
professionals, academics' livelihoods depend upon the decisions of those who control the funds. He went on to observe,
however, that most trade unions are not interested in increased, better, or cheaper production, or in enhancing service
aspects of their work for the larger society. In a university the
situation is different; trustees do not enhance their own pecuniary status by keeping salaries down, and the funds they dis-
pense are not their property, but tax-free funds intended for
public use. Lovejoy's conclusion was that there is a congruence
of employer-employee relations in academe and that unionism
would seriously split the ranks of the academic profession.

Until 1972, this was the general position of the AAUP,

when the outgoing president, Sanford Kadish, expressed opposition to unionization, collective bargaining, and strikes as representing a subordination of service ideals and the purposes of the university to selfish personal interests. He felt that unionization would split the university into worker-professors on the one hand and manager-administrators and governing boards on the other. His contention was that collective bargaining

> imperils the premise of shared authority, encourages the polarization in interests and exaggerates the adversary concerns over interests held in common. . . . Moreover, the process itself as it functions tends to remit issues which faculty should themselves determine to outside agencies, such as state and federal boards, arbiters, and union bureaucracies. In addition, since unions rest on continued support of their constituency, the process becomes susceptible to essentially political rather than essentially academic decision-making.[13]

Ironically, however, a fall meeting of the AAUP's Council in 1971 had already voted to adopt the following position: "The AAUP will pursue collective bargaining, as a major additional way of realizing the Association's goals in higher education, and will allocate such resources and staff as are necessary for a vigorous selective development of this activity beyond present levels." By a vote of 373 to 54[14] at its annual meeting in May, 1972, the Association officially adopted the recommended position. Despite the assertions made by some persons in 1973 to the effect that internal opposition to the new policy had vanished, a lack of unanimity in views was reflected in the fact that more than a tenth of its members had withdrawn from the organization during the previous year.

The National Education Association, founded in 1857, is the oldest and largest organization of its kind. Its membership has always been comprised largely of public school teachers, however, and many academics have felt that throughout most of its history the group's concerns with colleges and universities were secondary. The NEA's higher education department was established in 1870, dropped in the 1920s, reestablished in 1943, and eliminated as a separate office in 1977 with the announcement that "all services for college professors would be provided through the same units that serve school teachers." In the past, incidentally, most of the academics belonging to its higher education division were drawn from junior colleges, teachers colleges, and university schools or departments of education.

Like the AAUP, the NEA has undergone a transformation of purposes, with the intent since the early 1960s of developing more political and economic leverage as a bargaining organization. Spurred on by the growing strength of its rival, the American Federation of Teachers, the Association espoused collective bargaining and sanctioned strikes even though it initially called them "collective negotiations" and "work stoppages" or "denial of services." Giving less attention than in the past to broad studies of educational issues and problems, it allocated more resources to lobbying in Washington and in state capitals.

As Ladd and Lipset have pointed out,[15] the NEA in 1973 joined efforts with the American Federation of State, County, and Municipal Employees to form a new organization, the Coalition of American Public Employees, for the purpose of coordinating endeavor in such activities as collective bargaining and political action. Also, it cooperated with the AFT in various situations and was even a party to the merger of locals in some cities. By the spring of 1977, it had more local units with campus bargaining rights than did either of the other two national associations.[16]

Despite the fact that the AFT, an affiliate of the American Federation of Labor, was founded only a year after the AAUP, it was an unfamiliar organization to most academics until the 1960s. In my 1942 book, however, I noted the AFT's existence and quoted this statement from its official publication, *The American Teacher*.[17]

The American Association of University Professors does not perform the functions which the teachers' federation aspires to perform. Although it offers a junior membership to assistants and instructors, it has never made an appeal to this group. The professors' organization for the most part does not focus upon local campus issues. It offers no protection to its members so far as their economic status is concerned. The organization is a strictly professional one and has no outside affiliations. Most important of all, perhaps, the Association has no point of view and holds no opinions regarding economic institutions. As previously stated the teacher's federation has a point of view and does take a side on at least some very fundamental economic issues.

Following union successes in organizing public school teachers for more aggressive collective bargaining, unionism began to spread more rapidly on the higher education level, particularly in some metropolitan areas of the northern and eastern part of the United States. By May 31, 1977, there were bargaining agents on 544 campuses, as it indicated in detail in Table 7.1.

Table 7.1 Faculty Unionization in 1977

| | SUMMARY OF BARGAINING AGENTS | | | | | | |
| | Four-Year Campuses | | | Two-Year Campuses | | | Grand |
	Public	Private	Total	Public	Private	Total	Total
A.A.U.P.	21	24	45	2	2	4	49
A.F.T.	71	17	88	108	6	114	202
N.E.A.	29	12	41	164	2	166	207
A.A.U.P.–A.F.T.	1	0	1	0	0	0	1
A.A.U.P.–N.E.A.	4	0	4	7	0	7	11
Other	18	11	29	44	1	45	74
Total agents	144	64	208	325	11	336	544
Bargaining rejected	22	39	61	10	3	13	74

Source: Chronicle of Higher Education, May 31, 1977, p. 11.

With regard to the spread of unionization among college and university faculties, several observations are apropos. When the previous summation was made, there were twenty-six states that did not allow collective bargaining for public employees. Moreover, press coverage of particular campuses might have led to the erroneous impression that unionization was sweeping through academe like a tidal wave, when the fact of the matter was that only 17.8 percent of the nation's 3,055 institutions were unionized, and with junior colleges excluded from the count, only 10.8 percent. It is also significant that few of the faculties of major universities had chosen collective bargaining, and none of those in the Association of American Universities had made that choice.[18]

Ladd and Lipset have commented on some of the salient differences between academics who are for and those who are against unionization within their own ranks. In general, those favoring unionization are younger, less-productive scholars, lower paid, teachers with heavier instructional loads, employees of less prestigious institutions, and so on. Since unionization tends to minimize the salary differences among those engaged in similar tasks and accords seniority a higher priority than merit in individual status advancement, it stands to reason that academics who feel themselves to be disadvantaged should object less to being treated as interchangeable parts and should be predisposed to opt for more egalitarianism. Ladd and Lipset's data indicate, indeed, that among those academics favoring a bargaining agent, 81 percent do not want salary increases to be based on merit, 81 percent prefer age and seniority as the prime factors for allocating salary increases, and 80 percent oppose using the most demanding national standards for tenure determinations.

As Dael Wolfle has remarked, "If the bargaining brings higher pay, some members of the faculty will consider the exchange a good one, but the stature of the professoriate will have been diminished in the process."[19] In a commentary reprinted by the Carnegie Commission on Higher Education,

Joseph W. Garbarino has questioned the net benefits of the trade-off to members of the academic profession.[20] He has pointed out that on single campuses with fairly homogeneous faculties, where unionism was primarily defensive, salaries merely kept in step with those of other civil servants. A common outcome has been the extension of many faculty privileges to nonacademic employees, with core faculty often gaining less than others. Furthermore, among public institutions within a state there is often a drive for parity of pay among all senior-grade institutions, with a nominal leveling upward turning out in fact to involve also a leveling downward. Insofar as the public sector is concerned, this conclusion was reached:

> The conversion of academic employment policies into a version of the civil service that may otherwise occur will undoubtedly operate to reduce favoritism and arbitrary administrative domination in some institutions and may be a net gain. In those institutions, however, in which the imperfect processes of peer evaluation have worked on balance to reward merit, the introduction of procedures that can be defended before an arbitrator or a judge will incur a cost in quality. The pressures toward egalitarianism from both inside and outside the university are strong and to date academic unionism seems to have worked to reinforce them. Unionism need not mean standardization and bureaucratization of procedures and policies, but it will require intelligent and persistent effort on both sides of the bargaining table to avoid the result. [pp. 16–17]

Whether the unionization of academics will grow, level off, or recede in the years immediately ahead is as yet uncertain. Whatever the outcome, the movement on many campuses has already had effects on the academic's status as an employee, as a professional, and as a longtime partner in collegial governance. In an increasingly egalitarian social order where the long-range public interest is often ignored in the scramble of organized self-interest groups for an ever larger share of the total "pie," it is understandable why many academics may feel they face a Hobson's choice. Many others, nonetheless, do not agree, and are unwilling to barter away what they deem to be their intellectual birthright as professionals for a dubious mess of pottage as trade unionists.[21]

Professional Status and Academic Freedom

Like doctors, lawyers, and engineers, university professors have considerably more autonomy in their jobs than do the members of most other occupational groups. Simply stated, the tasks they perform as professionals are of such a nature that surveillance inhibits efficiency and effectiveness. Academic freedom, accordingly, is not a professorial fetish, but a necessary condition for the advancement of higher learning.[22]

Our purpose here will be to focus on how academic freedom interrelates with the professional status of the average academic. "Average" professors, of course, are probably so accustomed to time-honored privileges that they take them for granted; their professional behavior is such that they seldom put to test the outer limits imposed upon them. As indicated by the AAUP's record of 119 censured administrations in the 47-year period from 1930 to 1977, the total number of apparently serious institutional breaches of academic freedom averages out at slightly more than two and a half a year, which might be viewed as a not particularly disturbing record for an educational universe that now includes more than 3,000 colleges and universities.

This statistical record, however, does not portray the unrelenting struggle of academics and their institutions to countervail those who at various times would censor books, impose loyalty oaths, brand nonconformist political views as un-American, abolish tenure as a sinecure, or disqualify for faculty employment such an internationally distinguished philosopher as Bertrand Russell. The record also does not reveal how the cloak of academic freedom may be used at times by academics whose colleagues privately acknowledge them to be troublemakers of dubious professional competence. Nor does it disclose the inordinate amount of sufferance academe will undergo to avoid the public embarrassment and increasingly involved litigation entailed in the discharge of employees who really deserve short shrift.

As Robert Hutchins remarked a good many years ago, in some respects professors pay for everything that goes on in the university. Academic freedom and tenure are generally considered to be worth the price, but professors pay for poorly made appointments, for the unnecessary multiplication of staff, for keeping on those who should be let go, and for other practices that are wasteful of resources.[23] Although many of the academic freedom and tenure cases of earlier times involved ideological issues, with the most publicized cases sometimes centering on the most celebrated professors, in recent years this has happened less frequently. The most publicized case of late, for example, involved a teacher of philosophy (Angela Davis) who was previously unheard of in the profession. With the trend toward proletarianization in the ranks, the issue in dispute is more often job security or tenure, and the more unconventional the personality concerned the greater the likelihood that academic freedom will be brought into the dispute.

Another recent change is increased concern about _internal_ subversions of academic freedom. In 1970, the AAUP's Council felt called upon to make a statement on freedom and responsibility which asserted:

> ... there is need for the faculty to assume a more positive role as guardian of academic values against unjustified assault from its own members. The traditional faculty function in disciplinary proceedings has been to assure academic due process and meaningful faculty participation in the imposition of discipline by the administration. While this function should be maintained, faculties should recognize their stake

in promoting adherence to norms essential to the academic enterprise.

Three years earlier, at an annual meeting of the American Council on Education, W. Allen Wallis, then president of the University of Rochester, stated in an address that academic freedom on some of the nation's campuses was being "conspicuously eroded" by letting a Stokely Carmichael or Timothy Leary speak without hindrance while in effect circumstances ruled out even an invitation to the Secretary of Defense or the President of the United States. In an article called "Academic Freedom in America," Fred M. Hechinger made much the same kind of comment, noting that in the know-nothing attacks of the 1950s the enemies of academic freedom were easy to identify, and that the enemies during the McCarthy era had virtually no campus allies, but adding, "What makes the current situation different—and probably more dangerous—is that academic freedom . . . is embattled not only by the hostility of the repressive right wing throughout the country, but also by the coercive and occasionally violent radicalism within academia."[24]

Recalling the "intensity and perseverance" with which academics combatted "the first Senator McCarthy and his ilk," the University of Chicago's Distinguished Professor of American Institutions, George J. Stigler, felt impelled to take academics to task for being a party to new forms of thought control. He remarked:

> The students naturally shout down a Jensen or Herrnstein—after all, for a long time no respectable sociologist or psychologist or educationalist would say anything that hinted at differences among races.
>
> If American university faculties had indeed been open to strongly divergent viewpoints, the students would hardly have bothered to harass a visiting lecturer for saying things similar to what they were constantly hearing from their own faculty. But no: they had learned from the pronouncements of their faculties that certain views are beyond the pale.[25]

As further evidence of what he regarded as predominant biases in certain kinds of faculty attitudes, Stigler went on to attach significance to the fact that only 10 percent of the academics in major universities voted for the successful candidate for president in the national election of 1972, and suggested that there is an intramural need "to protect the individual scholar from the pressures of his fellow professors."

In addition to the campus harassments experienced by Berkeley's Professor Jensen and Harvard's Professor Herrnstein, Edward C. Banfield, a well-known urbanologist from the University of Pennsylvania, also was shouted down here and there in his speaking engagements for expressing conservative views. Another central figure in campus altercations of the early 1970s was Stanford's Nobel prizewinning physicist, Dr. William Shockley, whose views as an amateur geneticist were widely and at times violently criticized.[26] Following his unsuccessful effort to give an invitational address at Yale, where interference from the audience prevented his doing so, few faculty members spoke out about the violation of academic freedom, and the *Yale Daily News* even criticized the administration for "sanctioning" the intended talk. Repercussions followed, however, and the Yale Corporation named a committee of five faculty, chaired by Professor C. Vann Woodward, to make a report. In its introductory part, the Woodward Committee's report had this to say:

> The primary function of the university is to discover and disseminate knowledge by means of research and teaching. To fulfill this function a free interchange of ideas is necessary not only within its walls but with the world beyond as well. It follows that the university must do everything possible to ensure within it the fullest degree of intellectual freedom. The history of intellectual growth and discovery clearly demonstrates the need for unfettered freedom, the right to think the unthinkable, discuss the unmentionable, and challenge the unchallengeable. To curtail free expression strikes twice

at intellectual freedom, for whoever deprives another of the right to state unpopular views necessarily deprives others of the right to listen to those views.

We take a chance, as the First Amendment takes a chance, when we commit ourselves to the idea that the results of free expression are to the general benefit in the long run however unpleasant they may appear at the time. The validity of such a belief cannot be demonstrated conclusively. It is a belief of recent historical development, even within universities, one embodied in American constitutional doctrine but not widely shared outside the academic world, and denied in theory and in practice by much of the world most of the time. . . .

Without sacrificing its central purpose, [a university] cannot make its primary and dominant value the fostering of friendship, solidarity, harmony, civility, or mutual respect. To be sure, these are important values; other institutions may properly assign them the highest, and not merely a subordinate priority; and a good university will seek and may in some significant measure attain these ends. But it will never let these values, important as they are, override its central purpose. We value freedom of expression precisely because it provides a forum for the new, the provocative, the disturbing, and the unorthodox. Free speech is a barrier to the tyranny of authoritarian or even majority opinion as to the rightness or wrongness of particular doctrines or thoughts. . . .

Shock, hurt and anger are not consequences to be weighed lightly. No member of the community with a decent respect for others should use, or encourage others to use, slurs and epithets intended to discredit another's race, ethnic group, religion, or sex. . . .

[But] even when some members of the university community fail to meet their social and ethical responsibilities, the paramount obligation of the university is to protect their right to free expression. This obligation can and should be enforced by appropriate formal sanctions. If the university's overriding commitment to free expression is to be sustained, secondary social and ethical responsibilities must be left to the informal processes of suasion, example and argument.

The eloquence of this defense of academic freedom has a ring that reminds one of similar statements made years ago when the barricades were mounted to combat outside on-slaughts. It seems ironic that internal erosions of free thought and expression in one of our leading universities in the 1970s should have made necessary this kind of justification.

That things both change and remain the same in academe, and in some instances have run a full circle between the early 1940s and the late 1970s, was illustrated recently by a longtime defender of academic freedom, Sidney Hook, emeritus professor of philosophy at New York University.[27] Discussing the faculty members in the department of political science at Brooklyn College, CUNY, who felt that one of their colleagues should be dismissed because he had talked to one or more federal officials after returning from a trip to do research abroad, Dr. Hook said that the situation was reminiscent of efforts in 1940 to bar Bertrand Russell from teaching at City College. In that instance, suit was brought by a Brooklyn housewife who believed that his unorthodox views on sex and marriage rendered him unfit to teach mathematical logic. Dr. Hook's conclusion was, "The connection is as recondite in one case as in the other."

8

Economic Status

Although academics are obviously not engaged in the higher learning for the primary purpose of making money, they are in the main no less interested in their paychecks than are the employees in business and industry. Like the clergy, to be sure, their success is not judged in pecuniary terms, but to-day's professors no longer accept rationalizations about the dignity and importance of their calling as a sop for low pay. For them, no less than for most other workers, earned income is the main determinant of their economic status.

To get at the economic status of academics, some basic questions need to be answered: What is the monetary reward system in academe? How does faculty compensation compare with that of other professionals? In a time perspective, how have academics fared? What has inflation done to their economic status? What are their fringe benefits? How significant are their extra earnings as sources of income? Do women academics and ethnic minorities experience differential treatment? What problems appear to lie ahead?[1]

To begin, one should note that the typical professor is a male with a family to support.[2] Aside from the intangible satisfactions of his job, he expects to earn enough to be able to maintain a reasonably good level of living. Academics know, of course, that identical salaries are often paid to employees of different worth to their employing institutions, and they are aware that nobody can equate in monetary terms a discovery in Shakespearean sources with one in atomic structure. In general, academics appear to be satisfied with a scheme that pays salaries close to a fixed scale, within a framework that lets every professor do "as good work as he can." They also realize that an academic biologist, for example, being paid a five-figure income, may make a discovery capitalized upon by a physician with a six-figure income.

Yet there is no way of completely offsetting income as a status denominator. In university circles, as in most other spheres, the most highly valued jobs are usually the best paid, and in the long run a university gets about the caliber of academic talent it pays for. Leading institutions have long paid their professors better-than-average academic salaries, and professional schools typically have higher scales than nonprofessional schools. The correlation between faculty pay scales and institutional quality was first demonstrated a good many years ago, and the finding has been repeatedly verified by numerous studies since then.[3]

Comparative Compensation

Not only do compensation practices vary considerably among the heterogeneous institutions comprising the universe of American higher education, but also the opportunities afforded academics for extra earnings differ from one institution to another and by fields within the same institution. As Howard Bowen has pointed out,

> The measurement of faculty salaries or incomes is complicated because of ambiguities arising from nine-month versus twelve-month appointments, part-time service, fringe benefits and perquisites, contributed service, supplemental pay-

ments for special services, opportunities for outside income, and variations in types of institutions. Also, the term "faculty members" includes a wide variety of qualifications, abilities, and responsibilities. In measuring change through time, these problems are partly—but not wholly—obviated if consistent definitions are followed one year to the next.[4]

In comparing academic incomes with those of other occupations, accordingly, there may be the added difficulty of not being able to ascertain just what the available data include or omit. A study made by the Social Science Research Council and two federal agencies several decades ago of earnings in selected professional occupations for the period from 1929 to 1954, for example, showed that the average annual salaries of college-level teachers exceeded those of public school teachers but that they were lower than the average annual net incomes of nonsalaried lawyers, physicians, and dentists, and of the average annual pay and allowances of commissioned army officers throughout the entire period.

At a later point in time (1966), Seymour Harris[5] showed that educational institutions then paid most scientists at lower rates than did the federal government, other governments, the military, and business and industry. Self-employed scientists had the highest median salaries, and those working for nonprofit organizations other than educational institutions had the lowest.

Incidentally, for the highly trained specialist looking mainly for job security and top compensation, the most bountiful employing organization consistently has been the federal government. Between July 1, 1966, and the fall of 1973, the average federal worker had been given nine successive raises (including two boosts in 1969 alone, for a total of 15.1 percent in that year), with the median for all federal white-collar workers rising by 79.4 percent.[6] Since 1973, federal pay raises have generally exceeded those of academe.

Further evidence of federal benevolence is witnessed in

the fact that during the ten-year period prior to the spring of 1973, HEW increased the number of its GS-16 through GS-18 supergrade employees ($31,203 to $36,000) from 84 to 414. To top this inflationary trend, Congress in early 1977 raised its own salaries by 29 percent to $57,500, increased the pay of certain federal judges 48 percent, and that of top-career federal employees 24 percent, bringing these latter up from $39,600 to $49,000.

In its survey of average salaries for academics in 1976–77, the AAUP reported that the range in all institutions having ranks was from $11,920 for instructors to $23,930 for professors; in doctorate-granting institutions the corresponding figures were $12,150 to $25,670.[7] Unlike the federal government and some other employers, moreover, few colleges and universities have annual cost-of-living increases which automatically adjust wages and salaries to changes in the Consumer Price Index. Thus, as will be noted shortly, some of the increases going to academics in recent years have been more illusory than real in terms of purchasing power.

Faculty Compensation in a Time Perspective

In 1955, Beardsley Ruml and Sidney G. Tickton published a fifty-year comparison of academic salaries with those in various other occupations and industries, and with the rise in living costs.[8] Their conclusion was that for the teaching profession as a whole there had been little or no absolute deterioration except at the top; the serious losses, they found, had occurred in the compensation of educational executives at all levels and among the highest-ranking professors. Between 1904 and 1953, the real purchasing power of presidents of large universities had declined by 2 percent, as had that of full professors in such institutions. The rise in purchasing power for persons "in the field of education was less, generally, than in industry and the rate of increase slower" (p. 36).

Although the common misconception is that inflation

has been a phenomenon mainly of the 1960s and 1970s, Ruml and Tickton noted that in 1953 a salary of $11,200 would have been required to match the purchasing power of a $3,000 salary in 1904, and one of $54,600 to equal a $10,000 salary at the earlier time. They further showed that despite inflation, the earnings of physicians increased by 48 percent and of dentists by 40 percent in "real" purchasing power between 1929 and 1953, whereas those of large university presidents declined by 26 percent and those of similarly situated professors by 10 percent.

Bowen's findings were that faculty salaries in current dollars increased from 1912–13 to 1965–66 at an average annual rate of 3.5 percent, and in constant dollars at a rate of 1.0 percent. For the period 1939 to 1965–66, for which interval he considered the data to be more reliable, the corresponding rates were 4.5 and 1.4 percent, and over the period between 1949 and 1966, 5.0 and 3.0 percent. In brief, things improved in the later years under study.

Although a general trend may blur or conceal variations by kinds of institutions, Bowen found some surprising similarities. He observed that salary variations by rank and class of institution retain a high degree of pattern constancy, and he concluded that salary policy everywhere is heavily influenced by formula, seniority, and custom as well as by market conditions.

Although the long-term trend of faculty compensation throughout the twentieth century does not show marked improvement, there can be no question about relative as well as absolute gains from 1949–50 to 1965–66. During this period, salaries more than doubled, the gap between institutions narrowed, and, as Bowen has reported, faculty incomes appear to have risen more rapidly than family incomes for the whole population. The circumstances described in Chapter 1 all contributed to an expansionist movement in higher education. Economic prosperity made it easier to raise money both publicly and privately to finance what was already foreseen as an enrollment boom during the 1960s, and funds were more readily forthcoming than in prior years to train, recruit, and compensate more adequately the faculties required.

As Bowen has pointed out, however, there are "certain anomalies that raise questions about why changes in faculty salaries occur." The 1955 take-off was *after* the big drop in GI enrollment and *before* the enrollment increases of the 1960s. The production of doctorates in the years just prior to 1955 had risen rapidly, and faculty members were easy to recruit. I would agree with Bowen that the most important cause of rapid salary rises was the changed values that made possible improved financial support for higher education, research, and development.

It should be noted also that in 1958 the AAUP designed and introduced its widely publicized annual salary surveys. Renumeration goals were set, salary ranges by ranks were openly reported for named institutions by the hundreds, and findings were scrutinized avidly by faculty members and administrators, who called them to the attention of trustees, legislators, and others. For the first time, academics now had some meaningful data to show where their institutions stood in the matter of compensation. Although there were complaints here and there about some of the bases of comparison (e.g., the weights given to miminum salaries), virtually every college and university could annually view its relative gain or loss of standing. The precise influence of the AAUP project cannot be gauged, of course, but there can be no question about its bringing into the open and intensifying salary competition.

In 1970, the AAUP modified its grading scheme and began to use descriptive rather than normative ratings. About that time, or a little earlier, the association also expressed concern about the "first signs" of erosion in the purchasing power of faculty salaries.[9] It is no wonder that the AAUP entitled its economic status report for 1972–73 "Surviving the Seventies," its 1973–74 report "Hard Times," its 1974–75 report "Two Steps Backward," and its 1976–77 findings "No

Progress This Year." The academic profession was being hit by the combined blows of recession and inflation. For the seven-year period between 1969–70 and 1976–77, average annual increases in monetary compensation ranged between 5.0 percent and 6.4 percent during every year except one. Increases in *real* terms, however, varied between 0.2 percent and 1.0 percent during the first three years of the period, and during the next four years there were in effect decreases each year, ranging from a low of -0.3 to a high of -4.2.

Ladd and Lipset have maintained, nonetheless, that in terms of total *family income* academics in the mid 1970s were "not doing badly." They reported as follows:

> The median family income for all faculty members in 1974 was about $23,000. In addition, more than one-fourth reported income over $30,000, and one-tenth took in more than $40,000 from all sources.
>
> This income structure compared rather favorably not only with that of the general public where the 1974 family median was $12,836, but also with the income of the most highly compensated professional and managerial cohorts in America.
>
> Forty-three percent of the professors reported 1974 family income above $25,000, a level reached by just 30 percent of all families whose heads had finished four or more years of college.
>
> The median for faculty families was about $3,500 higher than that of families generally where the head occupied a professional position.[10]

How the various categories of institutions and ranks of academics stood in 1976–77 may be seen in Table 8.1.

From the figures set forth in Table 8.1, it is clear that the doctorate-granting institutions compensate all four ranks of academics at higher rates than do any of the other categories of institutions. Shown elsewhere in the AAUP's 1976–77 report is a tabulation indicating a considerable difference in average compensation of academics by ranks between the ninth-decile and the first-decile universities in Category I (doctorate-granting), as follows: professor, $34,270 and $23,000; associate professor, $24,420 and $18,790; assistant professor, $19,640 and $15,740; and instructor, $16,090 and $11,980.

Fringe Benefits

Fringe benefits are today, of course, important components in the total compensation of employees, whether wage earning or salaried. The AAUP has calculated that in 1975–76 such benefits approximated 15 percent of average academic salaries. Another calculation (made in 1975) for the major state universities in California, Illinois, Indiana, Michigan, Minnesota, North Carolina, Ohio, Washington, and Wisconsin showed that the range was from a low of 10.7 percent to a high of 19.6 percent.[11]

Fringe benefits include quite a range of items, such as retirement plans, insurance programs, paid leaves, vacation, sick leaves, leaves without pay, and what not. As a former colleague of mine said in reviewing a book on the subject:

> And what a grab-bag it is! Sixty percent of the institutions queried are landlords for faculty families, 15 percent are mortgage brokers, 93 percent of private colleges provide tax-free scholarships in the form of tuition waivers, 75 percent provide emergency medical treatment to faculty and families, one-fourth grant personal loans to employees, two-thirds pay moving expenses for tenure appointments, etc. Others, in varying numbers, provide family bonuses for children, free faculty lunches and morning coffee, free baby-sitting services, two-thirds of foreign travel expenses, and run holiday camps for faculty families. Over half of the institutions have regular sabbatical leave policies, and others have informal leave-with-pay arrangements. Six hundred institutions provide faculty parking spaces. Some, like Princeton, house half their faculty in university-owned property or in houses where the university has advanced all the money and requires no payments on principal.[12]

Table 8.1 Weighted Average Salaries and Average Compensations by Category, Type of Affiliation, and Academic Rank, 1976–77 (standard academic year basis)

Academic Rank	SALARY				COMPENSATION‡			
	All Combined	Public	Private Independent	Church-related	All Combined	Public	Private Independent	Church-related
CATEGORY I**								
Professor	$25,670	$25,210	$27,810	$23,640	$29,410	$28,680	$32,650	$27,000
Associate	18,890	18,830	19,350	18,520	21,670	21,530	22,600	21,320
Assistant	15,400	15,380	15,470	15,530	17,740	17,690	17,960	17,780
Instructor	12,150	12,010	12,510	13,310	13,980	13,840	14,370	15,010
All Ranks*	19,630	19,360	21,300	18,310	22,530	22,120	24,910	20,960
CATEGORY IIA**								
Professor	22,580	23,190	22,020	19,060	26,110	26,780	25,580	22,150
Associate	17,980	18,380	17,410	15,880	20,870	21,330	20,270	18,350
Assistant	14,770	15,060	14,340	13,420	17,090	17,450	16,550	15,380
Instructor	11,910	12,120	11,660	10,780	13,670	13,980	13,240	12,140
All Ranks*	17,400	17,810	16,850	15,300	20,140	20,620	19,510	17,630
CATEGORY IIB**								
Professor	19,340	20,650	20,780	17,620	22,470	23,330	24,430	20,530
Associate	15,490	17,120	15,850	14,390	17,940	19,480	18,540	16,710
Assistant	13,120	14,400	13,220	12,330	15,060	16,420	15,310	14,130
Instructor	10,880	11,680	11,020	10,290	12,330	13,350	12,530	11,540
All Ranks*	14,790	15,720	15,530	13,770	17,060	17,890	18,100	15,880

CATEGORY III**

Professor	21,560	21,860	16,620	12,840	25,100	25,460	19,020	14,660
Associate	18,230	18,420	14,570	12,140	21,180	21,400	16,820	13,910
Assistant	15,190	15,330	12,100	11,690	17,700	17,880	13,810	13,220
Instructor	12,410	12,560	10,150	8,900	14,320	14,510	11,200	10,040
All Ranks*	16,100	16,280	12,410	11,400	18,710	18,940	14,110	12,960

CATEGORY IV**

No Rank	16,080	16,520	11,820	10,870	18,140	18,610	13,510	12,540

ALL CATEGORIES EXCEPT IV

Professor	23,930	24,260	25,090	19,300	27,540	27,750	29,400	22,350
Associate	18,100	18,560	17,750	15,600	20,890	21,360	20,710	18,050
Assistant	14,820	15,210	14,420	13,210	17,110	17,570	16,690	15,120
Instructor	11,920	12,170	11,610	10,820	13,690	14,030	13,220	12,160
All Ranks	17,930	18,280	18,420	15,040	20,670	21,020	21,460	17,310

*Because of the weight any given rank may have, the "All Ranks" (overall) average figure should be used with caution. Sample includes all institutions participating in the survey.

**Category I—includes institutions that offer the doctorate degree and that conferred in the most recent three years an annual average of fifteen or more earned doctorates covering a minimum of three nonrelated disciplines.

Category IIA—includes institutions awarding degrees above the baccalaureate but not included in Category I.

Category IIB—includes institutions awarding only the baccalaureate or equivalent degree.

Category III—includes two-year institutions with academic ranks.

Category IV—includes institutions without academic ranks. (With the exception of a few liberal arts colleges, this category includes mostly two-year institutions.)

†"Compensation includes salary (adjusted to a nine-month basis, when necessary) plus countable fringe benefits. Where faculty members are given duties for eleven or twelve months, salaries are converted to a nine-month basis by applying a conversion factor of 9/11 or by the official factors used in a publicly announced formula."

Source: AAUP Bulletin, August 1977, p. 156.

No single institution has ever provided *all* of these perquisites, to be sure, but the reviewer estimated that in any number of faculty cases available benefits could easily add up to six or seven thousand dollars, or perhaps even ten thousand before taxes, for a family in the "right institution," with two children in college. Many professors persist in regarding themselves as an economically deprived group, nonetheless, and some of them would be surprised, as Irving Kristol remarked in the 1960s, to know that their total compensation equals that of vice-presidents of many banks.

Some of these fringe benefits (such as freely granted leaves of absence) are to be found mainly in academe, but one should note that executives in business and industry also have "arrangements"—company-provided club memberships, business entertainment allowances, chauffeured limousines, and so on—to help them lead a better life and minimize their income taxes. Moreover, academic retirement systems, to which professors themselves usually contribute, are less generous than those for the military, to which members do not contribute financially, and in which they may retire after twenty years at 50 percent of their base pay and after thirty years at a 75 percent rate, with no reductions in their military pensions when they go into other employment, even when the jobs they take are with the federal government. The nation's elected lawmakers in Washington are also provided with a considerable range of fringe benefits, including such items as the use of masseurs, reduced-rate food services, and free flowers for their offices.

Throughout business and industry between 1965 and 1975, moreover, the fringe benefits to workers above their cash pay increased by 165 percent, with the U.S. Chamber of Commerce estimating that by the end of the period the typical employing company was paying out $3,984 per year per worker. Companies with 5,000 or more employees were by then reported to be expending 38.1 percent of payroll on benefits. In 1976, workers on the Ford Motor Company's assembly lines, which at that time were strikebound, won a contract agreement which included a forty-day annual vacation. Elsewhere, factory laborers were getting such contractual provisions as dental care, more time for coffee breaks and wash ups, free legal advice, and, according to one compensation expert, even "lonely pay" for employees whose jobs involved isolation from other workers.[13]

Extra Earning and Outside Income

At least some academics have long been accustomed to extra earnings and outside income. More than half a century ago, earnings from extra teaching assignments, writing, lecturing, consulting, and various other activities were not unheard of, and, indeed, were frequently noted for academics in urban institutions. One study made in 1928 indicated that the median for supplemental earnings was $522. In later years, higher proportions of academics were doing better. Seymour Harris stated that by 1961–62 the percentage of faculty persons with outside earnings had increased, with average amounts earned having risen sharply.[14] For a wide variety of academic fields, he reported that the percentage with outside earnings ranged from a low of 44 in home economics to a high of 85 in psychology, with average amounts varying from $1,094 in home economics to $5,297 in law, and with an average of $2,165 for all fields. Outside earnings were from the following sources: summer teaching and other summer employment, other teaching, royalties, speeches, consultant fees, research, and a few other sources. (I do not have in hand any more recent data, but my guess would be that increased amounts would accrue from much the same sources, but with the addition of NEH summer institute earnings and other sources of income for some professors.)

Since approximately six out of ten faculty persons are paid their "regular" salaries for academic teaching (nine to ten months) rather than for the calendar year, for those who do summer teaching, sums earned constitute extra income, whether earned locally or elsewhere. About half of the institutions pay a fixed percentage of the academic year salary (with the median being about 22 to 23 percent). For those institutions basing payment on credit hours taught, the median amount per credit hour in 1969 for the top rank was $376 and for the bottom rank $228.[15]

Some academics also augment their incomes as paid consultants. In a 1972 survey, Ladd and Lipset found that in all fields 37 percent of the faculty were serving as paid consultants, ranging from a low of 17 percent in English and philosophy to highs of 70 percent in medicine and 78 percent in psychology.[16]

Although most academics who engage in scholarly and scientific writing get little or no income from their publications, the authors of textbooks sometimes do quite well. According to one estimate, there were at least fifty professors in 1975 who made upwards of $150,000 each in textbook royalties, and who would do as well in the two succeeding years.[17] About that time, an introductory textbook in accounting had sold over two million copies, and an art history book had similar sales. The head of a college division for a leading textbook publisher was quoted as guessing that at least several hundred academic textbook authors make between $15,000 and $25,000 annually from their royalties.

The outside earnings of faculty members have been a topic of some controversy, as one might guess, and as early as 1953 the Association of American Universities was expressing concern about the institutional obligations of academics, their proper compensation beyond regularly budgeted salaries for extra service, and the complications arising from dual employment. The federal government was also concerned about the strange phenomenon of the erstwhile full-time academic employee who in some institutions had become a five-fourths-time worker by virtue of what was calculated to be overtime given to research projects. A special committee of the Association drew up a list of ten recommendations as guidelines for member institutions. By now, most universities have their regulations and guidelines for employees, but even in the 1970s there were still some problems.

To give an extreme example, the State University of New York at Stony Brook had to demand the resignation of one of its full-time faculty who was found also to hold simultaneously—unbeknown to the Stony Brook administration—a full-time post at Yale.[18]

Economic Status Discrepancies

From the point of view of employing institutions, part-time academics facilitate staffing adjustments to unanticipated enrollment changes and may reduce somewhat the costs of an extended curriculum coverage. Many of the clinical faculty members in some medical schools, for example, are private practitioners whose university services are a fraction of their full-time work. In some other faculties, most of the women teachers may be on a part-time rather than a full-time basis. Insofar as the economic status of such persons is concerned, they are often paid at lower rates than the full-time faculty and may not be accorded any of the costlier fringe benefits. With increased numbers of universities experiencing financial exigencies and seeking ways to reduce instructional costs, it is no wonder that various professional groups, such as teachers unions and the AAUP, are disturbed by the prospect that more and more universities may be tempted to increase the fraction of their faculty who are on part-time (and presumably lower-paid) appointments.

Until recently, prevailing sentiments also sanctioned paying women less than men for doing the same work, and the entry of any considerable number of women into professional ranks was felt to be a depressing influence on average incomes. Changed attitudes and recent federal edicts have brought or presumably will bring an end to such discrimina-

tion, but women still constitute a minority on virtually all
university faculties. In 1976 they comprised 17 percent of the
total in public universities and 15.8 percent in private universities. Their percentage representation for each rank in public
and in private universities respectively was as follows: professor, 5.9 percent and 5.5 percent; associate professor, 12.3 and
13.9; assistant professor, 25.4 and 24.8; and instructor, 51.9
and 22.8. Not only is the percentage of women disproportionately low in the two top ranks, but also their salaries average
lower in all of the ranks, with the greatest discrepancy occur-
ring in the higher ranks. In all baccalaureate-granting institutions during 1975–76, the median salary for men was $17,001
and for women $13,934.[19]

In its annual report on the economic status of the profession for the academic year 1972–73, the AAUP made these
generalizations: 1) the size of the average salary disadvantage
of females tends to grow with years of postdoctoral experience
from about 6 percent for new Ph.D.s to about 25 percent for
those with twenty-five years of experience; 2) women tend to
be promoted more slowly; 3) women are more likely to be
employed in less prestigious institutions; 4) in disciplines
where data were adequate, the earning disadvantages of
women in government employment appeared to be less than
in academic or business employment. Whether the government is under greater scrutiny and does not discriminate as
readily or is simply less sensitive to individual productivity
differences was a question raised but not answered by the
AAUP.

Bayer's 1972–73 survey of a large number of academics, however, shows some fairly marked differences between
men and women which suggest that these differences rather
than institutional discrimination may be, at least in part, causes
of some of the discrepancies. In university faculties, 44.9 percent of the men hold Ph.D.s, as contrasted with 16.4 percent
of the women. With regard to reported hours per week in
research and scholarly writing, 19.4 percent of the men and

42.2 percent of the women either reported none or did not respond to the questionnaire item. Among all those queried, 19.8 percent of the men and 45.4 percent of the women had never published an article in a journal (or else omitted the item), and of those who had published eleven or more journal articles, 38.6 percent were men and 10.4 percent women. The findings were similar with reference to published books, manuals, or monographs.

The focus of women academics on teaching rather than research and writing was also witnessed in their spending more hours per week in preparation for teaching, their being more frequently engaged in nine or more hours per week of scheduled teaching, and in their being more predisposed than men to believe that teaching effectiveness rather than publication should be the primary basis of faculty promotion. Moreover, only about half as many women as men rated their most outstanding single accomplishment to be in research and writing as contrasted to teaching. In brief, it seems apparent that there are some sex differences in typical motivations and activity patterns, with women being more inclined than men to be predominantly interested in teaching rather than research.

Since the recognition and reward system of scholarship and science, and hence that of major universities also, is geared mainly to achievements in research or the advancement of knowledge, it is obvious that those individuals, regardless of sex, who have a somewhat different orientation should encounter competitive difficulties. Whether there should be varying ground rules for different categories of competitors, or a different set of ground rules for all, is, of course, another question.[20]

Prospects Just Ahead

It would be reassuring to forecast better days ahead economically for the academic profession, but there are no reliable indicators available to support such a prediction. As the

AAUP's 1976–77 report on the economic status of academics shows, in terms of salaries alone their purchasing power has diminished by over 5 percent during the last decade. Wage and salary employees in other lines of work have done better. Average salaries of all nonagricultural employees have risen by 48 percent since 1970–71, and those of faculty members by only 70 percent as much. In total compensation (salary plus fringes), the national average of other types of employees has increased by 36 percent more than that of faculty members since 1970–71. The AAUP data further indicate that in purchasing power terms, the average employee's compensation is now worth 3.5 percent more than it was a decade ago, whereas the average faculty member's compensation is worth 5.5 percent less.

In brief, inflation has been particularly damaging to the economic status of academics in recent years, and inflation shows no sign of letting up in the years just ahead. Regardless of their productivity, the expectations of employees in almost every kind of enterprise are now such than an annual increase in pay for all is taken for granted. Despite their complaints about rising prices, it is no wonder that large segments of the nation's population are not really inclined to participate in the stern measures necessary to halt inflation. In terms of their voting behavior, neither in effect are many professors whose political attitudes and behavior may seem to contradict their own self-interests.

With regard to the prospects for increasing professorial compensation by means of improved productivity, moreover, it should be observed that higher education is a labor-intensive endeavor, and that economies in production often entail reductions in the quality of education produced or in circumscribed opportunities for prospective students. Higher salaries for professors thus more often than not imply increases in production costs and in the pricing of various educational outputs. It is not surprising, therefore, that in recent years growing numbers of educational institutions (including some of the more prestigious) have confronted financial crisis and have had to struggle merely to keep abreast of price increases. Higher costs for energy, equipment, and supplies have on many campuses reduced the faculty salary share of total institutional budgets.

Some institutions have responded to changed circumstances in trying to adjust to the market by eliminating those programs least productive of tuition revenue, even at the expense of long-established academic values. For a number of years, both public and private institutions (particularly the latter) have been increasing their tuition charges, albeit with reluctance, and competition for students between the two sections as well as within them places limits on how far a given institution can go before reaching the point of diminished returns. Perhaps most important of all, the number of postsecondary "consumers" began to decline in the 1970s and will continue to drop off in the 1980s. Higher education is thus in a demographic sense no longer a growth industry.

Predictions made during the boom years about ever-increasing proportions of high school graduates seeking further formal education have already proved to be in error, and those of more recent origin about the vast numbers of adults who would like to enroll for continuing education are highly speculative. A more likely development under conditions of heightened institutional competition in the period just ahead will be the rise in influence of students as consumers, of governments as suppliers of financial support, and of administrators who will be held more strictly accountable for the allocation and expenditure of moneys. These circumstances unquestionably will impose tighter controls on faculties in the economic aspects of their jobs, no matter what may happen in collective bargaining.

As Howard Bowen foresaw back in 1968:[21]

> What are the realistic financial prospects of higher education? Can we mount ever-larger fund campaigns? Can we continue to raise tuitions? Can we secure ever-larger state

appropriations? Can we depend on ever-increasing federal support?

The nation can, of course, "afford" to provide increasing funds from all these sources, in the sense that there is plenty of unnecessry expenditure in our economy (both public and private) that could be diverted to higher education. But there are also insistent competing claims, aside from private consumption . . . among them: poverty programs, renewal of cities, cleaning up of air and water, improved elementary education and foreign aid. We must face the possibility that while higher education still has a place of great affection and high priority in the public mind [much less so now than then, I would interpose], it may be losing its preeminent position of the past ten years. It would not be surprising, then, if the rate of increase in funds available from all sources would taper off and if the shares of the other claimants would increase.

Considering Bowen's remarks retrospectively, one can see that federal support in constant dollars has already declined and that the rate of increase in state support of higher education is no longer soaring annually. While no universities of real consequence have as yet been forced to close their doors, the economic status of the academic profession as a whole can at best be regarded as disadvantageous during the years immediately ahead.[22]

9

Academic Profiles and Social Status

The university community's professionals traditionally refer to themselves in their governance rhetoric as a "body of peers," and in many respects they are. They have all undergone a certain professional preparation, possess expertise, and share responsibility and authority. Job stratification by formal gradations is certainly much less distended than in the military or in civil service, not to mention in large business or industrial corporations. A full professor's status is higher in the pecking order, of course, than that of persons in other ranks, and a professor of physics typically is accorded more colleague esteem than a professor of physical education. Every university has some brilliant lower-ranked faculty members with more personal prestige than many of their seniors in the top ranks, and everybody knows that the brightest stars in the academic galaxy are not necessarily those with the most longevity.

Insofar as internal social stratification is concerned, the community of academics is on the whole more democratic than the surrounding society. There are proportionately fewer order givers and order takers. More consistently than in the larger society, individual advancement and the award of kudos are tied to a merit principle based not on who you are but on what you know and do.

However this may be, academics additionally are members of the larger community where they also have statuses. Since the economic status of the professoriate has already been examined, our next concern will be with their social origins, some of their characteristics in statistical profile, and the positions they occupy in the surrounding society. To what extent have they risen above their fathers' statuses? How much more "advantaged" are some academics than others? What is their age distribution? Are their political opinions and attitudes about social issues as diverse as those of the general citizenry? Do they think of themselves primarily as intellectuals or as functionaries in the educational sector of the economy? How may their life styles be characterized? How much influence do they have outside their own bailiwicks? What are their social class positions? How accurate are stereotyped notions about them? Is the trend toward a more egalitarian social order upgrading or downgrading their social status?

The Professoriate in Statistical Profile

Since there are now upwards of half a million academics employed in American colleges and universities, their total group obviously includes a wide range of human diversity. When I published my first book about academics in 1942, the group was much smaller, but nationwide data about professors were too meager to permit many quantitative generalizations about them. Today, the U.S. Office of Education and other agencies regularly gather information about academics, and within the last decade some very extensive surveys have been conducted.[1] It is now possible to view the entire American professoriate in statistical profile.

In the open-class system of American society there is comparatively little social inheritance of occupational status, and this is certainly the case for academics. About 56 percent of their fathers never went to college, and of those who did, only 12.9 percent got advanced degrees. As Ladd and Lipset have shown, however, the probability that academics will be the sons or daughters of fathers who were college graduates varies with the selectivity in admissions and resources per student of the institutions in which professors are employed.[2] Ranking institutions into seven tiers with regard to these criteria, Ladd and Lipset found that 38 percent of the faculty in tier 1 institutions had fathers who were college graduates, ranging downward to 20 percent for tier 7.[3] The findings for those with fathers who were professionals or managers were quite similar.[4]

Ladd and Lipset also noted variations in paternal backgrounds of academics in various disciplines, with those in medicine and law, for example, more likely to come from higher socio-economic strata than those in education or agriculture. Academics with a Catholic upbringing were to be noted most frequently in the least selective institutions, and those with a Jewish religious background were found to have their greatest concentration in the most selective institutions. The women academics had their lowest percentage of representation in the tier 1 institutions and their highest in tier 7; with regard to their spread among the disciplines, their highest representation was in the humanities, fine arts, and education, and their lowest was in the physical sciences and in such professional fields as engineering, law, and medicine.

Although professors are popularly stereotyped as being for the most part elderly, Bayer's 1972–73 survey shows that about two-fifths of them are under the age of 40; 5.9 percent are 30 or under; and 12.2 percent over 60. (Halsey and Trow's data show, by way of contrast, that 28.9 percent of British academics are 30 or under and only 2.9 percent over 60.) Slightly more than half of all American academics are in the two top ranks, and two-thirds have tenure. In recent years, the percentage of blacks has shown a slight increase, but the proportion of women in academic ranks has increased only in the university sector, and not very appreciably there.

Both Bayer and Ladd and Lipset observe that with higher education moving into a "no growth" period, the median age of faculty members is rising and will rise still further in the years ahead, with one prediction that by 1990 the median age will be 48. Since age and experience affect the attitudes and values of academics no less than they do those of other persons, it is of interest to speculate about whether there will be a rise of conservatism among faculties in the future.

Faculty Attitudes and Values

Whatever the future may hold, Ladd and Lipset have ascertained that experience and age have marked effects on the attitudes of academics currently employed in colleges and universities, as may be seen in Table 9.1.[5]

Not only do experience and age affect faculty attitudes and values, but also academic discipline, sex, and type of institutional affiliation are factors. Professors in the social sciences are more liberal in their general outlook than those in the professional schools, and female faculty members are more so than their male counterparts. Ladd and Lipset concluded that the academic profession as a whole, while not predominantly radical, "is notably inclined to liberal and egalitarian social programs. Certainly no other large occupational group approaches its liberalism. . . . [Yet most of its members] entertain no notion of sweeping economic or political change."[6]

That self-interest does affect their attitudes toward egalitarianism, however, is demonstrated in Bayer's 1969 finding about the diversity of percentages agreeing that a professor at a junior college or state college ought to get the same pay as a university professor of equal seniority. Among junior college respondents, 84.9 percent agreed, compared with 61 percent of those in four-year institutions; among university professors, only 43.4 percent agreed.

Table 9.1 Attitudes of Faculty Members, by Age

	UNDER 35 %	35–44 %	45–54 %	OVER 55 %
Voted for McGovern	74	64	61	50
Republicans	18	25	29	37
Most conservative fifth	14	20	23	32
Nationalize big corporations	35	28	27	25
Ban homosexual teachers	14	25	27	40
Opposed to laws against pornography	66	51	48	40
Legalize marijuana	71	60	63	44
Expel disruptive students	56	67	65	72
Student demonstrations have no place on campus	13	24	26	42
Favor collective bargaining	79	69	70	57
Meritocracy is a smokescreen for discriminatory practices	46	46	40	45
Base salary increases on merit	51	47	44	49
Tenure should be awarded on basis of national standards	64	67	70	77
"Benign quotas" are justified	35	36	36	32
Reduce admissions standards to raise minority enrollments	63	64	64	59
Prefer research	35	26	23	16
No publications, last two years	43	46	52	58
Three or more publications	29	25	22	21
Prefer "hard" approaches	39	30	26	25
Like new and wild ideas	77	72	68	62
Attend religious services at least once a month	34	41	43	50
Own only American car	52	51	60	68
Own only foreign car	29	26	16	15
Own General Motors car	25	25	29	38
Own compact car	48	39	32	34
Own large car	30	37	39	44
Rarely or never attend concert	25	23	22	16
Rarely attend athletic event	38	38	41	47

As to religious attitudes and values, Bayer's 1969 survey found that Protestants, Catholics, and Jews alike included appreciably higher proportions of academics brought up in these faiths than were currently professing them; only

3.7 percent of the respondents in 1969 indicated no religious background, but the proportion indicating no "current religion" was 23.7 percent. Bayer's 1972–73 survey made no reference to particular religious affiliation or regularity of church attendance and simply had the item, "I consider myself a religious person." Responding to this statement, 60 percent of the academics considered themselves religious. Similarly, his 1972–73 survey had the item, "I consider myself to be politically conservative," and 44 percent of his respondents agreed with the statement.

Although self-designations of these kinds are interesting, they tend to obscure the fact that the concepts dealt with often have different meanings for different persons. There are, for example, varying kinds of radicalism in academe. One professional observer has identified three varieties of radical academics.[7] The educational, cultural, and political radicals may all be alienated from the status quo, but for each type it is a different status quo, and the conformist in one sphere may be a deviant in another.

By training, many academics have a high degree of critical acumen, and one of the university's traditional functions is to serve as a critic of society. As Bayer and others have noted, however, their dissatisfactions tend not to center on their jobs. Despite what has been said earlier in this book about faculty mobility, the 1972–73 survey being referred to here reported that only 12.0 percent had been in their current institutions for less than three years. If they were starting anew, only 13.5 percent would not choose to be academics, and only 18.2 percent would pick another discipline. In brief, most academics must experience many career satisfactions.

Professors as Citizens and Intellectuals

As Bayer's later study points out, average academics spend more time in unpaid public service consulting (41.8 percent of all academics report such extramural involvements) than in paid consulting (a comparable 37.7 percent are so engaged) outside of their own institutions. Ladd and Lipset have also shown that in their roles as citizens academics are more active politically than the U.S. population in general, and even more so than the college-educated portion of the total population. Professors are more likely than most other citizens to run for public office, involve themselves in political party affairs, assist candidates, and participate in groups formed to consider public policy questions.

The public backlash against academia and its denizens as a consequence of the widespread campus disorders of the 1960s and the early 1970s, a growing disenchantment with some of the anticipated but unrealized outcomes of higher education, and a slowdown in outside support have caused a good many academics of late, as Ladd and Lipset have noted, to feel undervalued and undersupported, uncertain about their proper missions, and doubtful about where they may be headed. Most of them remain committed, nonetheless, to egalitarian goals for the university and the larger society. Theirs may be a "peculiar profession," as Kenneth Eble has said, but they do share with most other citizens an increasingly democratic ethos.

As members of a traditionally dissenting academy now being called upon increasingly to serve more as society's servant than as its critic, professors who are or aspire to be intellectuals confront some dilemmas.[8] All academics are engaged in what is essentially an intellectual occupation, to be sure, as can be readily perceived by a comparison of their teaching and research functions with the tasks performed by most other gainfully employed workers. The Ladd-Lipset survey shows, however, that most faculty members think of themselves primarily as teachers. The next largest group consider the term *professional* the one word that best describes their work involvement. Some chose the term *scientist* and others the term *scholar.* Ladd and Lipset asked their respondents to pick the one designation among five that described them best and the one thought least suitable; the term *intellectual* came in last, with only 11 percent indicating that it best described their role. By disciplinary fields the percentages of those giving first preference to *intellectual* were social science, 14; humanities, 21; natural sciences, 6; and professional subjects, 5.[9]

Although intellectuals are obviously more likely to be found among persons who review scholarly books than among those who never read anything except the daily newspaper, it should be acknowledged that there is no specified and universally accepted procedure for identifying an intellectual. Some of the difficulties are illustrated, for example, in Kadushin's fairly recent book on Americans who were tagged as the nation's leading intellectuals.[10] By any set of reasonable standards, knowledgeable readers of the book would doubtless agree that the listing does include some very familiar names of individuals regarded in various circles as bona fide intellectuals. It is interesting to note that the book's author initially limited his purview to those persons (about 8,000) who between 1964 and 1968 had contributed to what were deemed to be the top twenty-two intellectual journals. When Professor Kadushin had by various means narrowed his list to 172 names, he found that about 40 percent of them were professors and another 40 percent editors or staff members of leading journals and newspapers. Only one physical scientist was included in the total, and more than half of the professors were at just four universities—Harvard, Columbia, Yale, and New York University. The author (a professor at Teachers College, Columbia) next asked the persons in his sample to name others on the list who had "influenced them on cultural or social-political issues, or who they believed had high prestige in the intellectual community." This procedure yielded the seventy finalists who were the presumed cream of the elite.

Professor Kadushin's disquisition, as one might have expected, brought forth some strong criticisms of his basic concepts, his methodology, and his findings. If for no other reason, however, his book is useful for its demonstration of the difficulty in getting at who the elite are among American intellectuals.

Life Styles

In my 1942 publication I had a somewhat lengthy quotation from Abraham Flexner's *Universities,* a book which had led to a good deal of discussion in academic circles. Flexner's view was that, with exceptions, "the American professoriate is a proletariat." He bemoaned the fact that professors of philosophy and Sanskrit were finding themselves more and more in the same boat with professors of advertising and extracurricular activities, and that "universities, by sacrificing intellectual purposes, have thus sacrificed the intellectual distinction which counts for more than money."[11]

It is doubtful that the professoriate has ever been a proletariat, I then commented, and now repeat. Although the professors in some European countries, like the mandarins of ancient China, have enjoyed more social prestige in some epochs than most academics have ever attained in the United States, a not inconsiderable number of American academics have achieved enviable life styles as well as high honors for their intellectual accomplishments.

As was noted in Chapter 1, academics lead less regimented lives than do the employees in most other lines of work. Several years ago a book was published by an anonymous Professor X entitled *This Beats Working for a Living: The Dark Secrets of a College Professor.*[12] It contained this quotation from another unnamed professor: "The life of a well-established, middle-aged professor in the Arts faculty of a modern university can, if he likes to make it so, be one of the softest jobs to be found on the earth's surface."

Also apropos are some remarks by J. Kenneth Galbraith. In 1976 he was awarded $10,000 in cash and a purple-and-gold Cadillac by the campus humor magazine for being "Harvard's funniest professor in 100 years." He made a spoofing commentary at the ceremony which included these remarks:

> An aspect of grim harassment also suggests deep devotion to one's work; gaiety, in contrast, could be thought to imply idleness. This is important because Harvard may be the only considerable community in the world, the Pentagon possibly excepted, where the effort to stimulate effort can exceed effort itself. After three months' vacation in the summer, a professor takes a sabbatical leave in the autumn so that he will be rested and ready for a winter's leave of absence to work up a course on the work ethic.[13]

True, there may be days between Monday and Friday when some academics are at home by the middle of the afternoon, and still others when they do not set foot on the campus at all. Oppositely, considerable numbers of professors spend long hours in the library or laboratory and may be busily engaged in their home studies well past midnight during the week and on weekends. Although their formally scheduled working hours may seem light to shop and office employees, the self-imposed schedules of many professors would be beyond the credence of those workers elsewhere whose work weeks do not exceed thirty-five or forty hours.

The distinctive behavior patterns of academics are also displayed in their avocational interests and pursuits. As to the general periodicals professors most commonly read, Ladd and Lipset have given the summation set forth in Table 9.2.

In analyzing the reading habits of academics, Ladd and Lipset were surprised to find that faculty persons tagging themselves "intellectuals" read no more widely among the twenty-five periodicals than those who considered themselves to be primarily "teachers," and that 22 percent of the professors at elite universities scored in the top fifth in range of reading, compared with almost as high a proportion (21 percent) of those in junior colleges. They found no differences in levels between professors spending much of their time doing

Table 9.2   Periodicals Ranked by Size of Faculty Readership

	ALL FACULTY MEMBERS	FACULTY MEMBERS AT MAJOR UNIVERSITIES
1.	Time	New York Times
2.	Newsweek	Time
3.	New York Times	Science
4.	Science	Newsweek
5.	Saturday Review	New Yorker
6.	New Yorker	New York Review of Books
7.	U.S. News	Saturday Review
8.	Wall Street Journal	Wall Street Journal
9.	New York Review of Books	U.S. News
10.	Harper's	New Republic
11.	Business Week	Harper's
12.	Playboy	Washington Post
13.	Atlantic	Atlantic
14.	New Republic	Playboy
15.	Fortune	Business Week
16.	Nation	Dædalus
17.	Washington Post	Commentary
18.	Dædalus	Fortune
19.	American Scholar	Nation
20.	National Review	Foreign Affairs
21.	Foreign Affairs	American Scholar
22.	Commentary	Public Interest
23.	Encounter	National Review
24.	Foreign Policy	Encounter
25.	Public Interest	Foreign Policy

Source: Chronicle of Higher Education, January 19, 1976, p. 14.

research and those primarily interested in teaching, or between those who publish a great deal and those who do not publish at all. They did observe that faculty political "activists" lean more toward periodicals of social, political, and economic discussion; that business school professors read more commentaries on economic affairs; and that the humanists rank higher than most in attention to the "cultural journals." Although the *New York Times* was reported as being read by 56 percent of professors in the Northeast, outside that region the figures were Midwest, 17 percent; South, 15 percent; and West, 9 percent.

The Ladd-Lipset survey was confined to general periodicals, of course, and did not include books, the vast range of scholarly and scientific journals, or the extensive array of professional journals. Likewise, the significance of the findings would be enlarged if there were comparisons with the reading habits and tastes of lawyers, doctors, business executives, and others. According to a publisher's survey made in 1971, faculty members spend an average of eleven hours a week reading nonprofessional matter, and fifteen hours on professional materials (six of these being for course-related books, five for journals, and four for reference materials).

Ladd and Lipset go on to characterize academics as "relatively heavy consumers of high culture."[14] More than a fourth of them report going to a concert at least once a month, and 22 percent see on average a play a month, but 40 percent report little or no attendance at athletic events. The Ladd-Lipset computer also turned up the statistic that, whereas only 18.5 percent of all automobiles in this country are of foreign manufacture, 42 percent of the academics report owning a foreign car. Among academics, moreover, the makes of cars owned proved to be "almost a proclamation of a social-political orientation or style of life," with the drivers of Saabs, Volkswagens, and even Mercedes being much more liberal in their general attitudes than the drivers of Plymouths and Buicks.[15] (My guess is that if in 1976 their categories had separated the long-haired and short-haired academics, their correlations might have been quite similar.)

Professional Stereotypes and Types

When he was Master of Clare College, Cambridge University, Sir Eric Ashby had this to say about changing stereotypes of the professor:

> The nineteenth-century professor, you remember, was absent-minded. You recollect, perhaps, the story of the profes-

sor who went to a seminar on Riemann geometry on a wet night. When he came home he put his umbrella to bed and stood in the umbrella stand all night. He had a gentle voice although his conversation resembled the footnotes of a German treatise on theology. He was impoverished, of course, with shabby shoes, and if he had a vest with six buttons on it, the top button was put into the second buttonhole and so on down to the bottom.

Then, sometime between the wars, this caricature changed. The modern concept of the professor is equally inaccurate, but quite different. If you want to meet him you do not go to his laboratory. You have to book a seat on a plane to Washington; or in my country, you have to get the 8:48 train from Cambridge to London. He dresses smartly, in a slightly Bohemian way; he has a split-level house and a Buick car. He has an effortless superiority of the nicest kind, but he does make you feel that he is a very charming member of a very exclusive club to which you don't belong.[16]

Sir Eric went on to characterize academic life as being anarchic, nomadic, and somewhat schizophrenic. By anarchic, he meant not that universities are lawless but that they (particularly in England) are conducted without much central control. Dissent is frequent among a class of professionals who are often predisposed to "think otherwise." By nomadic, he observed that in both England and the United States academics commonly migrate from one institution to another, the main difference between the two counties being that, because of very similar salary scales in all British universities, their academics gravitate elsewhere mainly for better research or teaching opportunities (the strongest pulls being exerted by Oxford, Cambridge, and London), or for such secondary reasons as better climate and better schools for their children, whereas in the United States universities use salary differentials to bid against one another for talent. The "schizophrenia" to which he referred relates to the conflict between teaching and research demands, and the split in faculty loyalty between a profession and an institution.

Irving Howe pointed out in an article he wrote in 1965 that the anti-intellectual tradition of American culture from the 1830s through the 1920s stereotyped the average professor as "a sort of amiable bumbler."[17] (A doctoral dissertation by Claude C. Bowman, *The College Professor in America,* privately printed in Philadelphia in 1938, culled and analyzed professorial stereotypes from twenty magazines over a period of forty-eight years, and in general derived a similar characterization.)

Howe further noted the drastic changes that came with the New Deal, the Cold War, and the trend toward mass higher education. Although "old-line scholars" still may be found on most campuses, "candor also requires one to admit that the strongest academic tendency, especially in the more amibitious universities, has been toward new types, far more snappy, aggressive, and up-to-date than the traditional scholar or intellectuals." Admittedly caricaturing to some extent, Howe has delineated three recently emerged types. First, there is The Research Magnate, usually a scientist and rarely a humanist, who supervises large projects and teaches less and less. He may at times be a "very troubled man," but he consoles himself with the thought that "he does the work of the world." Second, the Academic Enterpreneur is "the all-found grubber of univesity life; on a lower plane of distinction and status than the research magnate, he is a busy person as a conference arranger and attender," as a consultant, and as a writer of popular textbooks. Third, The Campus Org-Man is not much of a researcher and is not well known off the campus as an entrepreneur, but he "serves on twenty-seven commitees, 'advises' students endlessly, keeps in close touch with alumni . . . but as far as learning, writing, or even teaching is concerned, he simply fills a slot."

Howe concluded, however, by emphasizing that universities include thousands of academics who still care about intellect and the nurturing of student minds. A task at hand and ahead for universities is to reaffirm the value of pure scholarship and to "uphold the complex ideal of a balance between detachment and involvement." Howe's observations were made too early, of course, for him to caricature the faculty activists of the later 1960s and the early 1970s who found as much excitement as the student activists in new "involvements."

Under the influence of egalitarianism and the spread of mass education, the members of different occupations are less set apart from one another in appearance and social behavior than they once were. Professors, like public school teachers, are now emancipated from many of the limitations formerly prescribed for them. Excepting some of the clergy, the military, the police, and a few occupations that retain uniformed modes of dress as ready marks for identification, there has been a regression toward the mean in outward appearance. Inside the academic profession, it was once only a few of the senior professors in elitist colleges and universities who had beards or goatees as symbols of office; today, the senior professors are likely to be clean-shaven, with the younger academics more commonly bearded and resembling the undergraduates in casual modes of dress.

Academics and Social Class

Regardless of how loose or mistaken their criteria may be, Americans have their own means of identifying individuals as members of the so-called upper, middle, and lower classes. If this were not so, it would be difficult to say in what respect social classes "exist." Many aspects of social class phenomena are not readily perceived by the untrained observer, however, and this in part accounts for a considerable body of formal inquiry into the subject of social stratification.

Specialized views about what stratification means and what determines an individual's class membership differ. According to the Marxian conception, ownership or nonownership of the means of production is crucial, and in these terms alone most academics would be by definition "proletarians." Other definitions stress standard of living or style of life; still others, possession of a common ideology and shared attitudes. Some criteria play down economic determinants and emphasize "universal principles of intellectual superiority and inferiority"; in these terms alone, most academics would definitely be upper-class members.[18]

Even primitive societies may display some rudimentary social stratification, and in complex societies it is manifest that all jobs are not equally important, and that human abilities are not evenly distributed. It thus follows—according to the functional theorists—that responsibilities, rights, and perquisites must be unequally distributed; and some social analysts hold that this is precisely what stratification means.

American academics live in what is predominantly an open-class society: entry into their occupation is more accessible than in most other professions, and advancement in it is closely coupled with individual capability and effort. Kinship, fortuitous wealth, and other circumstances are of less importance in academe than in the larger society, but it must be borne in mind that here we are talking mainly about the academic's class position in the larger society.

In the United States during the past century, as in Great Britain and most of the Continent, there has been a trend toward more social equality. In 1966 in this country the average income of full professors in land-grant colleges and universities was 2.35 times (and of self-employed physicians, 4 times) that of full-time employees in all industries. It has been reported that in 1975 in Great Britain, the disposable income, after taxes, for a senior university professor or family doctor was not more than twice that of an automobile factory worker.

Contrary to what some persons in this country doubtless think, communist Russia is in certain respects less egalitarian in its occupational reward system than either the United States or Great Britain. Anthony Quinton, a philosopher at Oxford, in "Elitism: A British View" cites the experience of an eminent English physicist full of praise for the esteem in which his kind were held in the Soviet Union, from which he had just returned.[19] The scientist seemed particularly impressed by the fact that a man of his distinction in Russia would be getting seventeen times the wage of a manual worker—not merely four or five times the rate, as in Great Britain. Quinton's commentary is, in general, a defense of an elitism based on accomplishment rather than aristocratic inheritance of status, and he further notes that the movement in England toward equality of condition has been even more noticeable than income leveling.

Quinton has observed that during the 1930s in England there were three main classes—first: the gentlemen (land-owners), bankers, industrialists, professionals, and officers, second: the middle class of shopkeepers, office workers, and salesmen; and at the bottom, the lower classes. Some of the main differences among them in the 1930s and now are these: 1) *Auditory*. They spoke different kinds of English then. The gentry had more grammatical "gentility," and phonetic marks of class difference were prominent in vowel sounds. Under the impact of more education for the masses, together with the influence of radio and television as speech homogenizers, these linguistic indicators of stratification have lessened. 2) *Dress*. The mass production of clothing has made for more uniformity in dress styles, and there is no longer a readily identifiable way of determining social status at a glance, as there was in the 1930s. 3) *Similar changes*. Many persons now own cars, have the same style of home furnishings, engage in common leisure activities, and resemble one another in their habits and tastes of eating and drinking. For the majority, there has been upward movement rather than mere equalization. 4) *Equality of opportunity in education*. There has been more of it, with a trend toward eliminating the ossifying influence of social heredity as a main determinant of life changes.

By comparison with British society in 1930, individual mobility between classes in the United States was more fluid then, as it still is today. The laboring class there is more self-conscious, to be sure, has more political clout, and has pushed for the nationalization of industry to the extent that the British economy is much more socialized than our own. Mass education has been greatly amplified there in recent years, but the cleavage there between kinds of primary and secondary schooling is sharper than with us, and the opportunities for advanced education in Britain are more restricted than in this country.

In both nations, however, there has been a leveling up and down. Laboring class incomes have risen notably, and steeply increased income and inheritance taxes have reduced disparate extremes of life styles among the various social classes. A considerable portion of the population in both countries reads the same newspapers, watches the same television programs, and buys the same brands of mass-produced goods.

Although the forced busing of public school children in this country may have the unintended consequence of making lower-level education here more like that of the dual system in England, there can be no question about our real gains in equal opportunity on advanced levels of formal education. Race and sex discrimination are now illegal in the United States, and the covert quota schemes formerly practiced by many colleges and universities have virtually disappeared. Growing numbers of blacks and women may be seen in academic ranks, and Jews now have a proportionally higher representation in many fields of academic endeavor than any other ethnic category, including WASPs.

Bayer's 1969 report indicated that 58 percent of this nation's university professors felt that in the previous twenty years respect for their profession had declined. A poll conducted in 1977 indicated, nonetheless, that the public at large still ascribes a considerable amount of influence and power to educational institutions, ranking them near the midpoint among twenty-nine leading institutions, organizations, and social movements according to relative influence on "decisions and actions affecting the nation as a whole."[20]

In their roles as transmitters, advancers, and appliers of organized knowledge, academics have in the main gained rather than lost status in recent decades. They influence vastly more students than they once did, and serve as credentialers for a larger and larger array of occupations; and in addition the interpenetration of their thought modes into the extramural world has been greatly extended. Compared with government, business, and labor leaders they are not "men of power," as Parsons and Platt have observed,[21] but as indirect shapers of basic social decisions and actions their long-range influence is certainly appreciable. Their social status, accordingly, is, and undoubtedly will continue to be, a respected one.

10

3/10/79

University Prestige and Competition

Despite perennial debate about how universities should be organized or structured and what their goals should be, it is generally agreed that their basic functions are teaching, research, and public service. In the performance of these functions, they engage in both cooperation and competition. They cooperate to achieve the same or complementary shared objectives, and have many formal contacts with one another. Systems of institutions, course credit transfers, and similarities of policy and practice, for example, all display a patterning intended to further cooperation. Educational institutions also realize mutual advantages from less formalized modes of cooperation.

Since the material and human resources required for institutional growth and improvement are not unlimited, however, colleges and universities inevitably must compete with one another. Even when such resources are relatively abundant, acclaim and prestige are by definition scarce "commodities," and the pursuit of them as well as other forms of recognition and reward converts participants into competitors.

We have observed how students compete with one

another, as do professors and departments on the same campus. Our next step will be to examine the process of competition among universities. To what goals is the competition directed? Who competes with whom? By what means can the process be studied? How are accomplishments appraised? What are the costs and benefits to individual institutions and to American higher education?

Intellectual Competition among Universities

Unlike the open and publicized contests for determining institutional standings in intercollegiate athletics, modes of appraising the performance of universities in the intellectual sphere are not easily discernible or generally understood. Accrediting agencies give some assurance of minimal academic standards, but beyond this mere accreditation reveals little about the qualitative differences among colleges and universities. In the absence of systematic and comprehensive appraisals, the consumers and supporters of academic endeavor may thus lack objective knowledge about what they are getting for their investments, and the institutions themselves miss the potential benefit of having available detached and disinterested judgments on their relative strengths and weaknesses.

Although the application of research techniques to the identification and analysis of institutional merit is of fairly recent origin, efforts to uphold and protect high standards can be traced back to the beginning of this century. Institutional requirements for the Ph.D. showed a wide variation of standards in 1900, and in some places it was even awarded as an unearned or honorary degree. Such disparities, together with low regard in Europe for American advanced degrees, led Harvard's President Charles W. Eliot to invite representatives of fourteen institutions granting 90 percent of doctoral degrees at that time to meet to consider the whole matter. An outcome was the formation of the Association of American Universities. The growth in membership of this selective and prestigious organization from 1900 to 1969 brought its roster to forty-eight institutions—which was still the total in mid-1977.[1] Since being taken into the AAU fold is one indicator of the perceived quality and significance of a university's status in academe at a given time, it is pertinent to note in Table 10.1 the chronological sequence of admissions. Looking over the roster, an experienced observer will sense, of course, that some of the listed universities are no longer at the forefront of American higher education and that a few others are doubtless of less general significance than some universities that have more recently achieved prominence but are not as yet within the AAU fold.

Standards of judgment have long been a concern of the AAU. Just two years after its establishment, the organization's executive committee chairman raised some questions regarding AAU purposes and criteria for membership:[2]

> Is our body an organized association, intended to take in all who reach a certain grade of merit, and charged with the duty of establishing an objective grading and standing among universities? Or is it a club for mutual improvement and enjoyment, which can exclude members not likely to increase this improvement or enjoyment, without the necessity of telling them the reasons for this exlusion in a form available for publication?

Pertinent information about bases of selection is not available for the first two decades of the association's existence, but correspondence with members in 1928 indicates that four universities were proposed for consideration. The faculty members of fifteen selected departments in member institutions were asked to evaluate corresponding departments (including their named professors) in the institutions under consideration and "also the facilities for study which exist. . . ."

The tabulated responses to the inquiry indicate that the institution with the largest number of favorable ratings was admitted to membership the next year. Two others under con-

Table 10.1 Association of American Universities

1900	1926
1. University of California	27. McGill University
2. Catholic Univ. of America	28. University of Toronto
3. University of Chicago	1929
4. Clark University	
5. Columbia University	29. University of Texas
6. Cornell University	1933
7. Harvard University	
8. The Johns Hopkins Univ.	30. Brown University
9. Stanford University	1934
10. University of Michigan	
11. University of Pennsylvania	31. California Insti. of Tech.
12. Princeton University	32. Massachusetts Insti. of Tech.
13. University of Wisconsin	1938
14. Yale University	33. Duke University
1904	1941
15. University of Virginia	34. University of Rochester
1908	1950
16. University of Illinois	35. New York University
17. University of Minnesota	36. University of Washington
18. University of Missouri	37. Vanderbilt University
1909	1958
19. University of Kansas	38. Iowa State University
20. University of Nebraska	39. Pennsylvania State Univ.
21. Indiana University	40. Purdue University
22. University of Iowa	41. Tulane University
1916	1964
23. Ohio State University	42. Michigan State University
1917	1966
24. Northwestern University	43. University of Colorado
1922	44. Syracuse University
25. Univ. of North Carolina	1969
1923	45. Case Western Reserve Univ.
26. Washington University	46. University of Maryland
	47. University of Oregon
	48. Univ. of So. California

Source: Selden, "The Association of American Universities," p. 205.

sideration made it twenty-one years later, and the fourth prospect is still an outsider now. Similar modes of appraisal were employed in later years, but following publication of the American Council on Education's very comprehensive study of graduate departments in thirty academic disciplines in 1966 (the total number of departments surveyed was 1,663) and a similar inquiry and report made in 1970, the AAU had at its disposal and did utilize more meaningful data. (More will be said later about these ACE ratings.)

In my 1942 book I compared the rank order of the thirty leading graduate centers in the production of doctorates with their rank order in terms of various physical resources. It was noted that twenty-five of them were among the thirty-three members of the AAU, which suggested a close association between quantity and perceived quality in their doctorate productivity. For purposes of comparison, Table 10.2 reproduces the earlier information alongside the same kind of data for 1967–68, almost three decades later. Again, twenty-five of the thirty main producers of doctorates were AAU members, thus illustrating a maintenance of high standards over an extended period among the leading producers. Although the rank ordering has changed, and some institutions have been added to the productivity list of thirty while others have dropped out, the comparison demonstrates that leading universities manifest a remarkable stability in the husbandry of their physical resources, with newcomers to the ranks encountering strong competition from most of those already there.

Systematic Assessments of Quality

The general standings of universities become known to educated laymen largely through informal channels. Specialized excellence, while known to scholars and scientists within a field, is not widely disseminated as information even among undergraduates who contemplate entering the field. Harvard,

Yale, California, and other leading centers are accepted as symbols of scholarly prestige by many persons having only vague notions of how such standings are deduced. Even academics themselves are prone to be swayed by the magic of traditional renown, regardless of how meaningless it may be when applied to the merit of a particular department within a major university.

To provide interested individuals with a more rational basis for their impressions, numerous attempts have been made to rank colleges and universities in various orders of merit. In 1911, for instance, the U.S. Bureau of Education prepared a rating of 344 institutions at the request of the Association of American Universities. The list was first distributed semiconfidentially, but it aroused such a storm of protest that it was officially withdrawn. Despite objections from various sources to invidious comparisons, later rankings have been made. The best known of these in earlier years was undertaken by the American Council on Education.[3] This study relied upon the ratings of a presumably representative group of prominent specialists in thirty-odd fields (averaging about sixty-five judges to a field). The derived rank order of leading universities according to the number of distinguished departments was as follows (as of the year 1934): 1) Harvard, 2) Chicago, 3) Columbia, 4) California, 5) Yale, 6) Michigan, 7) Cornell, 8) Princeton, 9) Johns Hopkins, 10) Wisconsin, and 11) Minnesota.

Although institutional quality as such is the expression of a value judgment and is in some respects not quantifiable because of the lack of precise units for measuring quality, it has long been known to be associated with faculty and student capability and performance, adequacy of financial support, alumni accomplishments, library and laboratory facilities, leadership achievements, and so on.

One institutional rating of the 1930s, for example, showed a close correspondence between a university's standing and its share in the distribution of persons listed in *Ameri-*

Table 10.2 Comparison of the Physical Resources of the Thirty Leading Graduate Centers, 1939 and 1968

RANK ORDER IN TERMS OF DOCTORATES CONFERRED DECADE ENDING IN 1939 (A)	RANK ORDER IN TERMS OF DOCTORATES CONFERRED IN 1967–68 (B)	Value of Property 1939	Value of Property 1968	Endowment (Market Value) 1939	Endowment (Market Value) 1968	Educational and General Expenditures 1939	Educational and General Expenditures 1968	Centrally Budgeted Research 1939	Centrally Budgeted Research 1968	Size of Library (Bound Volumes) 1939	Size of Library (Bound Volumes) 1968
1. Columbia	1. Columbia	3	15	4	7	4	6	3	1	3	4
2. Chicago	2. Wisconsin	2	8	3	19	13	1	1	N.A.	5	11
3. Wisconsin	3. Calif. (Berkeley)	16	7	23	9*	10	10	6	+	6	6
4. Harvard	4. Illinois	N.A.	1	1	25	1	N.A.	7	6	1	3
5. Cornell	5. Harvard	8	10	11	1	5	N.A.	11	3	8	1
6. Yale	6. Michigan	1	2	2	16	7	3	9	2	2	5
7. Calif. (Berkeley)	7. Stanford	4	20	12	8	3	12	2	5	4	8
8. Michigan	8. Minnesota	7	6	17	17	2	4	14	12	9	12
9. Illinois	9. Michigan State	10	3	26	26	9	15	4	18	7	25
10. N.Y.U.	10. Ohio State	18	9	18	20	6	9	27	13	17	15
11. Ohio State	11. Indiana	17	4	25	24	12	18	13	16	18	13
12. Iowa	12. Calif. (L.A.)	19	5	27	9*	15	8	20	+	16	9
13. Johns Hopkins	13. N.Y.U.	14	12	10	15	19	7	5	4	15	16
14. Minnesota	14. Cornell	13	11	15	12	12	13	5	7	11	7
15. Pennsylvania	15. Purdue	9	14	13	22	11	20	10	23	10	29
16. Princeton	16. Texas	N.A.	18	9	3	21	5	15	8	12	14
17. Stanford	17. M.I.T.	12	26	7	5	16	19	23	4	13	27
18. M.I.T.	18. So. California	11	30	6	21	18	25	19	24	24	23
19. Pittsburgh	19. Chicago	20	24	21	6	23	2	16	9	28	10
20. Iowa State	20. Northwestern	24	27	28	11	20	27	8	28	26	19
21. Catholic U.	21. Washington (Seattle)	28	17	20	18	29	14	27	17	22	20
22. Northwestern	22. Pennsylvania	15	23	14	13	14	11	17	10	14	17

Rank	Institution (A)											Rank	Institution (B)
23.	Cal. Tech	23	15	19	2	N.A.	23	12	14	30	2	23.	Yale
24.	Texas	5	21	5	28	22	21	18	26	19	21	24.	Iowa
25.	Penn. State	27	13	30	27	27	17	25	15	29	22	25.	Penn. State
26.	Iowa State	25	28	22	29	28	24	21	22	23	30	26.	Iowa State
27.	Washington (Seattle)	22	22	29	30	24	22	26	25	21	24	27.	Florida
28.	Virginia	21	19	16	23	25	16	22	20	25	28	28.	Maryland
29.	Case-Western	6	29	8	14	17	28	27	19	20	26	29.	Case-Western
30.	Princeton	26	16	24	4	26	26	24	21	27	18	30.	Princeton

Note: Rankings with reference to physical resources for 1939 are for the institutions in column (A) and those for 1969 are for the institutions in column (B).

N.A. indicates that data either were not available or else were not reported in comparable form.

*The University of California (nine campuses) reported an endowment of $271,254,000, with no separation by institutions.

†The California system reported a total of $142,147,000 for its nine institutions.

Source: Doctoral output ranking for period ending in 1939 from Clarence S. Marsh, editor, *American Universities and Colleges,* Washington, American Council on Education, 1940, Table 13; physical resource data for same period from Henry G. Badger and others, *Abridged Statistics of Higher Education,* Washington, U.S. Dept. of the Interior, Bulletin No. 2, 1938. Data for 1967–68 rankings from Otis Singletary, editor, *American Universities and Colleges,* 10th edition, Washington, American Council on Education, 1968, and from unpublished reports in the files of the Association of American Universities.

can Men of Science. Another used a composite index of fellows of the Social Science Research Council and the National Research Council, the institutional affiliations of officers and committee members of various learned societies, and notation of the institutions where such persons took their degrees—together with other considerations—adding to a total of twenty-eight items for statistical comparison. That particular study yielded the following rank order of the sixteen leading Americn graduate centers in 1937: Harvard, Chicago, Columbia, Yale, California, Johns Hopkins, Cornell, Princeton, Michigan, Wisconsin, Pennsylvania, Minnesota, M.I.T., Illinois, Stanford, and Ohio State.[4]

Not until 1957 was another major evaluation study undertaken. Hayward Keniston at the University of Pennsylvania, which was then conducting a self-survey, wanted to ascertain how that institution's main departments were thought to compare with those at twenty-five other leading universities in the AAU. Accordingly, he queried department chairmen at those institutions, asking them to list, preferably in rank order, the fifteen strongest departments in their fields. Lists of the top twenty or so departments in the twenty-four disciplines included were published as an appendix to the Pennsylvania report.[5]

The first really comprehensive study was made in 1964–65 under the direction of Allan M. Cartter and the sponsorship of the ACE. It included a larger number of institutions (106), respondents (circa 4,000), and disciplines (30) than any of the prior inquiries, and a much more elaborate methodology. As I remarked in my Foreword to the Cartter report, the inquiry had three main purposes: 1) to bring up to date the information yielded by earlier studies; 2) to widen and improve the assessment of certain graduate programs in all major universities in the United States; and 3) to examine critically the available techniques of evaluation. The report, of course, did not claim to be anything more than a survey and analysis of informed opinion, but it also affirmed that in effect the national reputation of a department or an institution is esssentially an aggregation of individual opinions. My prediction was that Cartter's monograph would provoke a great deal of comment and discussion—and it did.[6]

In his overview, Cartter noted that foundations, government agencies, and other groups engage continuously in the assessment of educational quality. Select panels, study teams, site visits, and other procedures for making appraisals are in common use. University presidents, deans, department chairmen, and special faculty committees necessarily make comparative evaluations in allocating institutional resources. Whether rendered by individuals or by groups, the judgments on which such evaluations are based are frequently criticized as being subjective and impressionistic. There are those who argue that "hard" data about endowments, library holdings, faculty publication records, salary schedules, and educational expenditures per student are more objective indicators of quality. Admittedly, there are no universally adopted units for measuring or gauging quality in higher education. Institutions differ in role and scope, and the ingredients of excellence are not invariably additive. The California Institute of Technology has a small library and Rockefeller University (then called Rockefeller Institute) has no offerings at all in many major fields of graduate education. At the time of the Cartter study, Michigan and M.I.T. had no Nobel laureates on their faculties, and Parsons College[7] ranked next to Harvard in top faculty pay.

After using a variety of techniques for testing the reliability of his survey findings, however, Cartter concluded that "a survey based on the opinions of well-informed scholars within the academic community is as reliable a guide as one can devise in attempting to measure the elusive attribute of quality." He was understandably reluctant either to equate the importance of all disciplinary fields (e.g., Spanish and English, entomology and zoology) in aggregations to rank entire institutions, or to attach rank order of "disciplinary importance" to the relative number of doctorates granted in the various fields.

(For example, for the ten-year period ending in 1949, should chemistry have been considered more than nine times as important as classics because of proportional differences in the numbers of Ph.D.s granted, and weighted accordingly in institutional comparisons?)

Despite these complications, however, various graduate deans and others did derive institutional rankings from the Cartter report—most of which were unpublished and intended for limited circulation. The dean of the Graduate Division of the University of California at Los Angeles, H. W. Magoun, was less hesitant. He published an analysis of institutional and divisional standings compiled from the report.[8] In a footnote to his article, Dean Magoun made this comment:

> The Cartter Report's objection to overall standings obtained by summating scores rests on the presumptive ground that this might imply an equation of the importance of the subject fields involved. Additionally, it is proposed, summation would penalize an institution which did not offer work in each of the fields under review.
>
> In contrary opinion, the qualities of faculty and programs, which the report has assessed, are or should be just as important for graduate study in one field as in another. In the present article, the assessment of these qualities is considered to be quite independent of the comparative merits of the different fields. Moreover, insofar as could be determined from available catalogues, the overall standing of each institution is based on the assessment of these qualities only in fields in which graduate work was offered.

The general validity of this contention tends to minimize the significance of a division of labor between public institutions in some states, as, for example, between Indiana University and Purdue or the University of North Carolina and North Carolina State University, but Magoun appropriately stressed the importance of showing changes when he quoted Keniston's remark:

It is true that departments inevitably suffer ups and downs. A strong or a weak chairman may be the explanation of some of the shifts. But when an institution as a whole is gaining in strength, it can be explained only by the vigilance and vision of the central administrative officers, whether they are presidents or deans. The present study may be of some use to them in identifying the subjects and the divisions which need consideration.

Although institutional leadership undoubtedly affects the resources made available to a university and the use made of them in the competition for excellence, it does not determine the relative affluence or lack of it in particular geographic regions. The poverty of the South during earlier decades of the twentieth century had definite bearing on the relatively low standings of its universities,[9] and their rise in repute after their locales had become "Sunbelt states" in later years reflected to a considerable extent changes in the socioeconomic status of their region.

Regardless of the changing circumstances of regions and of the whole economy, nonetheless, many of the top-ranking universities of the nation exemplify what a leading social scientist has called "the Matthew effect."[10] As the Gospel According to St. Matthew puts it: "For unto everyone that hath shall be given, and he shall have abundance: but from him that hath not shall be taken away even that which he hath" (Matt. 13:2).

"The Matthew effect" is by and large illustrated in Table 10.3, derived from Magoun's analysis. Harvard, U.C. Berkeley, Yale, Princeton, Chicago, Michigan, Wisconsin, and Columbia in 1964 were still among the top ten universities in terms of faculty quality. Two West Coast universities, Stanford and U.C.L.A., nonetheless, had displaced two other institutions. Unlisted among the universities with top faculties in 1957, Texas, North Carolina, Brown, N.Y.U., Washington University, and Duke had joined the upper ranks in 1964.

Table 10.3 Institutional Standing in Letters and Sciences of Universities in Group A

KENISTON REPORT (1957)	CARTTER REPORT (1964)	
	Faculty	Program
1. Harvard	1. Harvard	1. Harvard
2. U.C., Berkeley	2. U.C., Berkeley	2. U.C., Berkeley
3. Columbia	3. Yale	3. Yale
4. Yale	4. Princeton	4. Princeton
5. Michigan	5. Chicago	5. Stanford
6. Chicago	6. Stanford	6. Wisconsin
7. Princeton	7. Michigan	7. Michigan
8. Wisconsin	8. Wisconsin	8. Chicago
9. Cornell	9. Columbia	9. Columbia
10. Illinois	10. U.C.L.A.	10. Cornell
11. Pennsylvania	11. Johns Hopkins	10. Johns Hopkins
12. Minnesota	12. Cornell	11. Illinois
13. Stanford	13. Illinois	12. U.C.L.A.
14. U.C.L.A.	14. Pennsylvania	13. Pennsylvania
15. Indiana	15. Minnesota	14. Minnesota
16. Johns Hopkins	16. Indiana	15. U. of Washington
17. Northwestern	17. Northwestern	16. Northwestern
18. Ohio State	18. U. of Washington	17. North Carolina
19. N.Y.U.	19. Texas	18. Texas
20. U. of Washington	20. North Carolina	19. Indiana
	21. Brown	20. Duke
	22. N.Y.U.	21. Brown
	23. Ohio State	22. Ohio State
	24. Washington U.	23. N.Y.U.
	25. Duke	24. Washington U.

Source: Magoun's "The Cartter Report on Quality in Graduate Education," p. 484.

Note: In Magoun's classification, Group A refers to the highest-rated 25 universities according to his analyses of Cartter's departmental classifications. Ties are given the same numbers. (Cartter's "Program" ratings were determined by respondents' replies to this questionnaire item: "How would you rate the institutions below if you were selecting a graduate school to work for a doctorate in your field today? Take into account the accessibility of faculty and their scholarly competence, curricula, educational and research facilities, the quality of graduate students and other factors which contribute to the *effectiveness of the doctoral program*.")

For ratings of universities in various professional fields, see Appendix E.

In more detail, Dean Magoun went on to compare the divisional strengths of universities, as shown in Table 10.4. Dean Magoun's analyses were made during the expansive years of graduate education in the mid-1960s, and he quoted President Johnson's words to the effect that half the federal expenditure for research was going to only twenty major universities, and that the number of strong centers in regions previously not well served ought to be increased. Another commentator of the time contended that the Great Society would require at least one great graduate institution for each of the nation's hundred metropolitan areas. During those boom years, however, few persons were giving close study to the matter of how many distinguished graduate centers the nation really needed, what the costs would be, and whether the required support would be forthcoming.

Moreover, aside from the National Science Foundation's program of substantial assistance to a selected group of universities in the "promising" category, not much attention was being paid by the federal government to augmenting the strengths and offsetting the weaknesses of what Magoun classified as the Group B universities, which showed up as being good but not distinguished in the Cartter report for 1964.[11] (At the same time, the federal government and some state governments were encouraging many institutions of lesser quality to establish new graduate programs.)

To give an extended time dimension to the Cartter report of 1965, the ACE had committed itself to a similar inquiry five years later, and in 1970 it brought out *A Rating of Graduate Programs* by staff members Kenneth D. Roose and Charles J. Andersen. The Roose and Andersen study enlarged the number of disciplines covered to thirty-two and shifted psychology from the biological to the social sciences in its divisional categories, but the approach in general was very much like the Cartter query in methodology and coverage.

Comparing institutional standings in 1964 with those reported for the *same* fields in letters and sciences in 1969,

Table 10.4 Ranking of Divisional Strengths in Letters and Sciences of Universities in Group A, 1964

HUMANITIES Faculty (3)	HUMANITIES Program (4)	SOCIAL SCIENCES Faculty (3)	SOCIAL SCIENCES Program (4)	LIFE SCIENCES Faculty (3)	LIFE SCIENCES Program (4)	PHYSICAL SCIENCES Faculty (3)	PHYSICAL SCIENCES Program (4)
1. Harvard	1. Yale	1. Harvard	1. Harvard	1. U.C., Berkeley	1. U.C., Berkeley	1. Harvard	1. Harvard
2. U.C., Berkeley	2. Harvard	2. U.C., Berkeley	2. U.C., Berkeley	2. Harvard	2. Harvard	2. U.C., Berkeley	2. Stanford
3. Yale	3. U.C., Berkeley	3. Chicago	3. Chicago	3. Stanford	3. Stanford	3. Princeton	2. U.C., Berkeley
4. Princeton	4. Princeton	4. Yale	4. Princeton	4. Michigan	4. Michigan	4. Stanford	3. Princeton
5. Columbia	5. Michigan	5. Princeton	5. Yale	5. Illinois	5. Wisconsin	5. Chicago	4. Wisconsin
6. Michigan	6. Columbia	6. Wisconsin	6. Wisconsin	6. Wisconsin	5. Yale	6. Yale	5. Yale
7. Chicago	7. Chicago	7. Michigan	7. Stanford	6. Yale	6. Illinois	7. Columbia	6. Chicago
8. Johns Hopkins	8. Cornell	8. Columbia	8. Michigan	7. Pennsylvania	7. Minnesota	8. Wisconsin	7. Columbia
8. Wisconsin	9. Pennsylvania	9. U.C.L.A.	9. Columbia	8. Cornell	8. Johns Hopkins	9. Michigan	8. Michigan
9. Pennsylvania	10. Wisconsin	10. Cornell	10. Northwestern	8. Johns Hopkins	9. Pennsylvania	10. Johns Hopkins	9. Johns Hopkins
10. Cornell	11. Johns Hopkins	11. Northwestern	11. Johns Hopkins	9. Princeton	10. Cornell	11. U.C.L.A.	10. Cornell
11. Stanford	12. Stanford	12. Minnesota	12. Cornell	10. Minnesota	11. U.C.L.A.	12. Illinois	11. Illinois
12. U.C.L.A.	13. North Carolina	13. Pennsylvania	13. U.C.L.A.	11. U.C.L.A.	11. U. of Washington	13. Minnesota	12. U.C.L.A.
13. Illinois	14. Illinois	14. Johns Hopkins	14. Pennsylvania	12. Columbia	12. Princeton	14. Cornell	13. U. of Washington
14. Texas	14. U.C.L.A.	15. U. of Washington	15. Minnesota	13. U. of Washington	13. Indiana	15. Northwestern	14. Minnesota
15. North Carolina	15. Indiana	16. Indiana	16. U. of Washington	14. Indiana	14. Chicago	16. Ohio State	15. Northwestern
16. Indiana	16. Texas	17. North Carolina	17. Indiana	15. Duke	15. Duke	17. Indiana	16. Indiana
17. Brown	17. Brown	18. Illinois	18. Illinois	16. Washington U.	16. Columbia	18. U. of Washington	17. N.Y.U.
18. N.Y.U.	18. Northwestern	19. Washington U.	19. Ohio State	17. Northwestern	17. Texas	19. Brown	18. Texas
19. Minnesota	19. Minnesota	20. Duke	20. Duke	18. Texas	18. Northwestern	20. N.Y.U.	19. Brown
20. U. of Washington	19. U. of Washington	21. N.Y.U.	21. N.Y.U.	19. Brown	19. Brown	20. Pennsylvania	20. Ohio State
21. Northwestern	20. Ohio State	22. Texas	21. Washington U.	20. North Carolina	20. North Carolina	21. Texas	21. Pennsylvania
22. Ohio State	21. N.Y.U.	23. Ohio State	22. Brown	21. N.Y.U.	21. Ohio State	22. Duke	22. Duke
23. Washington U.	22. Duke	24. Brown	22. Texas	22. Ohio State	22. N.Y.U.	23. North Carolina	22. Washington U.
24. Duke	23. Washington U.				23. Washington U.	24. Washington U.	23. North Carolina

Note: This table is a compression of Magoun's Tables 2, 3, 4, and 5.

one may note the rank orders (based on quality of faculty) in Table 10.4 alongside those set forth in Table 10.5, which I have derived from the Roose Andersen report. From a comparison of institutional standings in terms of faculty quality ratings, it is obvious that no very drastic changes were perceived as having occurred during the five-year period. The rankings of four institutions were the same in 1964 and 1969, nine had declined, and twelve had risen, with the change either way ranging from 4 to 12 percent. Going back to the ACE 1934 ranking of the eleven institutions with the largest number of distinguished departments, however, comparison shows that Stanford, UCLA, and Illinois had displaced three of the universities included in the preeminent group thirty-five years earlier. A few universities that were prestigious in the early part of the century, as will be recalled from the chronological sequence of admissions to the AAU, have survived but no longer even rank among the top fifty institutions.

Components of Quality

From the Cartter study, these generalizations were derived about the patterns and components of quality within and among institutions:

1. There was a moderate amount of evidence to support the view that good, strong, or distinguished departments show some tendency to cluster by divisions or allied fields. For example, no university had a distinguished department of economics that did not also have a distinguished or at least a strong political science department, and vice versa. Strengths in mathematics, chemistry, and physics appeared to be mutually reinforcing. Even so, distinguished or strong departments of mathematics at N.Y.U., German at Texas, geography at Louisiana State, philosophy at Pittsburgh, and anthropology at the University of Arizona were not flanked by other superior allied departments in their own institutions.

2. Some institutions displayed a concentration of field

Table 10.5 Institutional Standings, Letters and Sciences in Group A, 1969, by Same Divisions and Disciplines as in 1964 Report

INSTITUTIONAL STANDINGS, LETTERS & SCIENCES IN GROUP A, 1964, CARTER*	INSTITUTIONAL STANDINGS, 1969, ROOSE-ANDERSEN SURVEY				
	Humanities	Social Sciences	Life Sciences	Physical Sciences	Letters/Sci.
1. Harvard	2	1	1	1	1
2. U.C., Berkeley	1	2	2	2	2
3. Yale	3†	5	5	8	4
4. Princeton	3†	9	16	4	7†
5. Chicago	9	4	14†	5	7†
6. Stanford	5†	6	3	3	3
7. Michigan	6†	3	11	11	6
8. Wisconsin	6†	7	10	7	5
9. Columbia	8	11	21	6	12
10. U.C.L.A.	16	8	6	12	9
11. Johns Hopkins	15	15	7	14	14
12. Cornell	10	14	9	10	10
13. Illinois	14†	17	4	9	11
14. Pennsylvania	11	12	12	15	13
15. Minnesota	24	10	13	13	15
16. Indiana	12	18	17	16	16
17. Northwestern	20	13	24	18†	19†
18. U. of Washington	21	19	8	18†	17
19. Texas	13	20	20	20	18
20. North Carolina	17	16	23	25	21
21. Brown	18	21	19	17	19†
22. N.Y.U.	19	25	22	22	24
23. Ohio State	22†	23	25	21	25
24. Washington U.	22†	24	18	23†	23
25. Duke	25	22	14†	23†	22

*Standings in 1964 and 1969 based on quality of faculty.
†Tie is nob.

interest and effort. Six of Chicago's eight departments in the social sciences were rated distinguished, and its institutional rank by quality of faculty was third, whereas in life sciences its rank was tenth. M.I.T. had seven of its nine distinguished ratings in engineering and the physical sciences. (M.I.T., of course, like Cal. Tech., is a specialized type of institution.)

3. The top ten universities had a heavy concentration of national fellowship holders who would be accepted by the institutions of their choice.

4. In the matter of geographic distribution of institutional eminence, distinguished departments were to be found mainly in thirteen states, with 80 percent of them in only five states. The Northeast was the most overrepresented, and the Southeast and Rocky Mountain states the most underrepresented.

5. The price tag for high quality was greater than for average quality in faculty salaries and income per student. Large universities (30,000 or more students) appeared better able to achieve distinction with only average per-student income than were those with smaller total enrollments. Economies of scale were fairly marked in increased enrollments up to 20,000, but beyond this point were much less evident.

6. With regard to minimum and optimum sizes for departments, the dearth of university cost data collections by departments made generalizations uncertain, but it was noted that an outstanding physics department of relatively small size appeared to require at least six to eight outstanding senior physicists, an excellent research library, and expensive equipment. A department five times larger and of equal quality would not necessarily require a multiplication of these factors by five.

7. As to library resources, no other single nonhuman factor was as closely associated with high quality in graduate education. All institutions with superior offerings in all areas had major national research libraries. The top seventeen universities (not including the three leading science and technol-

ogy institutions) averaged 2.7 million volumes in their hold-ings, whereas the bottom twenty averaged 465,000.

8. Both faculty and student honors, awards, and special recognitions were proportionally much more numerous in the leading universities.

Although the outside support of graduate school en-deavor increased and interinstitutional competition intensified between 1965 and 1969, the overall rankings of institutions did not change markedly. The Roose-Anderson study showed a somewhat higher proportion of faculties in 1969 to be at least adequate for their advanced assignments, and also larger percentages were rated as strong or distinguished. The South, in particular, had moved forward qualitatively to the point that 73 percent of the rated university faculties were considered to be adequate or better, compared with an earlier 58 percent.

Even so, in both studies about 70 percent of all the faculties in disciplines common to both studies were rated at 2.0, or "adequate plus," and few of the faculties being scored for the first time were rated high. The proportion of programs in the top group remained relatively constant, but of those in the bottom group improvement was more noticeable than de-terioration. The Northeast still led other regions in quality, but its share of excellence was reduced somewhat, with in-creased shares being more marked in the South and West.

Incidentally, in the Roose-Andersen study, respondents were asked to rate particular programs in individual institu-tions as "better than 5 years ago," "little changed in last 4 years," or "worse than 5 years ago" when they had sufficient information to judge. Most of the favorable judgments were ascribed to an increase in the perceived quality of the graduate faculty.

The Importance of Departmental Productivity

What has been observed about the prestige of major universi-ties makes it evident that their academic standings are determined in the main by their productivity in scholarship and science. Institutional eminence is thus an aggregative phenomenon resulting largely from the cumulative contributions to the advancement of knowledge made within disciplinary departments. The prestige of departments within a university relates directly, in turn, to the institution's material and human resources, and its demonstrated capacity to recognize, attract, retain, and encourage creative talent. We have noticed that such factors as faculty salary scales and library holdings are closely associated with variations in levels of accomplishment, and that basic evaluations of productivity are made by scholars and scientists themselves. In the next chapter attention will be directed to who does the appraising and how, the prevailing modes of recognition and reward, the norms shaping research endeavor, and how determinations are reached about what is important and what unimportant.

Since contributions to the advancement of knowledge are not only numerous but also widely scattered in time and place, it is obvious that the results of inquiry must be communicated to be of any value. Less formal modes of communication are not unimportant, of course, yet the "publish or perish" dictum is as essential to the forward movement of systematic research as it is to recognition of the individual researcher. Despite overemphasis here and there on sheer quantity of output, moreover, there is apparently some necessity for a critical mass of activity to yield high quality of output at the top.

As Carter noted in his 1965 study, the repute and publication productivity of departments show some variation by fields. The association of the two is less close in English, for example, than in the social or physical sciences; highly productive scholars in English literature are occasionally found in smaller colleges and lesser universities, whereas well-known economists or physicists are seldom situated outside the leading universities. His general conclusion, however, was that the most productive scholars and scientists are concentrated in the leading departments, which in turn are mostly in the more prestigious institutions, with comparatively little productivity to be observed at the other extreme.

In his *Little Science, Big Science* (New York, Columbia University Press, 1963), Derek J. de Solla Price refers to Alfred J. Lotka's pioneer investigation of eminence which led to the formulation of an inverse-square law of productivity, that is, the number of people producing n papers is in the proportion of $1/n$, with about one-third of the literature and less than one-tenth of the researchers in a given field associated with high scores. Price goes on to remark:

> About this process there is the same sort of essential, built-in *undemocracy* that gives us a nation of cities rather than a country steadily approximating a state of uniform population density. Scientists tend to congregate in fields, in institutions, in countries, and in the use of certain journals. They do not spread out uniformly, however desirable that may or may not be. In particular, the growth is such as to keep relatively constant the balance between the few giants and the mass of pygmies. The number of giants grows so much more slowly than the entire population that there must be more and more pygmies per giant, deploring their own lack of stature and wondering why it is that neither man nor nature pushes us toward more egalitarian uniformity. [p. 59]

Within the last several decades there have been a number of intensive studies of the productivity of academics in various disciplines. The American Psychological Association in 1952 initiated "a major investigation of a number of interrelated questions of psychological personnel, education, and employment, and an appraisal of the state of development" in that field, under the direction of Kenneth E. Clark.[12] Albert Somit and Joseph Tanenhaus have published a similar inquiry about political science.[13] Following publication of the Cartter report, more than a dozen articles on various aspects of prestige and competition in the field of sociology appeared in publications of the American Sociological Association. From these different approaches, the following conclusions emerge:

1. In the main, the prestige or perceived qualitative differences among departments of sociology correspond fairly closely to "objective measures" of similarities and dissimilarities.

2. The leading departments tend to cluster in the more prestigious institutions and to attract a disproportionate share of the abler sociologists, who in turn attract a high proportion of the most promising graduate students. (The Matthew effect.)

3. In terms of department size, a minimum "critical mass" of faculty is apparently necessary for substantive coverage and accomplishment in view of one finding that a decrease in department size was correlated with a diminution of quality ranging downward from an average of 20.8 members in distinguished departments to 8.3 members in the "other" or lowest category.

4. Faculty "stars" enhance the prestige of individual departments more than does "good" performance by the majority of their members.

5. Prestigious departments initially recruit mostly their own graduates or those of other prestigious departments.

6. The most productive sociologists manifest this propensity early in their careers; correspondingly, slow starters seldom gather much momentum in later years.

7. Sheer quantity of published output by departments and individuals in the field of sociology influences appraisals more than it does in such fields as mathematics, physics, and the "exact" sciences.

Still other studies have been made of productivity and high-level research activity in such disciplines as chemistry and physics. They have found that in these fields the most significant research tends to be concentrated in particular universities, rather than in college or nonacademic research laboratories, and in academia rather than in industry or government. In both fields some of the most prolific producers also tend to author the most significant papers. Jonathan R. Cole and Stephen Cole have noted, for example, through an analysis of the 1965 *Science Citation Index,* that 60 percent of the eighty-four most frequently cited physicists were situated in the top nine departments, and that 43 percent of them had sixty or more citations each as contrasted with only 8 percent of a sample of 1,308 university physicists.[14]

Although these miscellaneous findings demonstrate a quite noticeable stratification by performance levels among universities and departments in the realm of scholarship and science, it should be acknowledged that there is still no universally accepted definition of "quality" and no single yardstick for measuring it. An extended recent inquiry in the field of psychology, for example, questions the validity of ratings based on reputation and opinion. It has ranked institutional programs according to the frequency of publication of their faculties in the thirteen journals sponsored by the American Psychological Association to derive a composite rating and separate ratings by major subfields.[15]

For the period from 1970 to 1975, the authors noted that average annual rejection rates of the thirteen journals rose from 66.6 percent to 76.4 percent, and they assumed that all of the published articles met "high standards of research and scholarship." This is a reasonable assumption, of course, but it does introduce editorial judgment as a subjective element, and their procedure of "measuring" productivity gives equal weight to all published items. However this may be, the authors did show that there are marked differences among departmental rankings from one area of specialization to another, and that discrepancies are frequently to be observed between their own "objective" rankings and the subjective rankings of the Roose-Andersen survey. In terms of reputational standings, they found that a number of older departments in private universities were overrated, whereas the opposite was true of newer departments in many public universities.

From the perspective of public interest, it is unfortunate that no definite answers can be given to many questions concerning the costs and benefits derived from the competition of universities and their departments for recognition and acclaim. Various regions of the United States have unquestionably benefited from improvements in the quality of their graduate centers, and a wider recognition of the importance of research productivity to the forward movement of society has undoubtedly been worthwhile. The extent to which this diffusion has also entailed trade-offs at the expense of established centers has not yet been determined. To use Derek Price's analogy, there is a great deal that we do not know about what the relationship is or ought to be between the "pygmies" and the "giants" in intellectual enterprise.

As the economist Kenneth Boulding has pointed out, [16] one of the problems of education in general is that we cannot measure all of the returns from various modes of utilizing our intellectual resources or even spell out the production function of much intellectual activity. Colleges and universities are typically nonprofit institutions, deriving most of their support from the grants sector of the economy, producing some outcomes which have no obvious prices in the marketplace, and yielding intangible dividends. Although the price of competitive excellence may appear to be high, the cost of neglect and a collective lapse into mediocrity of performance would undoubtedly dull the cutting edge of creative scholarship and science in this nation and impede the forward thrust of our whole society.

11

Individual Prestige and Competition

Evidence already presented clearly indicates that most academics give more time to teaching than to research and scholarly writing. Although the assigned teaching loads of those employed in universities normally allow ample time for research, the majority consider teaching to be more important than research and believe that their services should be evaluated primarily in terms of their teaching effectiveness. Except in major universities, many professors neither "publish nor perish," and it is obvious that their local recognition and rewards as faculty members do not depend significantly upon their contributions to the enlargement and improvement of knowledge in their fields.

The wider repute of academics, however, is another matter. The extent to which they are valued on their campuses may have little bearing on their standing in wider circles, and only the more exceptional among them gain the recognition and rewards accorded for creativity in scholarship and science. The ways in which exceptional academics differ from the majority in native ability, motivation, drive, and opportunity are not always specifiable, of course, but in recent years systematic inquiry into this whole matter has revealed certain characteristics of the scholarly and scientific elites of academe.

Even though money does count in academe, it has less significance as a denominator of individual success than it does in the realm of commerce and industry. This being true, it is important to know what the common denominators of achievement are among academics. How is "success" perceived? In what ways do the behavior patterns of highly creative academics differ from those of average members of the profession? How do academics gain recognition in their fields, and what kinds of prestige symbols are attached to unusual accomplishments? Who are the referees and "gatekeepers" in the elaborated system of honors and awards? What values and norms influence individual competition?

Indicators of Prestige

The desire for visibility and recognition is not confined to competition in the university sphere alone, to be sure, and ambitious scholars and scientists are probably no more vainglorious than the doers in many other fields. Despite the egalitarianism of our era, society still places a high premium on many forms of individual accomplishment. Someone has estimated that there are in this country almost 750 halls of fame to "enshrine" an astonishing variety of individual achievements, and even public malefactors may achieve the backhanded compliment of notoriety.

Excepting the Nobel laureates and a few others, however, outstanding academics seldom get much public acclaim and rarely become popular celebrities. They are judged mainly by their peers, and their accomplishments may be unappreciated outside their areas of specialization. Although this lack of popular acclaim probably does not bother most of the high achievers, their endeavors are by no means private concerns. They are impelled to make known their research results not just to satisfy their egos, but to augment the common fund of human knowledge and understanding. Communicating the outcomes of inquiries has long been recognized as an obligation of scholars and scientists because of its indispensable function in the advancement of learning.

Mainly through publication, the works of academics and other researchers become known and their authors are evaluated as contributors. In connection with his *American Men of Science,* James McKeen Cattell, a noted psychologist of the early twentieth century, undertook a statistical study of those scientists who were reputed by fellow specialists to be outstanding.[1] Some years after Cattell's study, when I became interested in prestige patterns in scholarship and science, I followed up Cattell's investigations and made an inquiry based on queries to a large sample of academics and others in twelve different fields: biology, botany, chemistry, economics, English, history, mathematics, philosophy, physics, political science, psychology, and sociology.[2] My purpose was to find out which living persons were thought to have made the most valuable contributions in those fields, why they were so considered, and how criteria and distributions varied among different categories of respondents from one discipline to another.

Although I ascertained that the amount of consensus differed from one field to another, there was a high percentage of agreement in each specialty regarding the most eminent contributors, with physicists showing the most consensus and English scholars the least. Respondents in the physical sciences tended to single out their confreres for discoveries and inventions stemming from experimental work, whereas the humanists and social scientists paid more attention to breadth of scholarship and volume of publication output.

That eminence tends to come late in life for most scholars and scientists was suggested by the fact that the average age of the 256 leading persons in all fields ws 62.5. Incidentally, of the 256 individuals ranked among the top twenty in their fields, 238 were in the employ of colleges and universities, and 73.9 percent of the latter were concentrated in ten institutions.

Then as now, of course, academics were judged largely by the recognition resulting from what they had to communicate to others and how it was evaluated by informed specialists. Since most of the scholarly and scientific media, such as the learned journals, have rather high rejection rates, the mere appearance in print of a paper or the invitational presentation of one at an important professional meeting is some indication that experienced evaluators considered the contribution to be worthy of further attention. Numerous publications by the same author, in turn, may earn a high "productivity" rating when sheer numbers of titles are counted to arrive at quantitative appraisals.

Realizing that this measure of productivity can be quite misleading, various researchers have attempted to devise weighting procedures to obviate some of its obvious shortcomings. A short research note may count for less than a full-length article, and an article in a leading journal for more than one in a lesser journal. The quantifying evaluators may consider a book to be the equivalent of "x" number of articles, with a theoretical or research monograph being given a heavier weighting than a textbook, and a textbook more than an edited collection.

A further refinement of the last two decades is the citation measure of productivity as exemplified in the *Science Citation Index,* originated in 1961 by the National Science Foundation, the National Institutes of Health, and the Institute for Scientific Information, which in 1964 covered 700 journals in fifty different fields. Although this index has its imperfections, citation data do afford presumptive indication of the influence of an author and strongly suggest a correlation with quality in his cited work.

As we have noted, institutions vie with one another to attract the high achievers to their faculties, and because the more prestigious universities benefit from their bargaining positions they generally can offer more than the lesser universities. Thus, an individual's occupancy of a post in a renowned institution is in itself an indicator of at least some prestige. The exceptional performers also are more likely than the average to be appointed to important national committees and boards; to be named to offices in the learned and professional societies; to be chosen for membership in a very selective academy of luminaries; and to receive medals, prizes, and honorific awards as symbols of prestigious recognition in the domain of scholarship and science.

Characteristics of the High Achievers

Social scientists in recent decades have inquired extensively into the circumstances relating to outstanding professional achievement. Attention is usually focused on eminent scholars and scientists who are matched, for controlled comparisons, with less renowned academics with regard to social origins, intelligence, formal education backgrounds, work habits, occupational positions, and publication records.

As to social origins, the high achievers tend to come from more advantaged socio-economic backgrounds than do most professors. A study of eminent physicists and biologists showed, for example, that more than half of them came from upper-class, white-collar, professional, and business families. Zuckerman's findings about the backgrounds of Nobel laureates were quite similar, with the largest single proportion of them having professionals as fathers, but with very few coming from opulent families.[3]

Although there is a predisposition among some social scientists to play down the significance of differences in native ability or talent and to play up social determinism in accounting for stratification, virtually all of the research into scholarly and scientific eminence recognizes the importance of "innate" ability as a factor in creativity. In their book on stratification in science (pp. 68–72), the Coles considered it to be the most obvious factor, and held that a scientist's success or failure is determined largely by intellectual capability. Where information is available about intelligence test scores, IQ standings are reported as being high. Bayer, Folger, and others, however, have been unable to establish meaningful correlations between IQ scores and output among productive scientists. One of the difficulties is that the intelligence tests thus far devised are poor instruments for getting at the "creativity," motivations, and stamina of those being tested.

Most studies of the educational backgrounds of high achievers show that in some fields they developed their interests early and persisted in them, and that in the main the departments in which they specialized for advanced-level training were of high quality. Since high quality departments attract a disproportionately large share of the ablest students, however, the greater productivity of their graduates may be "a function of ability rather than simply a function of the educational experience."[4]

For the highest-level achievers in American science, the Nobel laureates, Zuckerman found that about 60 percent of them had their baccalaureate degrees from Ivy League colleges (25.3 percent), other elite colleges (4.2 percent), or from the undergraduate colleges of top universities (29.4 percent). They were all products of the graduate schools of twenty-one universities, and forty-eight of the total ninety-two Nobel laureates who had done their prizewinning research in the United States by 1972 had worked at one time or another during their student years, or later as postdoctorates and junior collaborators, under one or more Nobel laureates. Twenty-five more of the American Nobel winners had worked under eminent scientists who were members of the National Academy of Science but had not received Nobel awards. These findings seem to make it evident that the highest-level achievers often perform important teaching functions for the potentially creative, and that the significance of the traditional master-apprentice relationship is wrongly slighted by those educational enthusiasts who frequently endorse mass production techniques of higher learning.

As to the work habits of the creative, we have already noted that productive scholars and scientists, of whatever repute, simply spend more time engaged in research than do most academics. Close inquiry into the behavior of those who achieve renown reveals that many have been hardworking to the extent of appearing to be obsessed with their tasks. The physical scientists, in particular, have been described as being less gregarious than many of their colleagues and more autonomous in their activities. Robert K. Merton has pointed out, in referring to James Watson's *The Double Helix* and to the career patterns of many other notables in the pantheon of science, that the high achievers are often intense competitors with strong desires to gain "reassurance by recognition" of their work.[5]

In the matter of occupational placement, the scholars and scientists who later become most prominent are likely to take their Ph.D.s at earlier ages than most academics, more likely to begin publishing even before obtaining their doctorates, and more likely to obtain their first posts in prestigious universities. Such initial placement, of course, frequently means lighter teaching loads, more stimulating colleagues, and better facilities for research and other creative activity. The equally able who are less advantaged at the start inevitably must overcome more obstacles to attain academic visibility, recognition, and reward. Open competition gives impermanence to all starting statuses, however, and thereafter what happens to young academics relates closely to what they are able to make of themselves in their careers.

Publication Media

Admittedly, those academics who are handicapped locally by meager library resources for many kinds of research in the humanities, inadequate facilities for much creative work in the sciences and engineering, lack of funds for research assistance and travel, and so on, are seriously impeded, but the publication media of scholarship and science are freely open to all. Moreover, virtually all of the manuscripts submitted to learned journals must undergo similar processes of review, so that a significant contribution from an unknown author stands a better chance of getting into print and being recognized for its worth than does something of low quality from a well-known figure.

Even though many academics complain about the paucity of publication outlets for their writings, it was estimated in 1962 that in science fields alone there were some 30,000 periodicals throughout the world, with a total output of six million papers.[6] *Ulrich's International Periodical Dictionary, 1975–1976* shows that on a worldwide basis there were 330 periodicals in sociology, 480 for chemistry, and 250 for philosophy. A report from the editor of the *American Sociological Review* during 1975–76 showed that it published only 154—roughly 15 percent—of the 1,056 items submitted, and one may suspect that in this field and others complaints about the inadequate number of outlets may emanate largely from those who experience rejections. (Still others complain, oppositely, about the superfluity of material of mediocre quality which does get into print from academe.)

However this may be, the rising costs of publication have caused some university presses to fold and others to cut back, many learned journals to reduce the number of pages per issue (e.g., *PMLA* and the *American Political Science Review*) and to request "processing fees" from contributors, and so on. Widespread efforts by publishers to cut costs and increase marketability may mean not only fewer papers and books, but also shorter ones, with less footnoting, shorter bibliographies, and more concise styles of writing. These trends dismay some of the expositors, but my guess is that a good many readers of academic discourses will not regard the outcome as altogether disastrous.

The number of journal publications varies considerably by fields, as does the number of academics in the diverse disciplines; the American Psychological Association, for example, publishes thirteen periodicals and the American Sociological Association five. Regarding book production, economics and sociology led the fields in 1975 with 5,219 titles, while "science" (not including medical science and technology) brought forth 2,461 titles, and history 1,119. Proportionally more of the items published in hard science fields, to be sure, are published in article, abstract, or note form than is the case in the social sciences and humanities. Note should also be made that in those subfields where knowledge is advancing very rapidly, specialists interested in communicating quickly with their peers and in getting prompt reactions may form "invisible colleges" which are often initiated by an eminent figure who facilitates informal meetings and furthers the circulation of preprint papers within limited circles.

Honors and Awards

Most academics with high prestige have published extensively and have been cited frequently, but by no means do all of the prolific publishers achieve the most coveted honors and awards. Studying the relationship between the quantity and quality of scientific output of 120 university physicists, two investigators arrived at this conclusion:

> Although these two variables are highly correlated, some physicists produce many papers of little significance and others produce a few papers of great significance. The responses of the community of physicists to these distinct patterns of research publication were investigated. Quality of output is more significant than quantity in eliciting recognition through the receipt of awards, appointment to prestigious academic departments, and being widely known to one's colleagues. The reward system operates to encourage creative scientists to be highly productive, to divert the energies of less

creative physicists into other channels, and to produce a higher correlation between quantity and quality of output in the top departments than in the weaker departments.[7]

Although less consensus exists in many other fields than in physics about what constitutes high quality of output, and as a consequence less likelihood that it will be unmistakenly differentiated from quantity, studies of productivity and recognition in other disciplines demonstrate a correlation between quality and quantity. Among those referees who make the judgments determining the bestowal of nationally and internationally significant honors and awards, some of the special recognitions they accord are for spectacular discoveries or single achievements, but most are given as symbols of esteem for prolonged efforts and cumulative achievements.

An individual's visibility and recognition are largely the cumulative product of what other individuals know about his or her work and how they regard it, but the formal recognition gained through honors and awards is accorded institutionally, and usually in a ceremonial way. Honorary degrees, for example, are normally granted only at commencement exercises where there is an emphasis on pomp and circumstance; medals and prizes are customarily given out at banquets or other special occasions where spectators are assembled to join in the plaudits. On such occasions, outstanding academics may find themselves sharing the podium with others who are being honored for reasons having little to do with intellectual achievement, but professors are more often than not singled out solely on the basis of their contributions to scholarship and science.

One investigator has divided honors and awards into two prestige categories.[8] The higher category includes presidencies of national scholarly organizations and professional associations; membership in such highly selective organizations as the National Academy of Sciences, the National Academy of Engineering, and the American Academy of Arts and Letters; honorary degrees from institutions that did not graduate

the recipients and do not currently employ them; and, to top
the list, the Nobel Prize. In the lower prestige category are
awards from Guggenheim, Rockefeller, National Research
Council, National Science Foundation, the Center for Advanced Study in the Behavioral Sciences, and so on. Also included in the second category are lesser prizes, service on
government advisory boards, and membership in study sections or committees and on the editorial boards of journals. In
addition, there is mention of holding endowed chairs, being
named to distinguished lectureships, and being starred for unusual distinction in *American Men and Women of Science.*

It should be noted, however, that there is no pronounced consensus among academics about the degrees of
prestige associated with the great variety of recognitions and
awards. Within the forty years after his Nobel award, Harold
Urey received twenty-one prizes and twenty-three honorary
degrees, but the Coles found that of 632 physicists employed
by the top twenty departments in 1960, only one-third mentioned any award in their *American Men of Science* listings.

The inclusiveness of membership in the professional
associations stands in marked contrast with the exclusiveness
of the honorific organizations. By 1970, for example, the
Modern Language Association had 33,340 members and the
Americn Chemical Society 114,323. About that time the
American Academy of Arts and Letters had 50 members; in
1977 the National Academy of Science had a membership of
1,219; and in 1975 the National Academy of Engineering had
a roster of 571. From these figures, it is obvious that the most
prestigious recognitions in academe are not widely distributed
and that rigorous modes of selection are employed in singling
out those individuals to be honored.

Referees and Gatekeepers

Although a creative mathematician, novelist, or philosopher
may need only pencil, paper, and a quiet place to work to

become intellectually productive, most academics require something more substantial in the way of encouragement and support. That inquiries are not shoestring operations is suggested by the National Science Foundation's report that in 1975 research spending in the nation's top twenty universities alone amounted to $1,225,338,000. Physical scientists and engineers often must have expensive apparatus and teams of research assistants to conduct their enterprises, and it is no wonder that federal agencies have come to supply more than 70 percent of all university research funding, with foundations also making substantial contributions.[9] Most universities also have their own earmarked funds for faculty research, but these tend to be much more limited and usually for modest grants to individuals (particularly in the arts and humanities) whose projects are less likely to attract outside support.

Except in special cases, granting agencies do not solicit proposals or attempt to direct inquiry. Until recently, moreover, most researchers in favored fields experienced few difficulties in gaining support. Even so, the requests have always been more numerous than the grants, and granting agencies of all kinds have long made use of referees and gatekeepers to help determine who gets what. With the competition for funds becoming more intense, it should not be surprising, as Daniel S. Greenberg has observed, that

> . . . the granting business is probably one of the most nerve-racking, doubt-ridden activities going today. The big private foundations, such as Ford and Rockefeller, periodically go through self-induced upheavals concerning their general priorities and specific choices; at the same time, the federal government's big givers, mainly the National Science Foundation and the National Institutes of Health, endlessly engage in introspection about their methods for deciding who gets what. Meanwhile, in a world where performance and paycheck are standard for most jobs, the grant protrudes as an oddity somewhat akin to found money.[10]

In general, federal agencies have elaborate screening procedures. The National Science Foundation uses both peer-review panels and outside readers for judging requests, with usually three to five scientists, drawn mostly from major university faculties, evaluating applications for grants and fellowships and ranking those found meritorious. Program officers also mail out applications to special readers who make recommendations. NSF program officers next make their decisions on the basis of panel recommendations and pass them on to program managers for final action.

Even more ramified is the NIH review system. A series of study sections consisting of twelve to fifteen scientists, chosen as experts in a field, meet from time to time to discuss all applications within their area. Typically approving about half of the applications, they then pass them on to the next review level, comprised of statutory councils of science and lay members who consider the relevance of the proposals to NIH objectives and then make advisory recommendations to program officers.

Although these federal agencies rotate their advisory groups and attempt to make them fairly representative of the scientific community, the expertise on which they must draw is, of course, not evenly spread everywhere, and awarding grants on a merit basis inevitably funnels a high proportion of funds to the faculties of those universities where research productivity is most evident. As one might expect, this causes some members of Congress to make noises about inbreeding and favoritism, and to attempt, from time to time, to politicize the process. Likewise, some institutional groups, such as the Americn Association of Community and Junior Colleges and the American Association of State Colleges and Universities, feel slighted by what they perceive as an oligarchy and press for more equable modes of distributing public funds for research.[11]

Those academics most actively engaged in research, however, seem to believe that the established system is preferable to any alternatives at hand. They like the fact that it is highly competitive and reasonably insulated against political interference, and that it uses experts to judge proposals in terms of their merit. They believe that validation of the process has been demonstrated in evaluative studies conducted by the Rand Corporation and other independent agencies. Several such studies have shown that articles published as a result of agency-funded inquiries have higher citation rates than those published as outcomes of proposals turned down but carried forward by investigators through other means.

Referees and gatekeepers play important roles not only in determining who gets what for the funding of research, but also in deciding which reported results get published. In addition to employing their own editors, learned journals, university presses, and commercial publishers make use of consultants and special advisers to arrive at judgments on what to put into print. Everybody is aware, to be sure, that a great quantity of academic writing does get published, but there is less awareness that an even greater quantity of scholarly and scientific writing is rejected.

The significance of status-judges such as editors and referees is suggested in a compilation of rejection rates made by Zuckerman and Merton from a study of eighty-three journals in the humanities, social and behavioral sciences, mathematics, and the physical sciences. For the year 1967, they ascertained that the mean rejection rate in terms of percentages ranged progressively upward from fifty in mathematics and statistics to ninety in history, and downward from forty-eight in anthropology to twenty in linguistics.[12]

As Zuckerman and Merton point out, "Status-judges are integral to any system of social control through their evaluation of role-performance and their allocation of rewards for that performance. They influence the motivation to maintain or to raise standards of performance."[13] The authors further noted a high degree of concurrence among judges, a functional importance attached to the *imprimatur* of leading journals, and some interesting similarities as well as differences regarding the whole process from field to field and journal to journal.

The institutions that signalize outstanding scholars and scientists by naming them to membership or bestowing special honors and awards are too numerous and varied to generalize about here, but brief mention will be made of the National Academy of Sciences, one of the nation's oldest and most prestigious. Touching upon the matter of election to that body, its president commented in a recent annual report:

> The external world views us with a cocked eyebrow. Egalitarianism and populism are in flood. There are those who would urge upon us public nomination of candidates for membership in the Academy. . . . There are . . . those who would have the membership of the Academy reflect the proportion of various groups within the population; by states, by sex, by ethnic groups. And there are those who consider the Academy to be an elitist relic of the past.
>
> Perhaps so. . . . But the hallmark of the Academy must continue to be excellence in all things and we must, above all else, retain our single criterion for election. We do believe that in science the best is vastly more important than the next best.

In his article, "National Academy of Sciences: How the Elite Choose Their Peers,"[14] Philip M. Boffey quotes these remarks, describes the very involved sifting mechanism employed by the Academy, then notes how selection of members "in recognition of their distinguished and continuing achievements in original research" yields a roster consisting primarily of "post-middle-aged white males from a relatively small number of elite institutions" concentrated in the Northeast, in one section of the Midwest, and in the state of California.

Values and Norms

From what has been noted about the individual prestige, it might appear that its meaning can be described only in operational terms—that is, by describing the scholarly and scientific competition in which scholars and scientists engage, or the sifting and sorting mechanisms used to determine who excels whom, and then pointing to the "winners." But even the National Academy of Sciences, with its elaborate procedures for selecting members, has no specified guidelines setting forth just what criteria scientists must meet in order to qualify; and the same is true of many other institutions which single out the high achievers designated for special recognition.

It is obvious, however, that not all kinds of successful accomplishment are equally valued. Because of the probability that basic or "pure" research will have greater theoretical significance in the development of a field, it tends in general to be more highly regarded among academics than does applied research. Medical scientists thus like to think that what they are doing is more important for the advancement of medicine than are the daily rounds of the surgeons and physicians, even though the practitioners are indispensable in patient care, better paid, and highly respected by the public at large.

Pedestrian approaches to the solution of trivial problems, regardless of volume of output, never get the kudos accorded for the imaginative and ingenious solution of difficult and important problems. Thus scholars and scientists, in their overall scheme of recognition and reward, manifestly place a high value on the originality and significance of contributions. For the individual researcher, discovery and invention entail getting there first with new conceptions and gaining a priority not only of accomplishment but also of acclaim. The replicators perform useful but less prestigious functions.

Jonathan R. Cole has questioned the so-called Ortega hypothesis which holds that the multitudinous minor contributions by average scientists make possible the crowning achievements of the most creative and renowned. He has observed from an empirical study in the field of physics that the hypothesis simply is not borne out. His data support the view that the physicists who produce important discoveries are most influenced by and depend almost wholly on the research produced by a relatively small number of scientists. He goes on to point out that this raises questions about the number of scientists needed to support the current rate of advance in science, and about whether, if means could be found to identify the best individual prospects at an early age, large numbers of researchers are really needed. His conclusion, however, is that an egalitarian ideology of science upholds collective endeavor, and that since the outcomes of engagement for all scientists involve elements of uncertainty, maintaining widespread commitments to instrumental goals may ultimately count in the historical development of science.[15] To this conclusion, I would add the reminder that in physics, as in all other disciplines, the main function performed by most academics is that of diffusing rather than advancing knowledge.

Although the logical rigor and methodological precision required of all researchers in such a field as physics facilitate comparison of individual achievements, multidisciplinary comparisons of the kind just cited are apparently fraught with more uncertainties. In some fields it is undoubtedly more difficult than in others to perceive clear-cut demarcations of quality performance, and it is perhaps not just by chance that there have been more studies of prestige patterns in the sciences than in the arts and humanities. (Chapter 6 on status appraisal has set forth many of the problems of equating varied forms of faculty accomplishment among the diverse professionals of any given university.)

Whatever the research fields may be, however, academics are expected to conform to certain norms of behavior. As Robert K. Merton has noted, universalism prescribes that performance should be judged by the same standards of scholarship and science everywhere. The prescriptive norm of disinterestedness requires a commitment to the advancement of knowledge rather than to personal self-interest or pecuniary profit as the basis for decisions, and the norm of organized skepticism requires suspension of judgment about a contribution until the facts are at hand. Communality (or "communism" as Merton terms it) means that the results of inquiry must be fully disclosed and made readily available.[16]

As studies about researchers have demonstrated, there is an authority structure in the world of scholarship and science. Someone has remarked that there is no democracy, in the political sense of the term, in the field of physics, where it cannot be reasonably argued that "some second-rate guy has as much right to an opinion as a Fermi." Yet, it is important to know that such authority has to be earned; it is ascribed only after the fact of individual achievement and can be accorded only by those who can appreciate its meaning. In this critical respect, scholarship and science are indeed organized as an open social system.

All of the competitors in this system are afforded the satisfaction of participation in a collective undertaking of unbounded social significance. And regardless of their creative accomplishments as advancers of knowledge, all academics can experience the rewards of cultivating the minds of others, and thus also make their contributions to the higher learning. It is no wonder, then, that most academics find both challenges and rewards in their chosen profession.

Appendix A

Faculty Tenure and Contract Systems:
1972 and 1974 Highlights

Extent of Tenure

There has been no overall change between 1972 and 1974 in the general prevalence of tenure systems. Tenure systems are nearly universal among universities and four-year colleges and are found in about two-thirds of two-year institutions. Of the institutions utilizing a term or contract system of faculty appointment, very few (2.5 percent) reported any plans to establish a tenure system.

Between 1972 and 1974, there has been an upward shift in the percentage of full-time faculty holding tenure. By 1974, 59 percent of those institutions with tenure systems reported that half or more of their full-time faculty held tenure (compared to 43 percent in 1972).

Tenure Awards and Contract Renewals

As compared to 1972 data, somewhat fewer of those faculty formally considered for tenure in 1973–74 actually received tenure. Percentage differences were small, however.

Two-thirds of the institutions with tenure systems reported that they had renewed 80 percent or more of their term contracts expiring during the 1973–74 academic year (other than those whose renewal would confer tenure).

Of the institutions operating under term-contract systems in 1973–74, almost all (93 percent) had reappointed 90 percent or more of their faculty.

Probationary Periods under Tenure Systems

As in 1972, almost all tenure institutions have probationary periods, and two-year institutions reported shorter maximum periods for probation than did four-year colleges and universities.

There is some shift toward longer probationary periods for tenure. Four-year colleges and universities, particularly those under public control, showed the greatest amount of change.

In 1974, contracts during the probationary period were still typically for terms of one year. However a small shift can be noted toward two- or three-year contracts, primarily at four-year institutions.

Four-year colleges also reported an increase in the number of years of prior service creditable to the probationary period.

Review and Appeal Procedures

A third of institutions with tenure systems had made changes in their review policies during the previous two years. Further reviews of tenure systems were currently under way, particularly among public universities.

As was true in 1972, close to half of all institutions always provided written reasons to a faculty member when tenure was denied or a contract was not renewed. Only a small proportion never gave written reasons.

Appendix B

Summary of the Forty-seven Recommendations of the
Commission on Academic Tenure in Higher Education

1. Academic tenure, because of its value in maintaining academic freedom and faculty quality, should be recognized as fundamental and strengthened by all institutions.

2. The faculty should play a major role in developing an institution's tenure policies by recommending them for administrative review and adoption by the board.

3. Nontenured faculty members should be consulted in connection with decisions on reappointment and tenure.

4. Students should participate—but not have a controlling role—in making recommendations on faculty appointment, reappointment, and tenure.

5. Administrators should emphasize their role in ensuring that a formal and appropriate personnel policy is developed and kept under review, and should give special attention to faculty responsibility for maintaining high professional standards.

6. Governing boards should insist on strong personnel policies and should require regular reports on the institution's staffing plan.

In 1972, procedures for appealing adverse decisions had been available at almost all institutions with tenure systems, but at few institutions with contract systems. By 1974, most contract institutions—especially the private four-year colleges and public two-year colleges—had modified their procedures to allow faculty members to appeal adverse contract decisions.

(Source: Elaine H. El-Khawas and W. Todd Furniss, *Faculty Tenure and Contract Systems: 1972 and 1974,* Washington, D.C., American Council on Education, 1974.)

7. System-wide personnel policies should be stated in general terms, giving individual institutions maximum latitude.

8. In statewide or multicampus operations, tenure should be explicitly granted in a particular institution, not in the whole system.

9. The system's administration and individual institutions should develop procedures to protect the tenure and freedom of faculty members in transferring from one institution to another, and to permit responsible evaluation by the faculty to which transfer is contemplated.

10. Colleges and universities should develop their own policies and procedures on personnel problems, so as to minimize reliance on the courts.

11. The higher-education community should vigorously call attention to the importance of preserving institutional and faculty authority on tenure policy.

12. Each institution should develop methods of evaluating teaching effectiveness, and professional associations should expand their efforts to improve teaching.

13. Students should have an explicit and formal role in assessing teaching effectiveness.

14. Faculties should develop more sophisticated and reliable methods of judging scholarly competence and promise.

15. The positive attributes of academic citizenship should be given significant weight in tenure decisions.

16. Each institution's faculty should assume responsibility for developing a code of conduct.

17. Each institution should develop a staffing plan, to be reviewed annually, that is based on careful and realistic estimates of enrollments, budgets, and other variables over five to ten years.

18. Staffing plans should provide explicitly for a substantial increase, in virtually all institutions, in the tenure component of women and members of minority groups.

19. An appropriate number of tenure positions, when

they become vacant, should be available for allocation to any unit that needs them—or for suspension or elimination.

20. Most institutions should not permit their tenured faculty to constitute more than one-half to two-thirds of their total full-time faculty in the decade ahead. Policies should be flexible enough to allow for necessary variation among units. Institutions will need to proceed gradually in order to avoid injustice to probationary teachers.

21. Plans to improve teaching and scholarly skills might include new policies for leaves of absence, released time to develop new courses, in-service seminars, and programs in association with other institutions.

22. Institutions need more continuous and affirmative means to assist faculty members, especially those on probation, to improve their teaching, scholarship, and professional performance.

23. Every institution should develop a formal statement of its faculty personnel policy, with variations to meet the special needs of individual departments and other units.

24. Institutions should systematically communicate their personnel policies to their faculties, giving special attention to new appointees. The terms and conditions of service should be clearly spelled out, and the specific criteria to be used for evaluations during probation should be explained in writing.

25. The award of tenure should always be based on an explicit judgment of qualifications. Tenure should never be acquired by default, through the mere passage of time.

26. Prospective faculty members should be carefully screened before their initial appointments.

27. Departmental personnel recommendations should be reviewed above the department level and should involve faculty members outside the department concerned.

28. The probationary period should be no less than five years and no more than seven years.

29. Institutions should have explicit policies on the na-

ture and amount of prior service elsewhere that they may credit toward fulfillment of the probationary rule.

30. Faculty members not recommended for reappointment or tenure should always be given informal explanation by the department chairman and, if he requests it, a written statement of reasons.

31. Permissible reasons for nonrenewal of term appointments or for denial of tenure should meet these tests: they should not violate the faculty member's academic freedom or punish him for exercising academic freedom, either in performance of his duties or outside the institution; they must not violate his constitutional rights or punish him for exercising them; they must not be arbitrary or capricious; they must represent the deliberate exercise of professional judgment in the particular institutional circumstances.

32. Probationary teachers should be able to present evidence on their behalf well before the final decision on reappointment or tenure.

33. Those denied reappointment or tenure should be able to secure an impartial review if they believe the decision resulted from improper procedures. In such appeals, the burden of proof should be on the teacher.

34. In dismissal proceedings, "adequate cause" should be restricted to demonstrated incompetence or dishonesty in teaching or research, substantial and manifest neglect of duty, and personal conduct that substantially impairs the individual's fulfillment of his institutional responsibilities. The burden of proof here rests upon the institution.

35. Each institution should adopt sanctions short of dismissal for possible application in cases of demonstrated irresponsibility or professional misconduct. These sanctions and related due-process procedures should be developed initially by joint faculty-administrative action.

36. All institutions should adopt these standards for notice of nonreappointment: at least three months before the end of an initial one-year contract; at least six months before

the end of an initial two-year contract or a second one-year contract; at least twelve months before the end of a contract after two or more years of service at the institution.

37. If nonteaching professional personnel are to be made eligible for tenure, they should meet standards as rigorous as those for the teaching faculty.

38. Institutions should consider modifying their tenure arrangements to permit part-time faculty service, where appropriate, to be credited toward tenure.

39. Tenure should not be granted in administrative posts of department chairman and above. Faculty members serving full-time in administrative positions should retain tenure up to a stated maximum period (say ten years).

40. Institutions should develop attractive options for early retirement or reduced service so those who wish may leave tenured positions before the mandatory age.

41. If financial exigency or academic program changes make it necessary to reduce the size of the faculty, this should be based on guidelines developed in consultation with faculty and student representatives.

42. Institutions should develop standards and procedures to protect themselves and faculty members for whom disability is claimed as a ground for dismissal, change of assignment or salary, or early retirement.

43. Funds available to the institution on a short-term basis should not be used to support new tenure positions unless continuing support can be identified in the regular budget.

44. Collective bargaining should not extend to academic freedom and tenure and related faculty personnel matters. Grievances on freedom and tenure should be handled outside the bargaining process.

45. The American Council on Education and other associations should provide a clearinghouse for faculty personnel practice.

46. Institutions trying alternatives to traditional tenure

arrangements should invite evaluations by appropriate national professional groups.

47. Professional associations and research centers should expand their development of more sophisticated conceptions of teaching effectiveness and more reliable methods to evaluate teaching.

(Source: *Chronicle of Higher Education,* March 26, 1973, p. 6.)

Appendix C

Carnegie Commission on Higher Education Panel's
Twenty-six Recommendations on Academic Governance

1. State grants to institutions for general support should be based on broad formulas and not line-item control.

2. Academic policies set by state agencies should be of a broad nature and should not interfere with the more specific professional academic judgments about faculty appointments, courses of study, admission of individual students, grades and degrees for individual students, specific research projects, appointment of academic and administrative staff and leadership, and protection of academic freedom.

3. Innovations in programs and in policies should be encouraged by public authorities by influence and not by control.

4. Coordinating agencies at the state level should seek to establish, in cooperation with public and private institutions of higher education, guidelines defining areas of state concern and areas of institutional independence that avoid detailed control.

5. The American Council on Education may wish to

consider establishing a Commission on Institutional Independence to be concerned with policies affecting independence and the review of cases of alleged undue external influence. Such a Commission should include members drawn from the public at large.

6. Elected officials with the power of budgetary review should not serve as members of governing boards of public institutions over which they exercise such review because of the conflict of interest and the resulting double access to control, and because of the partisan nature of their positions.

7. Members of governing boards of public insitutions (where the governor makes the appointments) should be subject to appropriate mechanisms for nominating and screening individuals before appointments by the governor to assure consideration of properly qualified individuals, or to subsequent legislative confirmation to reduce the likelihood of purely political appointments, or to both.

8. Faculty members, students, and alumni should be associated with the process of nominating at least some board members in private and public institutions, but faculty members and students should not serve on the boards of institutions where they are enrolled or employed.

9. Board membership should reflect the different age, sex, and racial groups that are related to the concerns of the institution. Faculty members from other institutions and young alumni should be considered for board memberships.

10. Boards should consider faculty and student membership on appropriate board committees, or the establishment of parallel committees with arrangements for joint consultation.

11. Boards periodically should review the arrangements for governance—perhaps every four or five years—to be certain that they fit the current needs of the institution and are appropriate to the various functions being performed.

12. Boards should seek "active" presidents and give them the authority and the staff they need to provide leadership in a period of change and conflict.

13. Boards may wish to consider the establishment of stated review periods for presidents so that withdrawal by the president or reaffirmation of the president may be managed in a more effective manner than is often now the situation. Faculty members and students should be associated in an advisory capacity with the process of review as they are in the initial appointment.

14. Faculties should be granted, where they do not already have it, the general level of authority as recommended by the American Association of Univeristy Professors.

15. State laws, where they do not permit it, should provide the opportunity of obtaining collective bargaining rights by faculty members in public institutions. One alternative under such laws should be choice of no bargaining unit.

16. Faculties in each institution should undertake the most careful analysis of the implications of collective bargaining and, more broadly, they should choose which of the alternative forms of governance they prefer.

17. Representation and bargaining units should be composed of faculty members, including department chairmen.

18. The approach to contract coverage should be one of restraint, with the contract covering economic benefits and with academic affairs left (or put) in the hands of the faculty senate or equivalent council.

19. A separate federal law and separate state laws should be enacted governing collective bargaining by faculty members in both private and public institutions and should be responsive to the special circumstances that surround their employment. If this is not possible, then separate provisions should be made in more general laws; or leeway should be provided for special administrative interpretations.

20. The principle of tenure should be retained and extended to campuses where it does not now apply.

21. Tenure systems should be so administered in practice 1) that advancements to tenure and after tenure are based on merit; 2) that the criteria to be used in tenure decisions are

made clear at the time of employment; 3) that codes of conduct specify the obligations of tenured faculty members; 4) that adjustments in the size and in the assignments of staff in accord with institutional welfare be possible when there is a fully justifiable case for them; 5) that fair internal procedures be available to hear any cases that may arise; and 6) that the percentage of faculty members with tenure does not become excessive.

22. Persons on a 50 percent time basis or more should be eligible for tenure, but the time elapsed before a decision on tenure must be made should be counted on a full-time equivalent basis.

23. Governance arrangements should provide 1) adequate academic options from among which students may choose, and 2) the right to be heard on important campus issues.

24. Students should serve on joint faculty-student (or trustee-student or administrative-student) committees with the right to vote or should have their own parallel student committees with the right to meet with faculty, trustees, and administrative committees in areas of special interest and competence such as educational policy and student affairs. Students serving on such committees should be given staff assistance.

25. Students should be given the opportunity to evaluate the teaching performance of faculty members; and students should be involved in periodic reviews of the performance of departments.

26. Conduct codes should be prepared with student involvement in the process of their preparation; ombudsmen or their equivalents should be appointed and formal grievance machinery should be available and should end in impartial judicial tribunals.

(Source: *Chronicle of Higher Education,* April 23, 1973, p. 5.)

Appendix D

Table A.1 Average Salaries of Administrators at More Than 1,000 U.S. Colleges and Universities in 1977

	Universities			PUBLIC INSTITUTIONS Four-year colleges			Two-year colleges		
	Men	Women	All persons	Men	Women	All persons	Men	Women	All persons
President or chancellor	$48,902	$52,333	$49,024	*	*	$40,936	$33,243	$33,124	$33,214
Chief academic officer	42,301	37,500	42,073	33,922	35,009	33,979	26,575	27,549	26,614
Chief business officer	38,920	†	38,920	29,719	18,762	29,580	23,971	17,954	23,644
Chief development officer	*	*	32,218	26,194	23,170	26,034	22,342	21,399	22,255
Chief student-life officer	34,779	29,962	34,363	27,298	24,553	27,020	23,606	23,713	23,616
Director, computer center	31,047	†	31,047	22,194	18,273	22,060	20,029	19,290	19,984
Director, student counseling	25,147	23,994	25,044	20,726	17,586	20,127	21,459	18,940	20,912
Chief librarian	32,808	29,395	32,565	24,420	20,991	23,657	20,561	17,861	19,261
Director, admissions	25,464	21,731	25,194	21,457	18,175	21,062	20,434	17,762	20,159
Director, physical plant	28,441	†	28,441	*	*	20,814	17,574	13,557	17,520
Chief public-relations officer	32,113	27,439	31,472	21,542	16,215	20,795	18,748	14,625	17,420
Registrar	24,174	21,858	23,958	21,198	17,572	20,459	19,235	13,621	17,142
Director, student financial aid	21,437	22,339	21,480	17,864	15,383	17,418	17,880	14,325	16,916
Bookstore manager	20,272	15,742	19,944	15,233	11,111	14,157	14,043	9,927	11,913

PRIVATE INSTITUTIONS

	Universities			Four-year colleges			Two-year colleges		
	Men	Women	All persons	Men	Women	All persons	Men	Women	All persons
President or chancellor	$57,573	†	$57,573	$32,714	$32,343	$32,693	$25,078	$25,286	$25,095
Chief academic officer	*	*	44,490	24,724	22,352	24,496	18,788	17,461	18,576
Chief business officer	*	*	42,528	23,027	15,453	22,469	17,549	12,392	16,467
Chief development officer	39,509	†	39,509	22,017	18,227	21,745	17,084	15,669	16,931
Chief student-life officer	31,352	30,800	31,311	18,908	17,071	18,506	14,413	15,040	14,553
Director, computer center	*	*	27,162	17,555	13,378	17,026	16,342	†	16,342
Director student counseling	22,167	21,119	21,957	15,897	13,146	14,859	12,805	10,243	12,000
Chief librarian	29,458	25,633	29,203	17,230	13,743	15,665	12,547	11,152	11,688
Director, admissions	*	*	24,290	17,195	14,440	16,618	14,659	12,063	13,936
Director, physical plant	25,641	†	25,641	15,463	12,001	15,378	*	*	11,633
Chief public-relations officer	*	*	25,975	16,338	13,207	15,357	13,978	10,423	12,556
Registrar	22,042	22,482	22,111	15,930	12,248	14,199	13,282	10,087	11,073
Director, student financial aid	21,262	18,111	20,587	13,976	10,999	12,927	12,674	10,430	11,526
Bookstore manager	19,463	15,930	18,736	11,673	8,324	9,899	9,303	7,903	8,544

*Data not included because of the possible disclosure of individual salaries.

†No respondents in this category.

SOURCE: National Center For Education Statistics (Source: *Chronicle of Higher Education*, September 6, 1977, p. 4.)

Appendix E

Ranked Standings of Various Institutions in Selected Professional Fields in 1964, 1976, and 1977

Table A.2 Institutional Standings in Engineering of Universities in Group A

CARTTER REPORT (1964)

Faculty	Program
(1)	(2)
1. M.I.T.	1. U.C., Berkeley
2. U.C., Berkeley	2. M.I.T.
3. Stanford	3. Stanford
4. Cal. Tech.	4. Illinois
5. Illinois	5. Cal. Tech.
6. Michigan	6. Michigan
7. Harvard	7. Princeton
7. Minnesota	8. Wisconsin
8. Wisconsin	9. Purdue
9. Purdue	10. Cornell
10. Princeton	11. Harvard
11. Northwestern	12. Johns Hopkins
12. Columbia	12. U. of Washington
12. Cornell	13. Carnegie Tech.
13. Carnegie Tech.	14. Northwestern
14. Johns Hopkins	15. Texas
15. Texas	16. Minnesota
16. Ohio State	17. Brooklyn Polytech.
17. U.C.L.A.	18. Case
17. U. of Washington	19. Columbia
18. Brooklyn Polytech.	19. N.Y.U.
19. N.Y.U.	19. Ohio State
20. Rensselaer	19. Pennsylvania
21. Case	19. Rensselaer
22. Pennsylvania	20. U.C.L.A.

(Source: Magoun analysis, p. 489.)

Table A.3 Cartter's 1976 Rankings of Schools of Education, Law, and Business

EDUCATION	LAW	BUSINESS
1. Stanford	1. Harvard	1. Stanford
2. Harvard	2. Yale	2. Harvard
3. Chicago	3. Stanford	3. M.I.T.
4. U.C.L.A.	4. Michigan	4. Chicago
5. U.C. (Berkeley)	5. Chicago	5. Carnegie-Mellon
6. Wisconsin	6. U.C. (Berkeley)	6. U.C. (Berkeley)
7. Columbia, Teachers College	7. Columbia	7. Pennsylvania
8. Ohio State	8. Pennsylvania	8. U.C.L.A.
9. Michigan	9. Virginia	9. Northwestern
10. Illinois	10. U.C.L.A.	10. Cornell

In 1976, the late Allan M. Cartter, then director of the Laboratory for Research on Higher Education at U.C.L.A., headed a national survey of leading professional schools in these three fields, utilizing somewhat similar methods to those employed in the 1964 inquiry he conducted for the ACE. It was published in the January 1977 issue of *Change* magazine, and the tabulation here was reported in January 31, 1977, by the *Chronicle of Higher Education*.

Table A.4 Cole and Lipton's 1977 Ratings of the Perceived Quality and Visibility Scores of American Medical Schools

MEDICAL SCHOOL	PERCEIVED QUALITY SCORE	STD. DEV.	VISIBILITY SCORE	NUMBER OF RATERS
Harvard	5.71	0.54	87.3	509*
Johns Hopkins	5.11	0.92	84.7	494*
Stanford	5.11	0.84	81.2	151
California, San Francisco	5.01	0.76	75.1	145
Yale	5.00	0.79	82.0	478*
Columbia	4.93	0.86	79.2	462*
Duke	4.77	0.82	82.4	159
Michigan	4.74	0.82	76.2	147
Cornell	4.71	0.80	76.9	143
Washington, St. Louis	4.68	1.00	80.3	155
U. of Pennsylvania	4.66	0.84	75.6	146
Minnesota	4.62	0.82	69.0	402*
UCLA	4.61	0.81	74.4	434*
Albert Einstein	4.60	0.94	70.1	143
U. of Chicago, Pritzker	4.52	1.06	57.0	110
U. of Washington, Seattle	4.52	0.81	69.5	405*
Case Western Reserve	4.41	0.86	76.7	148
Rochester	4.37	0.79	69.4	134
Colorado	4.36	0.86	71.5	133
California, San Diego	4.27	1.01	60.3	123
Mount Sinai	4.22	0.94	67.9	131
NYU	4.18	1.03	60.8	113
Texas, Southwestern	4.11	1.00	48.2	93
Vanderbilt	4.10	0.90	61.8	126
North Carolina	4.07	0.76	59.8	122
Baylor	4.06	0.95	64.7	132
Tufts	4.05	0.91	68.6	140
U. of Wisconsin	4.02	0.85	59.3	121
Northwestern	3.98	0.87	67.7	126
Emory	3.95	0.97	63.2	129
Boston University	3.95	0.94	65.1	121
Iowa	3.93	0.82	63.7	123
U. of Virginia	3.89	0.85	58.0	112
Ohio State	3.79	0.84	64.0	119
Alabama	3.78	1.00	48.9	91
U. of Florida, Gainesville	3.77	0.88	60.1	116
Dartmouth†	3.73	0.91	59.5	347*
Illinois	3.70	0.89	59.7	111
Tulane	3.68	1.00	62.7	128
Georgetown	3.68	0.96	75.1	145
Utah	3.68	0.82	50.0	93
Cincinnati	3.68	0.87	55.9	114
California, Davis	3.66	0.85	50.5	94
Penn State	3.64	1.03	46.8	87
Pittsburgh	3.64	0.80	59.7	111
Vermont	3.62	0.80	50.0	102
Virginia Medical College	3.62	0.85	60.2	112
Oregon	3.58	0.85	48.2	93
State University of New York, Syracuse (Upstate)	3.57	0.89	58.6	109

Michigan State	3.54	1.20	49.5	101
Indiana	3.54	0.87	52.0	106
Buffalo	3.53	0.84	59.1	114
Texas, Galveston	3.48	0.94	48.9	91
St. Louis	3.48	1.19	60.8	124
Temple	3.46	0.79	61.3	125
Miami	3.43	0.92	65.6	122
Medical College of Wisconsin	3.43	1.05	52.8	102
Maryland	3.41	0.82	64.2	124
Kansas	3.40	0.84	52.2	97
Albany	3.37	0.75	56.4	115
Bowman Gray	3.37	0.87	59.7	98
Arizona	3.34	0.95	37.7	77
Missouri	3.33	0.87	50.5	94
California, Irvine	3.32	1.04	45.6	93
George Washington	3.31	0.95	67.2	125
State University of New York, Brooklyn (Downstate)	3.31	0.84	57.4	117
Texas, San Antonio	3.25	0.75	34.7	67
Wayne State	3.24	0.89	54.8	102
Chicago Medical School	3.21	1.21	55.2	322*
Oklahoma	3.20	0.76	43.9	256*
Kentucky	3.20	0.82	52.9	97
Jefferson	3.19	1.02	61.1	118
New Mexico	3.17	0.80	50.0	93
Georgia Medical College	3.12	0.81	42.0	81
Tennessee	3.12	0.92	45.2	84
Louisiana State	3.05	1.07	45.7	85
Arkansas	3.05	0.78	39.9	77
Connecticut	2.96	0.95	44.6	91
Louisville	2.94	0.90	52.8	102
Medical College of Pennsylvania	2.94	1.07	47.8	89
Hahnemann	2.94	0.96	52.5	107
Loma Linda	2.93	1.00	46.6	90
West Virginia	2.92	0.81	36.7	214*
Nebraska	2.92	0.86	38.7	79
New York Medical College	2.92	1.00	59.0	344*
South Carolina	2.91	0.83	36.3	70
Mississippi	2.86	0.95	41.5	80
Ohio, Toledo	2.84	1.02	29.9	61
Howard	2.69	0.93	52.9	108
Loyola	2.64	1.02	42.2	86
Creighton	2.48	1.04	45.7	85
New Jersey	2.40	0.90	47.7	92
Puerto Rico	2.29	0.75	17.2	35
Meharry	2.23	0.85	47.8	239*

*These 13 medical schools appeared on all three forms of the questionnaire. This accounts for the larger number of raters.
†Dartmouth, of course, provided education only in the basic sciences at the time of survey.

Source: Jonathan R. Cole and James M. Lipton, "The Reputations of American Medical Schools," *Social Forces* 32, March 1977: 662–84.

Appendix F

Table A.5 Divisional and Institutional Standings of Graduate Faculty of Universities in Group B as Compiled from the Cartter Report

INSTITUTIONAL STANDING	DIVISIONAL STANDING				INSTITUTIONAL STANDING
Letters and Science	Humanities*	Social Sciences†	Life Sciences‡	Physical Sciences§	Engineering
(1)	(2)	(3)	(4)	(5)	(6)
1. U. of Iowa	1. Bryn Mawr	1. Michigan State	1. U.C., Davis	1. Rice	1. Ill. Inst. of Tech.
2. Michigan State	2. Pittsburgh	2. Syracuse	2. U. of Iowa	2. Colorado	1. Iowa State
3. Rochester	3. U. of Iowa	3. U. of Iowa	3. Western Reserve	3. Rochester	1. Penn. State
4. Pittsburgh	4. Tulane	3. Oregon	4. Rochester	4. Brandeis	2. Lehigh
5. U. of Kansas	5. Colorado	4. Pittsburgh	5. Michigan State	5. Maryland	3. Yale
6. U. of Oregon	5. Rice	4. Vanderbilt	6. U. of Kansas	6. Michigan State	4. Rice
7. Rutgers	5. Rochester	4. Virginia	7. Rutgers	7. Iowa State	5. Syracuse
8. Western Reserve	5. Syracuse	5. Penn. State	7. Yeshiva	8. Penn. State	6. Michigan State
9. Syracuse	5. U.S.C.	5. Rochester	8. Pittsburgh	8. Virginia	7. Delaware
10. U.C., Davis	6. Brandeis	6. U. of Kansas	9. Iowa State	9. U. of Iowa	8. Georgia Tech.
11. Penn. State	6. U. of Kansas	6. Rutgers	10. Oregon	9. U. of Kansas	9. U. of Florida
11. Iowa State	6. Michigan State	7. Brandeis	10. Utah	9. Oregon	9. Maryland
12. Brandeis	6. Rutgers	7. Bryn Mawr	11. Oregon State	9. U.S.C.	9. No. Carolina State
13. Colorado	6. Virginia	7. Emory	11. Penn. State	10. Pittsburgh	9. Oklahoma State

13. Rice
14. U.S.C.
14. Tulane
15. Vanderbilt
16. Maryland
17. Yeshiva
18. Virginia
19. Utah
20. Emory
21. U. of Florida
22. Bryn Mawr
22. Oregon State

6. Western Reserve
7. Iowa State
7. Emory
7. U. of Florida
7. Oregon
7. Penn. State
7. Vanderbilt
8. Colorado
8. Maryland
8. Rice
8. U.S.C.
8. Tulane
8. Western Reserve

11. Vanderbilt
12. Emory
13. U. of Florida
13. Tulane
14. Brandeis
15. Maryland
15. U.S.C.
15. Syracuse
16. Colorado
17. Rice
18. Virginia
18. Bryn Mawr

11. Rutgers
11. Syracuse
11. Utah
12. U.C., Davis
12. U. of Florida
12. Tulane
13. Oregon State
13. Vanderbilt
13. Western Reserve
13. Yeshiva

10. Colorado
10. Oregon State
10. Pittsburgh
10. U.S.C.
10. Washington
11. U. of Arizona
11. Cincinnati
11. U. of Iowa
11. U. of Kansas
11. Missouri
11. New Mexico
11. U. of Oklahoma
11. Tennessee
11. Texas A. and M.
11. Utah

*Catholic falls between 4 and 5, and Fordham ties with 5.
†Louisiana State falls between 3 and 4, Claremont ties with 5, and U. of Arizona and New School tie with 6.
‡Tufts falls between 10 and 11, Washington State ties with 13, and Buffalo falls between 13 and 14.
§Notre Dame ties with 10, Wayne State ties with 11, and U. of Arizona and Louisiana State with 12.

Source: Magoun analysis of Cartter report in 1966, p. 490.

Notes

Introduction

1. Paul L. Dressel and Lewis B. Mayhew, *Higher Educaton as a Field of Study*, San Francisco, Jossey-Bass, Inc., 1974.
2. For an insider's view of what has happened to one well-known institution, see Theodore M. Gross, "How To Kill a College: The Private Papers of a Campus Dean," *Saturday Review*, February 4, 1978, pp. 13–20. (City University of New York's dean of humanities "reflects on the gains, the losses, and the meaning of the entire experience for American education.")

Chapter 1: Professional Recruitment

1. Charles V. Kidd, "Shifts in Doctorate Output: History and Outlook," *Science* 179, February 9, 1973: 538–43.
2. From Edwin Harwood, "Confessions of a Conservative Sociologist," *Wall Street Journal*, August 11, 1970. Figures to be given later on the economic status of the profession show that academic salaries did rise both absolutely and relatively during the 1960s. It is also true, however, that during this period many campuses became less pleasant places to work. Some observers

attribute the spread of unionism in academe during this same period to growing faculty dissatisfactions here and there with the factory-like atmosphere of their employment conditions.

3. *Gradute Education in the United States* (note especially pp. 129–55), New York, McGraw-Hill Book Co., 1960.

4. See John A. Creager, *The American Graduate Student: A Normative Description,* Washington, D.C., American Council on Education, Research Report, October 1971. This study, done in cooperation with the Carnegie Commission on Higher Education, is by far the most comprehensive statistical report yet made on the subject. The data in Table 1.1 are derived from Creager's Table 7, pp. 56–79.

5. See Reinhard Bendix and Seymour Martin Lipset, editors, *Class, Status, and Power,* New York, The Free Press, 1966, pp. 322–34.

6. Princeton, N.J. Princeton University Press, 1971.

7. From a report, "Path to College Narrow in Soviet," *New York Times,* September 3, 1974.

8. See Julie W. Munro's report from Peking, "A Major Turn-around in China," with the subcaption, "In a shift from the policies of Chairman Mao Tse-tung, new leaders reinstate entrance exams, play down role of party politics," *Chronicle of Higher Education,* November 7, 1977.

9. An example of the unfortunate and absurd consequences which could result from this kind of evaluative buck passing in secondary education was reported in the *Wall Street Journal,* August 26, 1976, as follows: "As valedictorian of his class and as a straight A student, the 18-year-old graduate of a Washington, D.C. inner-city high school figured to have no trouble qualifying for the college of his choice. But George Washington University turned down his application for admission when his College Board Exam scores were only about half of what the school expected and when he did poorly on a special battery of tests administered by the university to try to determine if the College Board results were misleading."

10. The other side of this coin is that fewer and fewer students flunked out. Whether professors also watered down course requirements, I do not know, but a news item in the November 7, 1974, issue of the *New York Times* carried the headline, "College Textbooks Are Being Simplified To Meet the Needs of the Poor Reader." The item referred to the special needs of community colleges and other open-door institutions but also mentioned that such a prestigious institution as the University of

California reported that some 45 percent of its students were taking remedial English.

11. Scattered reports of grade inflation between 1960 and the early 1970s were widely noted in the public press and systematically confirmed in a survey of 197 institutions made in 1974 by Arvo E. Juola, acting director of evaluation services at Michigan State University. He found that the average increase in grade points was .404, or about half a letter grade for the period (see "Grade Inflation," *Chronicle of Higher Education,* October 7, 1974).

12. Garden City, N.Y., Doubleday and Co., Inc., 1968.

13. See an article by Robert Trumbull, "Talent Edges Out Wealth at 'Big Three,' " *New York Times,* March 14, 1964. Note also E. Digby Baltzell's "The Protestant Establishment Revisited," *American Scholar* 45, Autumn 1976: 499–518.

14. For my further comments on this general topic, note "Carrots and Sticks in the Higher Learning," in my book, *Shaping American Higher Education,* Washington, D.C., American Council on Education, 1972, pp. 152–62.

15. *Op. cit.,* p. 139.

16. See John K. Folger, Helen S. Astin, and Alan E. Bayer, *Human Resources and Higher Education,* New York, Russell Sage Foundation, 1970, p. 189.

17. From his book, *A Statistical Portrait of Higher Education,* New York, McGraw-Hill Book Co., 1972, p. 83.

18. From *Key Reporter,* Autumn 1974, Washington, D.C., Phi Beta Kappa, pp. 1 and 4.

19. New York, Praeger Publishers, 1976.

20. Solmon's data about mean scores on the GRE specialty tests were obtained from the Educational Testing Service for all takers of the tests in 1971–72 and 1972–73, and appear in a tabulation given on pp. 44–45 of his book.

It should be noted that graduate students are by no means all headed toward careers in the academic profession. Some are at work on M.A.s or Ed.D.s and go into public school teaching or administration. Others are pursuing first professional degrees for employment outside academe. Some Ph.D. aspirants drop out. The data I cite from the Creager survey refer only to those graduate students expecting to get their Ph.D.s. The National Research Council in a summary report for 1970, *Doctorate Recipients from U.S. Universities* (Washington, D.C., NAS, 1971), states that for the year 1970, 71 percent of all doctorates entered the teaching profession.

21. *Op. cit.,* p. 134.
22. For Gene I. Maeroff's "Family Share of Higher-Education Costs Found To Have Dipped," a commentary on the Carnegie Report, see the *New York Times,* June 2, 1976.
23. *Op. cit.,* p. 94.
24. *Five and Ten Years after College Entry,* p. 97.
25. *Op. cit.,* p. 155.
26. See Lindsey R. Harmon, *Fourteen Years of Research on Fellowship Selection,* Washington, D.C., National Academy of Sciences, 1966.

Chapter 2: Students and Apprentices

1. In 1970–71, to give one institutional example, Mississippi State University awarded more Ph.D.s in sociology (12) than did any one of the following universities: Cornell, Duke, Harvard, University of Iowa, Johns Hopkins, University of Kansas, University of Michigan, University of Minnesota, and Princeton. Prior to 1962, Mississippi State had not conferred any Ph.D.s in this field; up to 1966 it had conferred only 5; but in 1970–71 its output almost tripled that of the previous year.
2. In descending order of the number of doctorates awarded during the decade ending in 1968–69, the top 30 institutions were as follows: University of California (all campuses), Columbia, Wisconsin, Illinois, Harvard-Radcliffe, Michigan, New York University, Ohio State, Stanford, Minnesota, Indiana, Michigan State, Purdue, Massachusetts Institute of Technology, Cornell, Chicago, Texas, Yale, Pennsylvania, Pennsylvania State, Iowa, Northwestern, University of Southern California, University of Washington, Iowa State, Princeton, Maryland, Florida, Missouri (all campuses), Case-Western Reserve.

   The next 30 were these institutions: Rutgers, University of North Carolina at Chapel Hill, Pittsburgh, Johns Hopkins, Colorado, Boston University, Kansas, Duke, Florida State, Syracuse, Oregon, Oklahoma, Catholic University, State University of New York (all campuses), Nebraska, Louisiana State University, Oklahoma State, Wayne State, Rochester, Utah, Tennessee, California Institute of Technology, Oregon State, Texas A&M, University of North Colorado, Virginia, Arizona, Connecticut, Carnegie-Mellon, Brown.

   (Source of data: John L. Chase and Elfrida L. Burnett, *Doctor's*

Degrees Conferred by All U.S. Institutions: By State, Academic Field, Sex, and Institution, 1959–60 through 1968–69, Washington, D.C., U.S. Office of Education, Bureau of Higher Education, 1971, pp. 8–9.)

3. "Today, approximately 60 percent of the presidents of American corporations hold a master's degree [probably the M.B.A.]. Thirty percent hold a doctor's degree, while only 10 percent halted their formal education with the bachelor's degree." Lewis B. Mayhew makes this statement in his *Reform in Graduate Education*, Atlanta, Ga., Southern Regional Education Board, 1972, p. 134.

4. For a critique of the D.A. and similar degrees, note John M. Howell, "A Brief against the Doctor of Arts Degree," *Journal of Higher Education* 42, May 1971: 392–99.

5. See J. S. Hunter, *The Academic and Financial Status of Graduate Students, Spring, 1965*, Washington, D.C., U.S. Office of Education, 1967, p. 42.

6. *Unemployment in the Learned Professions*, London, Oxford University Press, 1937.

7. See David G. Brown, "A Student Evaluation of Research Assistantships," *Journal of Higher Education* 33, November 1962: 436–42.

8. *Op. cit.*, p. 214. For more information about assistantships, note John L. Chase, *Graduate Teaching Assistants in American Universities* (an HEW publication), U.S. Government Printing Office, No. HE 5.258:580039, 1970

9. From Robert Dubin and Fredric Beisse, "The Assistant: Academic Subaltern," *Administrative Science Quarterly* 11, March 1967: 522–47.

10. Peggy Heim and Becky Bogard's "Compensation of Graduate Assistants, 1968–69," *AAUP Bulletin* 55, Winter 1969: 483–88, particularizes on this subject. According to an American Association of University Professors salary study, stipends paid to graduate assistants in 1970–71 ranged from an average of $2,130 for laboratory assistants to an average of $3,230 for research assistants in private universities. "Work week" averages for such jobs ranged from 15.5 to 17 hours. In addition to direct pay, private universities tended to pay almost 80 percent of tuition costs, with percentage tuition payments by public universities ranging from 41 to 69 for in-state and 56 to 72 for out-of-state residents.

11. A detailed report of what happened on the Madison campus of

the University of Wisconsin is set forth in a book edited by Philip Altbach and others, *Academic Supermarkets,* San Francisco, Josey-Bass, Inc., 1971.

12. Note Vincent Nowlis, Kenneth E. Clark, and Miriam Rock, *The Graduate Student as Teacher,* Washington, D.C., American Council on Education, 1968.

13. Jacques Barzun's *Teacher in America* (Boston, Little, Brown and Co., 1945), has an entertaining chapter called "The Ph.D. Octopus," pp. 195–208.

14. Under the auspices of the Carnegie Commission on Higher Education, Stephen H. Spurr has done an extensive investigation and analysis of academic degrees in his book, *Academic Degree Structures: Innovative Approaches,* New York, McGraw-Hill Book Co., 1970.

15. For a brief critique, see Jay L. Halio, 'Ph.D.s and the Oral Examination—Need for Revision," *Journal of Higher Education* 34, March 1963: 148–52.

16. A study made in 1965 indicated that only 22 percent of large numbers of Ph.D.s met foreign language requirements with no special preparation. Note also Robert G. Wiltsey, *Doctoral Use of Foreign Languages—A Survey,* Princeton, N.J., Educational Testing Service. 1972.

17. In 1960 there were reported to be 2,462 different designations of American academic degrees, with more than 1,600 in use that year. Aside from the Ph.D., there are other types of doctorates, such as Doctor of Science, Doctor of Engineering, Doctor of Juridical Science, Doctor of Jurisprudence, Doctor of Canon Law, Doctor of Law, Doctor of Medical Sciences, Doctor of Public Health, Doctor of Sacred Theology, Doctor of Letters, and Doctor of Education. The doctor's degree was originally conferred in schools of theology, medicine, law, and philosophy, and since the school of philosophy represented the broadest training, the Ph.D. has come to be the usual type of doctorate taken by the generic academic.

    For a 1977 commentary, see John W. Ryan's "Degree Designations at U.S. Graduate Schools, " Special Report No. 11, in the *Communicator,* September 1977, Washington, D.C., Council of Graduate Schools in the United States.

18. In his article, "The First Ph.D.s under Title IV," Gustave Arlt then president of the Council of Graduate Schools in th United States, noted that even with fellowship aid, only 1 percent of the fellows completed their doctorates in three co

secutive years in the new or expanded programs of graduate education. The length of all the dissertations produced ranged from 47 to 550 typed pages. Thirty-two of the 97 dissertations were under 100 typed pages in length, and 28 were over 200 pages. (See Arlt's article in the *Journal of Higher Education* 34, May 1963: 241–49.)

19. Note S. L. Pressey, "Some Data on the Doctorate," *Journal of Higher Education* 15, April 1944: 191–93.

20. Studies of graduate student sources of income in recent decades indicate that gainfully employed wives are much more numerous.

21. See Table 5.22 in Folger, Astin, and Bayer, *Human Resources and Higher Education*, p. 192.

In view of recent efforts to increase the number of black doctorates, it is pertinent to refer here to a Ford Foundation study made in 1968–69, entitled *A Survey of Black American Doctorates*. It indicted that the median number of years for blacks to obtain the Ph.D. was 13, compared to 7½ years for Ph.D.s in general in the humanities and social sciences, and 5 years in the physical sciences as of 1968–69.

22. *Reform on Campus: A Report and Recommendations*, New York, McGraw-Hill Book Co., 1972, pp. 137ff.

23. "Berkeley Doctoral Students Appraise Their Academic Programs," *Educational Record* 48, Winter 1967: 30–44. The summation also sets forth recommendations for changes. This study, it should be noted, came in the wake of campus disturbances at Berkeley.

24. The 1927–35 figures are from Edgar Dale, "The Training of Ph.D.s," *Journal of Higher Education* 1, April 1930: 198–202; 1970 figures are from *Doctorate Recipients from U.S. Universities*, Office of Scientific Personnel, NRC Summary Report, Washington, D.C., NAS, 1971.

25. It is also apropos to note here the field mobility of employed Ph.D.s. *Doctoral Scientists and Engineers in the United States, 1975 Profile*, a report issued by the National Academy of Sciences in 1976, states that of the approximately 279,400 Ph.D.s trained in these fields between 1930 and 1974, nearly 263,000 were employed in 1975. The percentage of Ph.D.s trained in this period who remained in their field of training ranged from 65.4 percent for physics-astronomy to 90.2 percent in psychology. The 1974 cohorts, with the exception of those in the earth sciences, showed almost the same field mobility as the 1930–1974 cohorts, with a slight increase among the former group

(5.1 percent) as contrasted with the latter group (4.9 percent) going into nonscience jobs.

26. *Report on the President of Harvard University to the Board of Overseers*, Cambridge, Harvard University Press, 1940, p. 17.

27. "Methods of Appointment and Promotion in American Colleges and Universities," *Bulletin of the AAUP* 15, January 1929: 178–79.

28. For detailed studies of the functioning of the academic marketplace during the 1950s and 1960s, note Theodore Caplow and Reece J. McGee, *The Academic Marketplace*, New York, Basic Books, Inc., 1958; also David G. Brown, *The Market for College Teachers*, Chapel Hill, University of North Carolina Press, 1965, and by the same author, *The Mobile Professors*, Washington, D.C., American Council on Education, 1967.

29. See *Doctorate Manpower Forecasts and Policy*, Washington, D.C., National Board on Graduate Education, 1973.

30. Note his article, "A New Look at the Supply of College Teachers," *Educational Record* 46, Summer 1965: 267–77, and also his more extensive analysis later for the Carnegie Commission on Higher Education.

31. These reports are all derived from news items appearing in various issues of the *Chronicle of Higher Education* between 1973 and 1976.

32. See *Outlook and Opportunities for Graduate Education*, Washington, D.C., National Board on Graduate Education, Publication No. 6, December 1975, pp. 48–49.

Chapter 3: Staff Members

1. In *Academic Women*, University Park, Pennsylvania State University Press, 1964. For another comprehensive treatment of women academics, see Helen S. Astin, *The Woman Doctorate in America*, New York, Russell Sage Foundation, 1969.

2. According to studies published in October 1977 by the Carnegie Council on Policy Studies in Higher Education and the National Association of State Universities and Land Grant Colleges, only 2.9 percent of the doctorates awarded in 1973–74 went to American blacks, and almost two-thirds of those were doctorates in one field—education (reported in the *Washington Post*, October 5, 1977).

3. Cambridge, Harvard University Press, 1939.

4. The recently enacted federal requirement that students may have access, unless they waive the right, to faculty evaluations of them renders letters of recommendation more suspect than formerly, and prospective academic employers are now more likely to make their inquiries by telephone and less by mail. Colleges and universities have objected to this federal requirement, particularly with regard to employment recommendations. My information is that the American Council on Education is setting up a special group to prepare guidelines to aid institutions.

5. An interesting exception to my generalization is illustrated in an item, "City U. Out-of-City Hiring Held Biased Against Jews," which appeared in the *New York Times,* March 10, 1975, and had this opening paragraph: "Quiet efforts by the City University to 'diversify' its faculty by hiring fewer New Yorkers have raised the concern of the American Jewish Congress, a City Council member and others who are disturbed by the policy's effects on New York-trained academicians, particularly Jews."

6. Compliance with federal fiats did in some instances entail curious shifts. Many colleges and universities, for example, had long-standing regulations regarding antinepotism which had been adopted for the sole purpose of upholding fairness and impartiality in employment practices. Now they were being informed by HEW that such regulations could on occasion involve sex discrimination, and hence were no longer acceptable.

7. The *Chronicle of Higher Education* reported both of these events—the one for Brigham Young University in its issue of October 28, 1975, and that for CUNY in its issue of April 11, 1977.

8. See Laurence R. Marcus, "Has Advertising Produced Results in Faculty Hiring?" *Educational Record* 57, Fall 1976: 247–50.

9. See Allan M. Cartter and Wayne E. Ruhter, *The Disappearance of Sex Discrimination in First Job Placement of New Ph.D.,* Los Angeles, Higher Education Research Institute, 1975.

10. The widespread concern of academe's scholarly societies and professional associations with equalizing employment opportunities, nonetheless, is suggested by the fact that sixty such organizations are reported to have committees, commissions, or offices giving special attention to the whole matter.

11. Note her commentary, "Women and Minority Scientists," *Science* 189, No. 420S, September 1975: 751.

12. As will be seen in Chapters 10 and 11, the most prestigious universities tend to recruit mainly from their own ablest young

doctorates and from a limited number of other high-ranking institutions. Many other universities, however, recruit from a greater diversity of sources. Although persons initially employed for lower-rank positions typically are not teachers of graduate level courses, it is interesting to note here the third-level research degree origins of the 275 members of the Tulane University Graduate School faculty as reported in 1976. Their degrees were conferred by 66 different American and 13 foreign universities. About three-fourths of the doctorates were from member institutions of the Association of American Universities, and of these 210 only 29 were from Tulane itself.

13. *Op. cit.,* Chapter 7, "Candidates Evaluate Their Jobs," pp. 166–75.

14. See a monograph by John E. Stecklein and Robert L. Lathrop, *Faculty Attraction and Retention: Factors Affecting Faculty Mobility at the University of Minnesota,* Minneapolis, Bureau of Institutional Research, University of Minnesota, 1960. (Although there doubtless have been numerus unpublished studies of this kind made for internal use at various universities, I am surprised at the apparent dearth of published research on this important subject.)

15. In a little book published in 1908, *Microcosmographia Academica: Being a Guide for the Young Academic Politician,* Francis M. Cornford wrote spoofingly for English readers about how to get ahead in the British university, particularly at Cambridge. In 1966, an American writer calling himself "Academicus Mentor" did a similar job for this country, entitled *Up the Ivy: Being Microcosmographia Revisited, a True Blue Guide on How To Climb in the Academic World without Appearing To Try,* New York, Hawthorn Books, 1969.

16. *Bulletin of the AAUP* 24, May 1938: 249; averages for member groups.

17. This change from earlier years may be noted in the percentage of teaching assistants (in terms of full-time equivalents) included in the total teaching staffs of these major state universities in 1974–75: California (Berkeley), 22; Illinois, 39; Indiana, 31; North Carolina, 14; Ohio State, 27; Texas (Austin), 19; U.C.L.A., 22; Washington, 26; Wisconsin, 29. (Data from *Institutional Self-Study: A General Report,* The University of Texas at Austin, 1975.)

18. Even in the military the graphic representation of the distribution of commissioned officers by ranks is not a perfect pyramid.

As of November 1971 in the Air Force, for example, the percentage distribution of officers by rank was as follows: general, .3; colonel, 5; lieutenant colonel, 12; major, 19; captain, 38; 1st lieutenant, 18; 2nd lieutenant, 12. Captains were thus more than twice as numerous as both grades of lieutenants, and lieutenant colonels about as numerous as commissioned officers in the lowest rank. (Data from *Armed Forces Journal,* March 1972, p. 14.)

19. At The University of Texas at Austin in 1975 about 10 percent of the 570 full professors occupied endowed chairs and professorships, with such posts being concentrated mainly in the professional schools. (Data from *Institutional Self Study: General Report.)*

20. See Floyd Reeves and others, *The University Faculty* (The University of Chicago Survey, Vol. 3), Chicago, University of Chicago Press, 1933, pp. 59–60.

21. Interestingly, the Harvard personnel study published in 1939 pinpoints the untenured rank problems of the present just as accurately as it did those of about four decades ago, and this is my reason for the particular reference. As I have mentioned earlier in these comments, however, one should bear in mind that Harvard and other leading universities are much more rigorous in their methods of selecting persons for tenured posts than are most institutions, and hence the uncertainties and strains of occupying temporary assignments are more severe.

22. Dr. Stigler also details the complications and uproars which resulted. (See *The Intellectual and the Market Place and Other Essays,* New York, The Free Press, 1963.)

23. In August 1974, Elaine H. El-Khawas and W. Todd Furniss did a follow-up of the 1972 ACE survey (*Faculty Tenure and Contract Systems: 1972 and 1974,* Washington, D.C., American Council on Education, 1974). The highlights of their findings regarding extent of tenure, tenure awards and contract renewals, probationary periods, and review and appeal procedures are reproduced in Appendix A.

24. The commission's forty-seven basic recommendations are summarized in Appendix B.

25. Todd Furniss has done some insightful analyses of these concerns in articles which have appeared in the *Educational Record,* as follows: "Is There a Perfect Faculty Mix?", Vol. 52, Summer 1971, pp. 244–48; "Steady-State Staffing: Issues for 1974," Vol. 55, Spring 1974, pp. 87–95; "Retrenchment, Layoff, and

Termination," vol. 55, Summer 1974, pp. 159–70. The Summer 1971 issue of the *Educational Record* also reproduces a memorandum from the provost to deans and academic chairmen at Cornell University regarding "Faculty Appointments, Promotions, and Extension of Appointments Beyond Age 65" (pp. 248–50). It specifies the practices at Cornell for dealing with the kinds of issues raised in the Furniss articles.

Chapter 4: Administrators

1. See his article, "Management: Intruder in the Academic Dust," *Educational Record* 50, Winter 1969: 55–59. Also, Harold L. Hodgkinson has asserted that during the institutional retrenchments of 1972–73, a number of colleges and universities "both *lowered* the size of the faculty, and *increased* the size of the administration. Lowering the faculty size was usually done in public with much weeping and gnashing of teeth, while the new administrative slots were added in a quieter manner." From "How Many Administrators are Enough? Too Many?", *Chronicle of Higher Education*, April 2, 1973, p. 7.
2. A. H. Halsey and M. A. Trow, *The British Academics*, Cambridge, Harvard University Press, 1971, pp. 114–15.
3. Prior to the concessions made in response to student activist demands for more voice in university affairs during the 1960s, the academic community's most numerous participants likewise had no direct share in campus power structures. It is important to add however, that as consumers, students have always had a strong influence directly as well as indirectly on the basic aspects of higher education. In an era of leveled-off and declining enrollments it is likely that many institutions will become even more sensitive to the wishes of students as consumers.
4. When J. Harris Purks was provost of the University of North Carolina he gave a conference address (unpublished) satirizing the tendency toward curriculum proliferation. Speaking presumably of a land-grant institution, he traced the evolution of a B.S. degree program in Alligator Farm Management. It began with a single course, somewhat reluctantly endorsed by a department chairman and committee on the curriculum. The courses were enthusiastically backed on the outside by alligator farm managers eager to enhance the prestige of their occupation, and student aids were soon underwritten by the Amalgamated Fabri-

cators of Alligator Hides, Inc. There was a mushrooming of course offerings, such as: The Alligator in the Modern World, The Adolescent Alligator, Alligator Ecology, Alligator Demography, and so on. As of the time of Dr. Purks's remarks there was still no separate school for the field, but he did note that the birth of a new profession was signified by the addition of a new code number in the national Roster of Scientific and Specialized Personnel.

5. From *The Confidence Crisis,* San Francisco, Jossey-Bass, Inc., 1970, p. 13.

6. Robert B. Macleod's "Confession of an Ex-Chairman" detailed his own feelings at Cornell University in the *AAUP Bulletin* back in 1954, when the times were less hectic than in more recent decades (vol. 50, Autumn 1954, pp. 40–43).

7. *The Organization of Departments,* Washington, D.C., American Association for Higher Education, Research Report No. 2, 1970. (Incidentally, when *The Academic Man* came out in 1942, almost no systemtic research had been done regarding departments; Peterson's 1970 brochure includes a bibliography listing forty-five researches of this kind.)

8. *Op. cit.,* note Chapter 6, "The Institute," pp. 120–31.

9. I do not have at hand any comprehensive data about the disciplinary backgrounds of academic deans in general, but the Council of Graduate Schools in the United States reported that 1,496 graduate deans serving 240 universities from 1872 through 1975, in descending order for the ten top disciplines represented, were from the following fields: chemistry, 159; education, 127; English, 126; history, 125; physics, 108; biology, 85; engineering, 75; economics, 70; psychology, 69; and mathematics, 63. Median length of service for all during the whole period was slightly less than four years.

10. From Victor E. Hanzeli, "The Educational Leadership of the Academic Dean," *Journal of Higher Education* 37, November 1966: 421–28. The cited table appears on p. 425 of the article.

11. For an impious and insightful treatment of academic administrators, see Chapter 4, "Administrators Above and Below," in Jacques Barzun's *The American University,* New York, Harper and Row, 1968. The general tone of the treatment is suggested by the first subheading, "The Rascals Have a Use."

12. This was illustrated in New York State in 1975 when the chancellor of the State University of New York and the commissioner for the New York Board of Education clashed over the

question of who had the authority to begin and terminate graduate programs. (See *Chronicle of Higher Education,* December 15, 1975, p. 3.)

Incidentally, Lee and Bowen's study for the Carnegie Commission on Higher Education in 1971 estimated that three-fourths of all public university enrollees are in schools that are part of multicampus institutions.

13. See Michael R. Ferrari, *Profiles of American College Presidents,* East Lansing, Michigan State University, 1970. Note also Robert Birnbaum's "Presidential Succession: An Interinstitional Analysis," *Educational Record* 51, Spring 1971: 333–45, for an explanation of why recruitment is usually from the outside, and why institutions draw their top officers from similar types of institutions.

14. For information about how college and university presidents are expected to measure up to certain qualifications, are searched out, and are chosen for office, see Frederick deW. Bolman's *How College Presidents Are Chosen,* Washington, D.C., American Council on Education, 1964.

15. Note his article, "The Job of a College President," *Educational Record* 48, Winter 1967: 68–78.

16. From Herbert J. Walberg, "The Academic President: Colleague, Administrator, or Spokesman?" *Educatonal Record* 50, Spring 1969: 198. Incidentally, presidents' secretaries reported somewhat the same distribution for them, but with a lower percentage for administrative problems, higher for external matters, lower for collegial concerns, and lower for individual activities. Of the presidents' total time involvement with persons, their secretaries said that 26.1 percent was with administrative personnel, 37.9 percent with board members and outsiders, 14 percent with faculty and students, and 22 percent with no other persons directly.

17. See my article, 'Academic Administration: Its Abuses and Uses," *AAUP Bulletin* 41, Winter 1955: 684–92.

18. Note his book, *The Academic President—Educator or Caretaker?,* New York, McGraw-Hill Book Co., 1962. It has been proposed that American colleges and universities should follow the European pattern of having the top administrative officers chosen for a limited term of only one or two years, with the expectation that they would then return to the professorial fold. I agree with those who maintain that this pattern would be ill-suited to the needs of most American institutions. I would

also add that the pattern is increasingly ill-suited to the needs of European universities.

19. See his article, "Management and Accountability in Higher Education," *AAUP Bulletin* 63, Summer 1973: 135–38.

20. Incidentally, in my paper, "Analyzing and Evaluating Costs," given at the ACE annual meeting of 1960, my cautions and conclusions were somewhat similar to those of Dr. Danforth in 1973. Although what I had to say was published in an article in 1961, I reproduced it in a 1972 book of some of my collected writings, my purpose being in part to illustrate that current problems and issues are not always as new as some persons may think. *Plus ça change, plus c'est la même chose.*

21. Dr. Millett, chancellor emeritus of the Ohio Board of Regents, later became vice-president and director, Management Division, Academy for Educational development. My references here are to what was in 1973 an unpublished manuscript of his entitled "Governance, Management and Leadership."

22. See James G. March and Michael D. Cohen, *Leadership and Ambiguity: The American College President,* New York, McGraw-Hill Book Co., 1974.

23. See his article, "The Anonymous Leaders of Higher Education," *Journal of Higher Education* 43, January 1972: 9–22.

24. For discussions of the cons and pros of extramural controls in American higher education, note Harold L. Enarson's "The Occasional Search for the Public Interest," and my own companion piece on "External Governance in Higher Education: Bane or Boon?" in *AGB Reports,* March/April 1975, Washington, D.C., Association of Governing Boards of Universities and Colleges, pp. 20–27 and 28–36.

Chapter 5: Academics and Governance

1. See his chapter, 'Politics of Academia," in Harold L. Hodgkinson and L. Richard Meeth, editors, *Power and Authority,* San Francisco, Jossey-Bass, Inc., 1971, pp. 54–65. Note also in the same volume T. R. McConnell's "Faculty Government" and various other commentaries.

2. *The Trusteeship of Colleges and Universities,* New York, McGraw-Hill Book Co., 1969.

3. John W. Nason's introductory and summary comment section

of *The Future of Trusteeship,* Washington, D.C., Association of Governing Boards of Universities and Colleges, 1974.

4. Kenneth B. Hare; see his published speech in *Affaires Universitaires* 8, February 1969: 3.

5. For a comprehensive treatment of policies and practices prior to the changes effected in the 1960s and 1970s, see John J. Corson, *Governance of Colleges and Universities,* New York, McGraw-Hill Book Co., 1960.

6. See Edward Gross and Paul V. Grambsch, *University Goals and Academic Power,* Washington, D.C., American Council on Education, 1968.

7. Table 5.1 is reproduced from p. 76. Two critics have pointed out, however, that in their judgment the data and methodology of this study really do not support this cheerful conclusion, and that "universities' stated goals may be in reality a justification for the accrual of large income, prestige, and security that over the long run may have critical impact on the achievement of other goals." The inference of these critics is that many professors and administrators may have a "Manichean attitude in line with the intellectualist rationality of Weber's 'ethic of conviction,' " and that strained relations do stem from dilemmas, contradictions, and conflicts with regard to university goals. See the commentary by Victor Thiessen and Mark Iutcovich, "Some Comments on Edward Gross's 'Universities as Organizations: A Research Approach' " *American Sociologist* 5, August 1970: 252–54.

8. Washington, D.C., American Council on Education, 1968.

9. *Atlantic,* September 1968, pp. 42–47.

10. For a detailed account of what took place at Columbia and some other universities with regard to reform of governance, see David D. Dill, *Case Studies in University Governance,* Washington, D.C., National Association of State Universities and Land Grant Colleges, 1971.

11. Reported in *The Campus Senate: Experiment in Democracy,* Berkeley, Center for Research and Development in Higher Education, University of California, 1974.

12. From a statement cited in *Danforth News and Notes,* November 1968, p. 6. See also Appendix C for the Carnegie Commission on Higher Education's twenty-six main recommendations on governing colleges and universities.

13. From my article in *AGB Reports,* March/April 1975.

14. Some federal concerns with higher education, however, date

back to the eighteenth century, as is witnessed in the Northwest Ordinance of 1785 and a contract in 1787 with the Ohio Company reserving two townships of land for the support of a university. The Morrill Act pertaining to the establishment of land-grant institutions was passed in 1862, and a department of Education was created in 1867.

15. See "Another Campus Revolt—This Time against Washington," *U.S. News and World Report,* July 5, 1976, pp. 91–94.
16. See "Medical Deans' Revolt," *New York Times,* November 16, 1976.
17. Note "Restoring the Partnership," *Cleveland Plain Dealer,* February 2, 1977.

Chapter 6: Status Appraisal

1. See my article, "Merit and Equality in Higher Education," *Educational Record* 51, Winter 1970: 5–13.
2. In "The Protection of the Inept," *American Sociolgical Review,* 32, Febrary 1967: 5–19.
3. Reported in "Tenure at City U. Seen as Routine," *New York Times,* April 11, 1974.
4. Carl Friedrich, "The Selection of Professors," *Atlantic* January 1938, p. 112.
5. See their chapter, "Age, Aging and Age Stratification in Science," in Matilda Riley, Marylin Johnson, and Anne Foner, editors, *Aging and Society,* vol. 3, New York, Russell Sage Foundation, 1972. Quotation from pp. 306–7.
6. *Scaling the Ivory Tower: Merit and Its Limits in Academic Careers,* Baltimore, Johns Hopkins Press, 1975.
7. Reported in the *AAUP Bulletin* 15, January 1929: 177 ff.
8. From "Evaluation of Teaching Performance: Issues and Possibilities," in Calvin B. T. Lee, editor, *Improving College Teaching,* Washington, D.C., American Council on Education, 1967, pp. 265–81.
9. *Op. cit.,* section entitled "Current Practices in the Evaluation and Training of College Teachers," pp. 296–311. Table 6.1 is from p. 298.
10. Fred Luthan, *The Faculty Promotion Process: An Empirical Analysis of the Management of Large State Universities,* Iowa City, University of Iowa, Bureau of Business Research, 1967.
11. *Op. cit.,* pp. 303–7. Astin and Lee's commentary about practices

in evaluation has an appendix called "Outstanding Teacher Awards" showing that they are to be noted in more than half of all the colleges in universities, but in only 13.3 percent of junior colleges, 26.3 percent of teacher colleges, and 29.8 percent of liberal arts colleges. These awards are variously entitled, often involve students as nominators or judges, and range from substantial cash prizes down to plaques and scrolls. Such awards, I would add, have multiplied in the last twenty-five years, particularly in universities. A possible explanation is that they represent one kind of response to a feeling that effective undergraduate teaching has not been formally accorded due recognition and reward through the usual channels of professional evaluation.

12. Reeve's book, pp. 158ff.
13. Alan E. Bayer, *Teaching Faculty in Academe: 1972–1973*, Washington, D.C., American Council on Education, 1973.
14. Paul f. Lazarsfeld and Wagner Thielens, Jr., *The Academic Mind: Social Scientists in Time of Crisis,* Glencoe, Ill., The Free Press, 1958.

Chapter 7: Professional Status

1. Many publicly supported institutions have to engage in repeated struggles with state legislatures to ward off attempts to set minimum teaching loads, however, and academic resistance to such interference is often resented by those legislators with limited conceptions of what a six or nine hour teaching load may entail.

2. This judgment leaves open the question as towhat disinterestedness and competence (knowledge and skill) are to be used for, so that from a pragmatic point of view, disinterestedness is merely an attitude serving as a tangential rather than an ultimate end.

"Generalizations, laws, hypotheses, do not, that is to say, proceed either by some self-revelation of phenomena, or by some equal and impartial treatment of them by the human mind, but by a method of approach and handling which is definitely 'interested,' in the sense of putting preconceived questions to which answers are sought. In this sense all Science is qualified by human interest. So when we speak of 'disinterested science' we mean, either that the questions are valued merely as knowledge, or that, if behind that knowledge lies the sense of the need to utilize it, that utility is conceived in terms of general human welfare, not in terms of some particular gain. Specific utilities must come as implications, or by-products. . . . " From J. A. Hobson, *Free Thought in the Social Sciences*, New York, The Macmillan Co., 1926, pp. 61–62.

3. From *Policy Documents and Reports*, Washington, D.C., American Association of University Professors, 1971, pp. 50–51.

4. See the piece by Paul Von Blum, October 21, 1974, p. 20.

5. For a mock-serious commentary on this subject, note "Sex and the Professor," by "Aristides," in *American Scholar* 44, Summer 1975: 357–63.

6. It is of interest here to note that in the early 1970s, the American Association of State Colleges and Universities dropped its endorsement of the AAUP's oft-quoted 1940 statement about the principles of academic freedom and tenure and formulated its own statement, giving as much emphasis to academics' responsibilities as to their freedoms.

7. See his article, "The Ethics of Higher Education," *Educational Record* 48, Winter 1967: 11–21. One should note, however, that a generally understood code of proper and improper behavior is apparent in the conduct of scientific research. Stealing other persons' ideas and not giving credit for sources of basic information are taboo in all fields. Certain kinds of experimentation with human beings are forbidden. The patenting of some kinds of discoveries is frowned upon, and the nondisclosure of techniques used to accomplish particular results, which is common among industrial laboratories, is definitely contrary to the ethics characterizing academic inquiry.

   In January 1977, the University of Southern California held a three-day conference on "Ethical and Economic Issues: University Policies for Consulting, Overload Instructional Activities, and Intellectual Property," Virginia V. Rolett, of U.S.C.'s Office of Institutional Studies, prepared a selected bibliography (in press) which lists various publications on recent issues.

8. Bayer's 1972–73 survey reports that 35.4 percent of teaching academics in universities are away from the campus from 11 to 21 or more days per year for professional activities (*op. cit.,* p. 28).

9. New York, McGraw-Hill Book Co., 1974.

10. *Academic Freedom and Tenure,* edited by Louis Joughin (Madison, University of Wisconsin Press, 1967), is a useful handbook of AAUP policies and practices. It also has a lengthy appendix with some individual commentaries on academic freedom, due process, and tenure.

11. New York, B. W. Huebsch, 1918.
12. *Bulletin of the AAUP* 24, May 1938: 409–17.
13. "The Theory of the Profession and Its Predicament," *AAUP Bulletin* 58, June 1972: 120–25.
14. Although voting at that meeting was entirely in accord with Association procedures, it is pertinent to remark that those present and voting represented a fraction of less than one percent of the total membership.
15. See Everett C. Ladd, Jr., and Seymour Martin Lipset, *Professors, Unions, and American Higher Education,* prepared for the Carnegie Commission on Higher Education; Washington, D.C., American Institute for Public Policy Research, 1973.
16. It has been reported that at the beginning of 1976, the AAUP had 80,000 members and 1,365 chapters, 35 of them with bargaining rights. The NEA then had 54,000 members from institutions of higher education in its 354 locals, 149 of which were bargaining agents; corresponding figures for the AFT were 40,000, 273, and 92. Bayer's cross-section of university faculties in his 1972–73 survey showed the following percentage of membership in each of the three groups: AAUP, 26.8; NEA, 12.0; AFT, 1.9 (*op. cit.,* p. 28).
17. 20, 1934; 253–54.
18. For the institutional membership roster of this association in 1977, see Table 11.1.
19. "Increased Pay, Diminished Stature," *Science* 179, January 1973: 1.
20. "Faculty Unionism: From Theory to Practice," reprinted from *Industrial Relations* 11, February 1972: 1–17.
21. Myron Lieberman in his article, "Professor, Unite!" *Harper's,* October 1971, pp. 61–70, attempted to forecast some of the outcomes of unionization. In addition to the Ladd and Lipset book, two other generalized treatises are Robert K. Carr and Daniel K. VanEyck's *Collective Bargaining Comes to Campus* and E. D. Duryear, Robert S. Fisk, and associates' *Faculty Unions and Collective Bargaining,* not to mention other monographs. Also the growing literature on the subject includes specialized treatises on court decisions, the role of labor organizations, the determination of "appropriate" bargaining units, what happens at the bargaining table, strikes, student reaction, and so on.

Incidentally, worth noting for purposes of comparison is Halsey and Trow's report that some 60 percent of British academics belong to a major association, with membership "less strong in the ancient universities and the higher ranks." In 1976, according to press reports, their organization (the Association of University Teachers), after debating the matter for four years, voted to affiliate with the Trades Union Congress, a labor union federation including about half of the total British work force.

22. For a history of academic freedom in this country, note Richard Hofstadter and Walter P. Metzger's *The Development of Academic Freedom in the United States,* New York, Columbia University Press, 1955. Robert M. MacIver's *Academic Freedom in Our Time,* New York, Columbia University Press, 1955, deals with the main issues of several decades prior to the publication date of the book.

23. See Hutchins's article, "The Processor Pays," *AAUP Bulletin* 18, January 1932: 22–23.

24. *Change* November/December 1970: 32–36.

25. From his article, "Thought Control on the Campus, *Chronicle of Higher Education,* August 13, 1973, p. 12.

26. These interferences with academic freedom, incidentally, were much less frequent on the campuses of lesser institutions than at such prestigious universities as Dartmouth, Toronto, Chicago, Harvard, Princeton, and Yale. Alan E. Bayer's comprehensive survey, *Institutional Correlates of Faculty Support of Campus Unrest* (Washington, D.C., American Council on Education, 1971), also found correlates between institutional quality and student unrest in the late 1960s, together with a close association between faculty and student attitudes.

27. "To Teach the Truth, Without Let or Hindrance," *Chronicle of Higher Education,* April 4, 1977; 40.

Chapter 8: Economic Status

1. Halsey and Trow's book, incidentally, covers most of these questions with regard to British academics.

2. Bayer's 1969 data for a large cross-section of academics report the marital status of males as follows (percentages): currently married, 87.0; divorced, separated, widowed, 3.0; and never married, 10.0; corresponding figures for females are 47.0, 12.4, and 40.1. The numbers of children for male and for female faculty are: none, 29.3 and 65.3; one, 16.7 and 12.3; two 26.3 and 12.9; and three or more, 27.7 and 9.6. The weighted pro-

portion of women faculty in all institutions is 19.1 percent; in two-year colleges, 25.6 percent; in four-year colleges, 22.7 percent; and in universities, 14.8 percent. (See Alan E. Bayer, *College and University Faculty: A Statistical Description,* Washington, D.C., American Council on Education, 1970, pp. 7 and 12.)

3. One of the most detailed demonstrations is set forth in Allan M. Cartter, *An Assessment of Quality in Graduate Education: A Comparative Study of Graduate Departments in 29 Disciplines,* Washington, D.C., American Council on Education, 1966.

4. From "Faculty Salaries: Past and Future," *Educational Record* 49, Winter 1968: 9–21.

5. *Op. cit.,* pp. 530–31.

6. See *U.S. News and World Report,* October 15, 1973, pp. 86–87, for summary data.

7. These figures are for salaries only and not for total compensation. See *AAUP Bulletin,* Summer 1977. For salary data on a wide range of administrative posts, see appendix D.

8. *Teaching Salaries Then and Now,* New York, Fund for the Advancement of Education, 1955.

9. The fact is that in the twenty-five year interval between 1942 and 1967, the Consumer Price Index had already risen from an assigned base of 100 to 205, thus reducing the worth of the dollar by more than half. Then between 1967 and 1976 the CIP soared to 349, and the purchasing power of the dollar dropped to less than a third of what it was in 1942.

10. Although Ladd and Lipset (*Chronicle of Higher Education,* October 6, 1975, p. 2) give no information about the proportion of employed spouses among the highly compensated professional and managerial occupations in general, Alan E. Bayer's *Teaching Faculty in Academe: 1972–73* shows that in all institutions 35.6 percent of the wives of the faculty men and 44.3 percent of the husbands of faculty women were employed (for university faculties only the percentages were 32.9 and 44.0). Also, more than one-third of the spouses of university teachers have attended graduate or professional school. In light of these facts, my guess would be that the likelihood is greater in the academic profession than in law, medicine, or in corporate management that both the husband and wife will be gainfully employed.

11. As reported in *Institutional Self-Study* (The University of Texas study cited earlier).

12. The late Allan M. Cartter was reviewing Mark H. Ingraham's *The Outer Fringe: Faculty Benefits Other Than Anuities and Insur-*

ance, Madison, University of Wisconsin Press, 1965; the review
was in *Science,* September 3, 1965, p. 1084. Another informa-
tive book on the subject is William G. Greenough and Francis
P. King's *Benefit Plans in American Colleges,* New York, Columbia University Press, 1969.

13. These comparative data are cited to demonstrate that in the
matter of fringe benefits, academics are by no means a privi-
leged class. The federal system of taxation being what it is,
virtually every organized occupational group finds it advanta-
geous to maximize tax-free benefits along with increases in direct income payments. As one might expect, the proportion of
fringe benefits included in total academic compensation has
risen steadily for more than a decade.

    For readers who want to know "how much can a person make
for a job like that?" an article bearing this title in the *New York*
magazine (May 1, 1972, pp. 28–35) identifies the occupations
and sets forth the salaries of hundreds of named New Yorkers,
ranging from nationally known to little-known individuals.

14. *Op. cit.,* pp. 532ff.

15. See *AAUP Bulletin,* Summer 1973, pp. 206–7.

16. Note figures on p. 351, Everett C. Ladd and Seymour Martin
Lipset, *The Divided Academy,* New York, McGraw-Hill, Book
Co., 1975.

17. As reported by Henry Stein, "Publish and Flourish," *Esquire,*
September 1976, pp. 66f. Although now being outsold by
another textbook, Paul Samuelson's textbook in economics was
said by Stein to have sold 3,500,000 copies and earned for its
author an estimated 6 million dollars in royalties since the appearance of its first edition in 1949. Unlike most textbook authors, Samuelson is a top figure in his field—adviser to presidents and a Nobel laureate. In general, however, most textbook
authors neither make much money not gain much prestige
thereby in the pecking order of scholarship and science.

18. See "Should Profs Be Allowed to Moonlight?" *New York Times,*
May 21, 1972. The article does not mention whether the Yale
administration was previously aware of the situation, or what
action it took. The article goes on to state, however, that in
April of that year the Board of Higher Education in New York
City had decreed that "supplemental activity" would be limited
in the city university faculty to the equivalent of one day per
school week, and that "no faculty member will engage in any

occupation . . . that would impair his services to the college or interfere with his ability to meet his commitments. . . . "

19. The data just set forth are from Charles Andersen, editor, *A Fact Book on Higher Education*, Third Issue of 1976, Washington, D.C., American Council on Education, 1976.

20. Incidentally, Bayer's data do not indicate whether the heavier teaching loads of many women teachers are a matter of choice or assignment; also, their being more frequently engaged than men in nine hours or more of teaching may at least in part result from the fact that women are more likely to be employed in institutions where the teaching load of the entire faculty is heavier than in the more prestigious universities.

   Insofar as I can ascertain, there are no comprehensive data of the kind just discussed about the employment experiences of blacks and other ethnic minorities. Their as yet rather limited numbers in university employment make statistical comparisons risky. Federal edicts regarding affirmative action have facilitated their opportunities for initial employment, to be sure, but how appreciable numbers of them have fared in their later advancement apparently has not been systematically surveyed.

21. *Op. cit.,* pp. 20–21.

22. For broad views on the problems of financing higher education note the following publications: The Carnegie Commission on Higher Education, *Higher Education: Who Pays? Who Benefits? Who Should Pay?* New York, McGraw-Hill Book Co., 1973; *The Management and Financing of Colleges,* New York, Committee for Economic Development, 1973; National Commission on Financing of Post-Secondary Education, *Financing Post-Secondary Education in the United States,* Washington, D.C., U.S. Government Printing Office, 1973.

Chapter 9: Academic Profiles and Social Status

1. A 1969 inquiry based on a very detailed questionnaire was conducted under the sponsorship of the Carnegie Commission on Higher Education and the American Council on Education. The questionnaire was sent to 100,315 regular faculty members in 303 institutions (junior colleges, four-year colleges, and universities); usable returns were received from 60,028 respondents. Bayer's *College and University Faculty: A Statistical Description* is

based on the findings of this survey; Bayer's *Teaching Faculty in Academe: 1972–73* repeated in part the earlier survey. In addition to their analysis based on the 1969 survey data, Everett C. Ladd, Jr., and Seymour Martin Lipset made a further survey using a smaller sample several years later and reported their results in a series of articles appearing in various issues of the *Chronicle of Higher Education* between the fall of 1975 and the spring of 1976. The statistics presented here are in the main from these several sources.

2. Reported in an article by the authors in the *Chronicle of Higher Education,* May 17, 1976, p. 11.

3. Bayer's 1972–73 survey reports a similar range of variation among junior college, four-year college, and university-employed academics, with the parental education level moving upward for each institutional category. Interestingly, Bayer's tabulation shows that the mothers of academics have more education than their fathers in each of the three institutional categories.

4. Incidentally, Halsey and Trow's book about British academics (*op. cit.,* p. 216) sets forth comparable observations about social origins. The academics at Oxford and Cambridge come from more advantaged family backgrounds than do those at other institutions.

5. From "The Aging Professoriate," *Chronicle of Higher Education,* May 24, 1976, p. 16. See also Lazarsfeld and Thielens (*op. cit.*) for a comprehensive study of faculty attitudes during the McCarthy era.

6. Fifty-one percent of Halsey and Trow's British academics placed themselves left of center politically, 27 percent in the center, and 19 percent to the right of center (3 percent did not respond.).

7. Note James Hitchcock's article, "A Short Course in the Three Types of Radical Professors," *New York Times Magazine,* February 21, 1971, pp. 30ff.

8. See Peter Schrag's "The Dissenting Academy," *Saturday Review,* February 17, 1968, p. 63.

9. This particular topic is dealt with by Ladd and Lipset in their article in the *Chronicle of Higher Education,* April 19, 1976, p. 14.

10. See Charles Kadushin's *The American Intellectual Elite,* Boston, Little, Brown, 1974.

11. New York, Oxford University Press, 1930.

12. New Rochelle, N.Y., Arlington House, 1973.

13. *New York Times,* April 30, 1976.
14. A defense of "highbrowism" in academe was wittily made several decades ago by Robert B. Heilman in "An Inquiry into Anti-Highbrowism," *AAUP Bulletin* 35, Winter 1949: 611–27.
15. As reported in the *Chronicle of Higher Education* by the authors in the issue of April 5, 1976, p. 18.
16. From his "Anatomy of Academic Life," *Educational Record* 48, Winter 1967: 45–50.
17. "Beleaguered Professors," *Atlantic,* November 1965, pp. 115–18.
18. For a detailed treatment of these general considerations, see a book I coauthored with William L. Kolb, *Sociological Analysis,* New York, Harcourt, Brace and Co., 1949, pp. 429–509.
19. The *American Scholar* 45, Winter 1975–76: 719–31.
20. See *U.S. News and World Report,ro* April 18, 1977, *p. 36.*
21. Talcott Parsons and Gerald M. Platt, *The American University,* Cambridge, Harvard University Press, 1973.

Chapter 10: University Prestige and Competition

1. For a brief treatment of the AAU's development, note an article by William K. Selden, "The Association of American Universities: An Enigma in Higher Education," *Graduate Journal* 8, No. 1, 1968: 199–209. (Quotation from Selden's article.)
2. It should be noted that beginning in 1913 the AAU developed a standardizing and accrediting service with an initial list of 119 approved institutions, and continued this function throughout more than half of its history.
3. *Report of the Committee on Graduate Instruction,* Washington, D.C., American Council on Education, 1934. Although this report was the most comprehensive up to that time, the sampling procedures were somewhat faulty, and the representativeness of the returns was not checked. Also, the inclusion of agricultural subjects (which were prominent in the curriculum of the institution whose president was chairman of the Committee) not even offered at about half of the institutions being compared was a distorting factor in the cumulative rankings.
4. See Walter C. Eells, "Another Ranking of American Graduate Schools," *School and Society* 46, August 28, 1937: 282–84. For a somewhat similar study using specified indices of faculty quality

and indices of institutional attractiveness several decades later, note Albert Bowker's "Quality and Quantity in Higher Education," *Journal of the American Statistical Association* 60, March 1965: 1–15.

5. Hayward Keniston, *Graduate Study and Research in the Arts and Sciences at the University of Pennsylvania,* Philadelphia, University of Pennsylvania Press, 1959.

6. See Allan M. Cartter, *An Assessment of Quality in Graduate Education* Washington, D.C., American Council on Education, 1966.

7. This institution's reported salary data were later proved to be rigged; as a result of its various dubious practices, Parsons College went out of business shortly thereafter.

8. See "The Cartter Report on Quality in Graduate Education," *Journal of Higher Education* 37, December 1966: 481–92. (Quotation from p. 482.)

9. See Allan M. Cartter, "Qualitative Aspects of Southern University Education," *Southern Economic Journal* 32, July 1965: 39–69.

10. See Robert K. Merton, "The Matthew Effect in Science," *Science* 159, January 5, 1968: 56–63. Merton's and Zuckerman's studies of Nobel laureates and other individual luminaries in scholarship and science confirm the assertion that the "rich tend to get richer and the poor poorer" in terms of repute. With some qualifiction, this tends to be true also of institutions, but some of the outstanding private and public universities of bygone periods have lost ground because their leadership and their resources have not kept pace with increased and changed competition.

11. Magoun's tabulation of Group B universities is given in Appendix F.

12. *America's Psychologists: A Survey of a Growing Profession,* Washington, D.C., American Psychological Association, 1957.

13. *American Political Science: A Profile of a Discipline,* New York, Atherton Press, 1964.

14. See their book, *Social Stratification in Science,* Chicago, University of Chicago Press, 1973.

15. Note W. Miles Cox and Viola Catt, "Productivity Ratings of Graduate Programs in Psychology Based on Publication in the Journals of the American Psychological Association," *American Psychologist* 32, No. 10, October 1977: 793–813.

16. In his chapter, "The Misallocation of Intellectual Resources in Economics," in Irving L. Horowitz, editor, *The Use and Abuse of Social Science,* New Brunswick, N.J., E. P. Dutton and Co., 1971, pp. 35–51.

Chapter 11: Individual Prestige and Competition

1. See his "A Statistical Study of American Men of Science," *Science* 24, 1906: 699–707, and "A Further Statistical Study of American Men of Science," *Science* 32, 1910: 633–48, 672–88.
2. "Prestige Patterns in Scholarship and Science," *Southwestern Social Science Quarterly* 23, March 1943: 305–19.
3. Harriet Zuckerman, *The Scientific Elite,* New York, The Free Press, 1977.
4. See Alan E. Bayer and John Folger, "Some Correlates of a Citation Measure of Productivity in Science," *Sociology of Education* 39, Fall 1966: 388.
5. In "Behavior Patterns of Scientists," *American Scientist* 57, No. 1, 1969: 1–23. Note also Merton's book, *The Sociology of Science,* Chicago, University of Chicago Press, 1973.
6. Figures from Derek Price, *Op. cit.*
7. See Stephen Cole and Jonathan R. Cole, "Scientific Output and Recognition: A Study in the Operation of the Reward System in Science," *American Sociological Review* 32, June 1967: 377.
8. Diana Crane, "Scientists at Minor and Major Universities: A Study of Productivity and Recognition," *American Sociological Review* 30, October 1965: 699–713.
9. Warren G. Hagstrom's *The Scientific Community,* New York, Basic Books, 1965, gives an extensive analysis of the social influences which bear heavily upon the directions of academic research.
10. See "The Edgy, Competitive World of Research Grants," *Washington Post,* October 18, 1977.
11. For a highlighting of these various political aspects, note Philip M.Boffey's "Peer Review Under Attack," *Chronicle of Higher Education,* May 25, 1975. (It may be recalled that the Endowment for the Humanities was similarly criticized in 1977 and that populist political forces apparently had the upper hand in the naming of a new director.)
12. From Harriet Zuckerman and Robert K. Merton, "Patterns of Evaluation in Science: Institutionalization, Structure and Functions of the Referee System," *Minerva* 9, No. 1, January 1971: 76.
13. *Op. cit., p.* 66.
14. *Science* 196, May 1977: 738–41.
15. See Cole's article, "Patterns of Intellectual Influence in Scientific Research," *Sociology of Education* 43, Fall 1970: 377–403.
16. See Merton's *Social Theory and Social Structure, Glencoe, Ill., The Free Press, 1957, pp. 550–61.*

Index

Academic degrees, number and variety of, 279

Academic freedom: as a correlate of professionalism, 166–67; sources of recent subversions, 167–69; its defense, 169–71; importance of disinterestedness to negate bias in scholarship and science, 291

Academics as professionals: distinctive characteristics of professions, 145–46; crosscurrents of egalitarian and elitist influences, 146–48; bureaucratic alterations, 148–49; ethics, 149–55, 292; professional asociations and learned societies, 155–59; status protection associations (AAUP, 159–61; NEA, 162; AFT, 163); unionism and collective bargaining, 163–66, 293

Academics in statistical profile: their upward social mobility, 193; age distribution, 193; political, social, and other attitudes and values, 194–95; religious beliefs, 196; roles as citizens and as intellectuals, 197–99; social behavior patterns and recreational interests, 199–202; professorial stereotypes, 202–5; class positions in society, 205–9; variations in characteristics by types of institutions, 298

Academicus Mentor, pseud., 367

Altbach, Philip, 279

American Academy of Arts and Letters, 214

American Association of Community and Junior Colleges, 246

American Association of State Colleges and Universities, 246, 292

American Association of State Universities and Land-Grant Colleges, 157

American Association of University Professors (AAUP), 50, 66, 76, 79, 85, 101, 104, 107, 128, 129, 152–54, 156, 159–61, 166–68, 175, 177–79, 185–86, 188, 278, 292, 293

American Astronomical Society, 156

American Bar Association, 157

American Chemical Society, 156, 158, 244

American Council of Learned Societies, 124, 156

American Council on Education (ACE), 78, 104, 107, 215, 282, 297

American Economic Association, 152

American Federation of Teachers (AFT), 80, 156, 159, 162–63, 293

American Historical Association, 157

American Indian Historical Society, 157
American Medical Association, 157
American Physical Society, 158
American Psychological Association, 230, 242
American Sociological Association, 61, 230, 242
Andersen, Charles J., 21, 223–25
Aristides, pseud., 382
Arlt, Gustave, 279
Ashby, Sir Eric, 202–3
Association of American Colleges, 79, 157
Association of American Medical Colleges, 157
Association of American Universities, 93, 150–52, 157, 184–85, 212–14
Association of Governing Boards of Universities and Colleges, 104
Association of Research Libraries, 45
Association of University Teachers, 294
Astin, Alexander W., 131–32, 290–91
Astin, Helen S., 281
Attrition factors and rates in graduate schools, 35–36

Bacon, Francis, 149
Bailey, Stephen K., 52
Banfield, Edward C., 169
Barnard College, 111
Barzun, Jacques, 279, 286
Bayer, Alan E., 136–37, 186–87, 193–97 passim, 208, 239, 293, 294–95, 297, 298
Berelson, Bernard, 14, 20, 22, 23, 29, 52
Bernard, Jessie, 57
Birnbaum, Robert, 287
Bisconti, Ann S., 27
Bloland, Harland G., 158–59
Bloland, Sue M., 158–59
Boffey, Philip M., 248
Bogard, Becky, 278
Bolman, Frederick deW., 287
Boulding, Kenneth, 233
Bowen, Howard, 173–74, 176–77, 189–90

Bowker, Albert, 300
Brewster, Kingman, Jr., 101
Brigham Young University, 59
Brown, David G., 62–63, 69, 281
Brown University, 221
Bundy, McGeorge, 110
Burkhardt, Frederick, 124
Burnett, Elfrida L., 277

California Institute of Technology, 219, 227
Cambridge University, 139, 203, 283, 298
Caplow, Theodore, 69, 72, 281
Carmichael, Stokely, 168
Carnegie Commission on Higher Education, 46, 96, 297
Carnegie Council on Policy Studies in Higher Education, 60
Carnegie Foundation for the Advancement of Teaching, 26
Carr, Robert C., 293
Cartter, Allan M., 52, 218–20, 225–31, 269, 295–96
Catt, Viola, 300
Cattell, James McKeen, 160, 236
Center for Advanced Study in the Behavioral Sciences, 244
Center for Research and Development in Higher Education, 113
Chase, John L., 277
Chronicle of Higher Education, 49, 79
City University of New York, 20–21, 23, 60, 79, 124, 171, 282
Clark, Kenneth E., 230
Cole, Jonathan R., 231–32, 238–39, 244, 249–50
Cole, Stephen, 231–32, 238–39, 244
College Entrance Examination Board, 18
Columbia University, 102, 107, 111–13, 198, 218, 221
Commission on Academic Tenure in Higher Education, 79
Commission on Human Resources, 1970 Staff Report, 20

Competition and prestige within and among universities: nature of intellectual competition, 210–11; importance of high quality, 211; appraising institutional accomplishment, 211; role of the AAU, 211–14; systematic efforts to assess institutional quality, 214–19; stability and change in institutional standings, 223–25; components of quality, 225–28; special relevance of departmental strengths, 229–32; public costs and benefits, 233

Conant, James B., 31

Conference Board of Associated Research Councils, 156

Cornell University, 218, 285

Cornford, Francis M., 283

Corson, John W., 289

Cox, W. Miles, 300

Crane, Diana, 301

Creager, John, 14–15, 24, 276

Curriculum proliferation satirized, 285–86

Danforth, William H., 94

Davis, Angela, 167

Dill, David D., 289

Dissertation Abstracts, 45

Doctorates granted by top sixty granting institutions, 1968–69, 277

Doctor of Arts degree, 35, 278

Dodds, Harold, 93

Dressel, Paul L., 2, 84, 86

Duke University, 221

Duryear, E. D., 293

Dykes, Archie, 109–10

Eble, Kenneth, 197

Ecoles of France, 32

Economic status of academics: income as a social denominator, 173; comparative compensation, 173–75; academic incomes and purchasing power, 1904–77, 175–79; fringe benefits inside and outside academe, 179–83; added earnings and outside income, 183–84; discrepant economic status of faculty women, 185–87; prospects just ahead, 187–90

Educational Testing Service, 276

Eells, Walter C., 299

Egalitarian thrusts, 82, 115, 117, 124–25, 127–28, 146–47, 165, 206, 301

Eliot, Charles W., 211

El-Khawas, Elaine H., 27, 253–55

Employed spouses, 295

Enarson, Harold L., 121, 288

Endowed chairs, 284

Ethnic minority academics, 24, 57–58, 61, 281, 297

Evaluating faculty services: pivot points of decision making, 122; merit principle and compromises, 123–25; basic criteria, 128–34; faculty work loads, 134–37; balances between teaching and research, 138–39; misconceptions about "publish or perish" dictum, 141; off-campus appraisals in scholarship and science, 141–43; major and minor university differences, 143

Excellence and "undemocracy," 230

Federal involvements of varied kinds, 27, 59–60, 119–21, 246, 282, 289–90, 297

Field differences in doctorates awarded in 1940 and in 1969, 48

Financing higher education, major problems in and prospects for, 297

Fiscal crunch and institutional responses, 79–80

Fisk, Robert S., 293

Flexner, Abraham, 199

Florida State University, 166

Folger, John K., 239

Ford Foundation, 79, 245, 280

Friedrich, Carl J., 126

Furniss, W. Todd, 79, 253–55, 284

Galbraith, J. Kenneth, 103, 199–200

Garbarino, Joseph W., 165

Gardner, John, 18

Glenny, Lyman, 96–97
Goode, William J., 123–24
Goodman, Paul, 103
Gould, John Wesley, 89
Governance of universities: professorial
    scope of authority, 100–101; autoc-
    racy, gerontocracy, and authoritarian-
    ism, 101; changes of the 1960s,
    102–5; varied faculty roles and am-
    bivalent attitudes, 106–10; senates,
    110–14; increased external controls,
    115–19; rising federal influence,
    119–21
Grade inflation, 18–19, 276
Graduate deans' disciplinary back-
    grounds, 286
Graduate Record Examination specialty
    test scores, 22
Graduate student aids and stipends, 37–
    39, 278
Graduate students: quality, 19–22; social
    backgrounds, 23–24; demographic
    characteristics, 25
Grambsch, Paul V., 108
Greenberg, Daniel S., 245
Greenough, William G., 296
Gross, Edward, 108
Gross, Theodore M., 274
Gustad, John W., 130–31

Hagstrom, Warren G., 301
Halio, Jay L., 279
Halsey, A. H., 82, 139, 147, 193, 293–
    94, 298
Harris, Seymour E., 20, 38, 174, 183
Harvard University, 58, 67, 70, 120,
    198, 218–19, 221
Harwood, Edwin, 274–75
Hechinger, Fred M., 168
Heilman, Robert B., 299
Heim, Peggy, 278
Heiss, Ann M., 47
Herrnstein, Richard J., 169
Heyns, Roger, 114
Higher education as a field of study, 2–3
Hobson, J. A., 292

Hodgkinson, Harold, 113, 285
Hofstadter, Richard, 294
Hook, Sidney, 98, 171
Howe, Irving, 204
Howell, John M., 278
Hume, David, 126
Hutchins, Robert M., 83, 167

Imbroglios of the 1960s, 101–5
Indiana University, 129–30, 220, 283
Individual recognition and reward in
    scholarship and science: indicators
    such as listings in American Men of
    Science and Science Citation Index,
    235–36; amount of consensus re-
    garding those considered eminent,
    236–37; characteristics of high
    achievers, 238–40; publication media
    and their importance, 241–42;
    awards and honors, 242–44; agencies
    and procedures for according special
    recognition and rewards, 245–48;
    values and norms affecting research,
    249–51
Inducements to enter the profession:
    general, 12–16; relative prestige of
    the profession, 16–17
Ingraham, Mark H., 295
Iutcovich, Mark, 289

Jencks, Christopher, 19, 92
Jensen, Arthur R., 169
Job placement of new Ph.D.s: general,
    49–50; currently depressed market,
    50–53; field mobility, 280; pros-
    pects for near future, 54–55
Johns Hopkins University, 218
Johnson, Lyndon B., 223
Joughin, Louis, 292
Juola, Arvo E., 276

Kadish, Sanford, 161
Kadushin, Charles, 198–99
Kant, Immanuel, 126
Keast, William R., 79
Keniston, Hayward, 218, 220–21

Kerr, Clark, 11
King, Francis P., 296
Knapp, David C., 81
Kolb, William L., 299
Kotschnig, Walter, 36
Kristol, Irving, 182

Ladd, Everett G., 162, 164, 178, 184, 193–97 *passim*, 200–202, 295, 298
Lathrop, Robert L., 283
Lazarsfeld, Paul F., 138–39
Leary, Timothy, 168
Lee, Calvin B. T., 131–32, 290–91
Lewis, Lionel S., 127
Lieberman, Myron, 293
Lipset, Seymour Martin, 162, 164, 178, 184, 193–97 *passim*, 200–202, 295, 298
Lotka, Alfred J., 230
Louisiana State University, 225
Lovejoy, Arthur O., 160

McCarthy, Joseph Raymond, 168
McGee, Reece J., 69, 72, 281
MacIver, Robert M., 294
Macleod, Robert B., 286

Macy, John, 79
Magoun, H. W., 220–24, 268, 272–73
Major changes affecting higher education and its expansion, 10–11
Massachusetts Institute of Technology, 218, 219, 227
Mayhew, Lewis, B., 2, 278
Merton, Robert K., 126–27, 141, 237–40, 247–48, 250–51, 300, 301
Metzger, Walter P., 294
Michigan State University, 276
Millett, John D., 94–95, 155, 288
Mississippi State University, 277
Modern Language Association of America, 156, 244
Moscow State University, 17
Munro, Julie W., 275

Nason, John W., 103
National Academy of Arts and Letters, 243
National Academy of Engineering, 243–44
National Academy of Sciences, 127, 239, 243–44, 248–49, 280
National Board on Graduate Education, final report summary of, 54–55
National Center for Higher Education Management Systems, 94
National Education Association (NEA), 80, 156, 159, 161–62, 293
National Institutes of Health, 245–46
National Research Council, 48–49, 61, 156, 244
National Science Foundation, 233, 244, 245–46
National University Extension Association, 157
New York Regents Advisory Committee on Educational Leadership, 91
New York University, 198, 221, 225
North Carolina State University, 220
Nowlis, Vincent, 279

Office of Civil Rights (HEW), guidelines and goals of, 58
Office of Scientific Personnel (National Academy of Sciences–National Research Council), award selection procedures of, 30
Ohio State University, 120–21, 218, 283
Opening of opportunity in American higher education, 17
Oxford University, 139, 203, 298

Parsons, Talcott, 209
Parsons College, 219
Peterson, Marvin, 85
Ph.D. requirements: course marks, 40; special examinations, 41, 45–46; foreign language tests, 42, 279; curricular and residence demands, 42; dissertation, 43–46, 280; time stretch-outs, 46, 280; student reactions, 47

Platt, Gerald M., 209
Price, Derek J. de Solla, 223, 230, 233
Princeton University, 218, 221
Professor X, pseud., 199
Public disenchantment with higher education, 8, 94, 95, 97, 121, 189, 197, 248
Purdue University, 220
Purks, J. Harris, 285–86

Quinton, Anthony, 206–7

Rand Corporation, 247
Rauh, Morton A., 103
Relaxed sifting methods: general, 18–19; unfortunate outcomes, 275; grade inflation, 20, 275–76
Riesman, David, 19, 92
Rockefeller Foundation, 245
Rockefeller Univeristy, 219
Rolett, Virginia V., 292
Roose, Kenneth L., 21, 223–25
Ruml, Beardsley, 175–76
Russell, Bertrand, 166, 171
Ryan, John W., 279

Samuelson, Paul, 389–90
Satisfactions afforded less creative academics, 251
Schockley, William, 169
Schrag, Peter, 298
Scientific Manpower Commission, 61
Selden, William K., 299
Simon, Herbert A., 90–91
Social Science Research Council, 156, 174
Solmon, Lewis, 21, 26, 276
Somit, Albert, 230
Spurr, Stephen H., 279
Staff hierarchy in academe: who is recruited and how, 56–58; affirmative action effects, 58–61, 282; experiences of new appointees, 62–65; seniority principle, 67; metabolism, 67–69; instructor or assistant professor, 69–72; associate professor,

72–73; professor, 73–74; tenure and status problems, 75–80; faculty mobility, 283; comparisons with military, 284; recent changes, 285
Staff turnover, 68–69
Stanford University, 218, 221, 225
State University of New York (SUNY), Binghampton, 102
State University of New York (SUNY), Buffalo, 67
State University of New York (SUNY), Stony Brook, 185
Stecklein, John E., 283
Stein, Henry, 296
Stigler, George J., 75, 168–69
Student participation in campus power structures, 285
Student recruitment policy issues on graduate level, 30–32

Tanenhaus, Joseph, 230
Teachers College, Columbia University, 111
Teaching excellence awards, 291
Thielens, Wagner, Jr., 138–39
Thiessen, Victor, 289
Tickton, Sidney G., 175–76
Trow, Martin A., 82, 111, 139, 147, 193, 293–94, 289
Tulane University, 283

Union Theological Seminary, 111
U. S. Chamber of Commerce, 182
U. S. Department of Labor, 60
U. S. Equal Employment Opportunity Commission, guidelines and goals of, 58
U. S. Office of Education, 11, 53, 81, 192
University administration: body of equals tradition, 81; departmental organization, 83–86; institutes, 86; schools and colleges, 87–88; deans and presidents, 87–93; management concepts, 94–96; conflicts regarding leadership and goals, 96–99

University of Arizona, 225
University of California, Berkeley, 38, 47, 59, 106, 218, 221, 283
University of California, Los Angeles, 220–21, 225, 283
University of Chicago, 67–68, 75, 134–35, 218, 221, 227
University of Illinois, 225, 283
University of London, 139, 203
University of Maryland, 29
University of Michigan, 38, 45, 58, 67, 218, 219, 221
University of Minnesota, 35, 64–65, 129, 218
University of North Carolina, 220, 221, 283
University of Pennsylvania, 218
University of Pittsburgh, 225
University of Southern California, 292
University of Texas at Austin, 67, 221, 225, 283, 284
University of Wisconsin, 279, 283
University syndrome, 33–34
Urey, Harold, 244

VanEyck, Daniel K., 293
Veblen, Thorstein, 160
Vetter, Betty M., 61

Walberg, Herbert J., 287
Wallis, W. Allen, 168
Washington University, 94, 221
Watson, James, 240
Western Interstate Commission for Higher Education, 94
Wilson, Logan, 1–2, 3–5, 7, 25, 34, 40–42, 44, 87, 165, 172, 198, 263, 281, 359, 374, 375
Wiltsey, Robert G., 279
Wolfle, Dael, 16, 164
Women in academe: scores on GRE tests, 21–22; allegations of discriminatory practices in admissions, 22; proportions getting aid and awards in training, 27–28; job market experiences, 57–61; distribution by ranks, 66; economic status discrepancies, 185–87, 297
Women's Equity Action League class action suits, 58
Woodward, C. Vann, 169–70

Yale University, 67, 169–70, 221

Zuckerman, Harriet, 126–27, 141, 238, 247–48, 300